The Personal and the Political

The Personal and the Political: How Personal Welfare State Experiences Affect Political Trust and Ideology

Staffan Kumlin

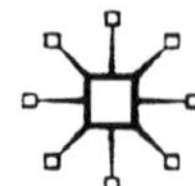

THE PERSONAL AND THE POLITICAL
© Kumlin, 2004

First published 2004 by PALGRAVE MACMILLAN™
175 Fifth Avenue, New York, N.Y. 10010 and
Houndmills, Basingstoke, Hampshire, England RG21 6XS
Companies and representatives throughout the world

PALGRAVE MACMILLAN is the global academic imprint of the Palgrave Macmillan division of St. Martin's Press, LLC and of Palgrave Macmillan Ltd. Macmillan® is a registered trademark in the United States, United Kingdom and other countries. Palgrave is a registered trademark in the European Union and other countries.

ISBN 1–4039–6451–3 hardback

Library of Congress Cataloging-in-Publication Data
Kumlin, Staffan
      The personal and the political : how personal welfare state experiences affect political trust and ideology / by Staffan Kumlin.
        p. cm. – (Political evolution and institutional change)
    Includes bibliographical references and index.
    ISBN 1–4039–6451–3 (hc)
      1. Welfare state—Sweden. 2. Allegiance—Sweden. 3. Trust—Sweden. 4. Party affiliation—Sweden. I. Title. II. Series.

HV338.K85 2004
306.2′09485—dc22   2003065608

A catalogue record for this book is available from the British Library.

Design by Newgen Imaging Systems (P) Ltd., Chennai, India.

First edition: June, 2004
10 9 8 7 6 5 4 3 2 1

Printed in the United States of America.

To my parents

CONTENTS

Figures

ACKNOWLEDGMENTS

The academic business first attracted me for all the wrong reasons. I was under the false impression that the only crucial keywords of good research are independence, solitude, isolation, peace, and quiet. But of course—as anyone who has tried it should know—in reality you are, and should be, dependent on others: colleagues, financiers, friends. In fact, this dependency is now one of the reasons why I enjoy being in the business. I would like to take this opportunity to thank those on whom I have depended the most.

The Department of Political Science at Göteborg University has a long and proud tradition in the fields of political behavior, public opinion, and political representation. This tradition—which by now dates back some 50 years—has been important for me: I think it is hard to overstate the benefits of learning the trade in a genuinely cumulative research environment. A collective round of thanks to everyone who continues to keep it alive.

My dissertation adviser Maria Oskarson introduced me to this environment, and suggested I should enter the business. Throughout the last seven years, she has been a constant source of fruitful discussion and pleasant company. Sören Holmberg—the grand old man of Swedish electoral research—served as my assistant dissertation adviser. I have benefited greatly from his vast knowledge in the field, as well as from his international contacts. Together, Maria and Sören have given me more constructive advice and moral encouragement than anyone could have asked for. For this I thank them most sincerely.

I would also like to extend my warmest thanks to Peter Esaiasson, Mikael Gilljam, and Henrik Oscarsson, because they share my enthusiasm for simultaneously talking about public opinion formation, democratic theory, and regression coefficients. They have furnished me with countless good ideas over the years, and have commented on numerous drafts at different stages of completion.

Several others have made equally positive contributions. Ever since my undergraduate days, Bo Rothstein has been, and continues to be, a great source of inspiration and new perspectives. Lennart Nilsson has been very helpful, not least during the planning of the 1999 West Sweden SOM Survey. Toward the end of the project, Folke Johansson and Jon Pierre provided valuable comments on the entire manuscript. Maria Jarl voiced constructive opinions on chapters 2 and 9. Marcia Grimes nicely checked and improved my use of the English language.

The social aspects of the business cannot be underestimated. In particular, during the first intensive years in the Ph.D. program, I thoroughly enjoyed the almost constant company of my four office mates in the "class of '96": Anna Bendz, Ann-Kristin Jonasson, Ylva Norén Bretzer, and Marie Uhrwing. My subsequent office mate Sverker Jagers offered stimulating conversation and showed me how to water the plants. Monika Bauhr has been a good friend, and has also commented on various chapter drafts.

Many other people have made everyday life at the department brighter. In fact, the list is too long to be printed here. Therefore, I would like to collectively thank everyone who makes me look forward to coffee breaks and lunches during long and lonely sessions in front of the computer. You know who you are.

If good friends matter, good datasets are absolutely crucial. And it has been difficult to be critical in this respect. Per Hedberg has never failed in helping me with the Swedish Election Studies. Similarly, I would like to thank Kerstin Gidsäter, Sophie Johansson, and Åsa Nilsson at the SOM Institute for their cooperative spirit and professional help with codebooks, questionnaires, and data files.

Several funding sources have made this research project possible. The Swedish Council for Social Research financially supported the project from which this book constitutes the main report (project F0029/1999). A second funding source has been the "TMR network" on Political Representation and Party Choice in Europe. This network, which consisted of electoral researchers from all over Europe, was directed by Hermann Schmitt, University of Mannheim, and financed by the European Commission. My warmest thanks to the participants in the network for making all the conferences, winter schools, and summer schools such rewarding personal experiences (including many good laughs!). A third funding source came from the Swedish Research Council in the form of a grant that enabled me to spend the summer of 1998 at the ICPSR Summer Program in Quantitative Methods of Social Research, University of Michigan.

The TMR network gave me the opportunity to spend 18 months at the Social Science Research Center, Berlin (WZB). At the research unit "Institutions and Social Change," directed by Hans-Dieter Klingemann, I received constructive comments on my work by Edeltraud Roller, Christian Welzel, and Bernhard Wessels. Also, I would like to thank the entire staff of the research unit for making my stay such an enjoyable period in my life. Not least John Garry, Philipp Harfst, Jutta Horstmann, Sybille Frank, and Kai-Uwe Schnapp made sure I was never bored.

Finally, I would like to express my deepest gratitude to my parents Barbro and Sven Kumlin. I think this book is partly the result of their ability to always support me without telling me what to do.

Research Problems

CHAPTER ONE

The Personal and the Political

The rise of the modern welfare state has transformed the relationship between citizens and the state. A century ago, many ordinary people had only infrequent personal contacts with government institutions and employees. Abstractions such as "the state" or "the public sector" were given more meaning by the picture of the king on the wall, than by direct experiences with concrete government policies and services.

Much of that changed throughout the twentieth century. Public social insurance systems were established and a broad range of human services were increasingly financed and produced by the public sector rather than by the family, by the market, or by civil society. Today, most citizens in developed nations have frequent personal encounters with one public service institution or another. Most of us are in regular contact with things like public health care, education, transportation systems, and public libraries. And at one life stage or another we receive parts of our incomes in the form of pensions, student aid, unemployment insurance, and so on.

From the outset, observers have suspected that in the emerging welfare state, personal contacts with public institutions would increasingly begin to affect people's lives, thoughts, and opinions. For instance, already in 1931 British political scientist Herman Finer exclaimed: "This is the problem of the twentieth century: the relationship between officials and the public."[1] In a nutshell, this is also the basic idea of the book you are about to read. It is an investigation of how personal welfare state experiences affect political orientations among the mass public.

The Welfare State as an Arena for
Public Opinion Formation

The character and causes of welfare state expansion have been a major topic in the social sciences.[2] For instance, considerable attention has been devoted to identifying causal forces behind the postwar welfare state growth (see Flora and Heidenheimer 1981; Baldwin 1990; Olsson 1993). Other studies have examined why the size of public spending on welfare arrangements is larger in some countries than in others (see Korpi 1983; Castles 1989; Hofferbert and Cingranelli 1996), and why the organization of such arrangements looks different across countries (see Titmuss 1974; Esping-Andersen 1990).

There has also been much research on attitudes toward the welfare state. Researchers have assessed the extent to which welfare state arrangements enjoy popular support in different countries, and whether such support has strengthened or weakened over time. Also, they have explored the socio-economic and demographic group bases of welfare state support (see Coughlin 1980; Taylor-Gooby 1985; Hadenius 1986; Svallfors 1989, 1996; Borre and Scarbrough 1995; Nilsson 1996b; Johansson, Nilsson, and Strömberg 2001).

This study looks at the welfare state and public opinion from a slightly different angle in that it deals explicitly with citizens' direct personal welfare state experiences. The aim is to shed light on whether and how such experiences affect political attitudes. In short, I investigate what happens when a person is discontent with some aspect of, say, the particular health services or the public kindergartens that she has experienced. Will she lose faith in the welfare state? Does she take her negative experiences as a sign that the political system and its politicians are not functioning very well? Will her inclination to support the governing party drop? And how strong is the impact of experiences compared to other explanatory variables?

Researchers have long sensed that some form of political impact of personal welfare state experiences is taking place. For instance, in their summary of the five-volume *Beliefs in Government* project, Kaase and Newton (1995:65) argued, "It is not just the scope of government that has expanded, but also the depth of its influence on the everyday lives of citizens. This combination of scope and pervasiveness gives the state its paramount significance in Western Europe." Or as Skocpol (1994:21) contends somewhat more explicitly: "public opinion does not come out of nowhere. Nor is it only rooted in current social and economic conditions—although it partly is. Public opinion is also influenced by the citizenry's experiences with pre-existing governmental institutions and programs." And Soss (1999:364) makes a case for "studying welfare programmes as sites of adult political learning [...] I argue that as clients participate in welfare programs they learn lessons about how citizens and governments relate, and these lessons have political consequences beyond the domain of welfare agencies [...] Because clients associate the agency with government as a whole, these program-specific beliefs, in turn, become the basis for broader orientations toward government and political action." Finally, Rothstein (1991:43–44) has ventured that "Weber's view, that the output side is especially important for the legitimacy of the state, is probably even more valid in the modern welfare state than it was in his own time. The simple reason is that citizen's lives, to a greater degree than before, are directly dependent on public sector programs and schemes. We are born, we play, we are educated, we are nursed [...] and we finally die under the aegis of public administration."[3]

A Deceptively Simple Research Question

The message is that a new arena for public opinion formation has arisen with the welfare state. In that arena, citizens can directly observe how the political system and its policies perform in practice. Personal welfare state experiences thus provide politically relevant information that might—or might not—influence political orientations.

More empirical studies of the link between personal welfare state experiences and public opinion are needed, however. More often than not, dramatic statements like those above lack references to empirical results that demonstrate the alleged effects. With important exceptions to be discussed, we still have surprisingly little empirical knowledge about what Herman Finer thought was the problem of the twentieth century.

The basic research question thus seems straightforward. In fact, some readers might now feel ready to delve into a theoretical discussion about what kinds of welfare state experiences may have what kinds of political effects. But it turns out that the research question is deceptively simple. As the remainder of this chapter will make clear, one cannot presuppose that personal experiences have attitude effects. In fact, much empirical public opinion research implicitly suggests the opposite: that citizen's personal experiences in adult life are typically not very consequential for political preferences.

This suggestion has two components. First, many influential studies on public opinion and political behavior a priori assume that people actually do not have many politically relevant experiences in adult life from which they can draw political conclusions. Political issues and struggles are (sometimes implicitly) regarded as located well beyond citizens' life spheres.

The second component consists of empirical research indicating that when people do have personal experiences from which they could draw political conclusions, they nevertheless typically fail to do so. While personal events like unemployment, short-term ups and downs in the private economy, or personal experiences of violent crime are of great personal importance, they often have proven to be of relatively minor importance to citizens' political reasoning (Schlozman and Verba 1979; Sears and Funk 1991; Mutz 1998). Instead, the literature suggests that perceptions of aggregated *collective experiences* of societal events and trends have much greater effects on political attitudes than direct personal experiences of the same events and trends. Such perceptions of collective experience—often called "sociotropic" perceptions—are seen as the results of information provided by political elites, experts, and the mass media. Judging by these findings, people are rarely willing and/or able to translate personal observations of social reality into political judgments. And the fact that the personal and the political seem to lead separate lives makes people dependent on the mass media and elite actors for politically relevant information.

This literature forces us to postpone the discussion about what kind of welfare state experiences may have what kind of effects. Instead, the remainder of this chapter addresses the more basic premise that welfare state experiences have effects *at all*. While previous research nicely points out that such a premise is not unproblematic, we will also discover that many studies have had certain biases in their research designs, biases that may have led to an underestimation of personal experience effects on political attitudes. More to the point, most previous research has actually dealt with personal *economic* experiences rather than with personal welfare state experiences; we devote the latter parts of chapter 1 to a discussion of why personal welfare state experiences may be more politically consequential than personal economic experiences.

Only after having addressed these basic issues will the time be ripe for developing a theoretical framework for thinking about political effects of personal welfare state experiences. Along which dimensions can personal welfare state experiences be conceptualized? And what kind of political orientations could be affected by such experiences? Do different kinds of welfare state institutions systematically generate different experiences and in turn different effects on political orientations? A framework addressing these and other questions is laid out in chapters 2–4.

A number of testable hypotheses will be presented as we go along through chapters 1–4. These hypotheses are tested in chapters 6–10, using mostly primary Swedish survey data described in chapter 5. Conclusions are drawn and implications spelled out in chapter 11.

The Political World: Out of Reach, Out of Sight, Out of Mind?

An implicit assumption that *the personal is separate from the political* can be traced back through the history of political behavior research. According to this assumption, politics and its results are things that people do not observe directly. Rather, citizens are to a large degree dependent on political elites and the mass media to notice and comprehend the political world. As explained by Heunks (1989:135), "Many observers have the impression that ordinary people are usually not interested in politics because it takes place at a level that is too abstract or too removed and inaccessible to them. People have their daily worries and pursuits which seem remote or irrelevant to the political issues of the day."

Especially American studies of opinion formation and political behavior convey the notion of a watertight partition between the personal and the political. Moreover, while there is—as we shall soon see—certainly evidence to support this notion, its source runs deeper than empirical results. In fact, American opinion researchers often start out with an *a priori assumption* that politics is something remote, something distant, an extraterrestrial phenomena having little to do with people's personal life spheres. Scholars tend to describe their basic research puzzles in questions like "how do people manage to arrive at political judgments in complex issues that they have no personal experience with?" These researchers sustain Lippman's feeling that "The world that we have to deal with politically is out of reach, out of sight, out of mind" (Lippman 1922:29).[4]

For example, Iyengar and Kinder's (1987:2) oft-cited study on mass media and opinion formation kicks off like this: "Our argument begins with the observation that Americans develop opinions towards an astonishing variety of issues that lie far outside their own experience [...] They reach such judgments without benefit of direct experience..." Similarly, Sears (1993:144) says that "For the most part, the political choices faced by citizens do not have a major impact on their lives." And in Kinder's (1998:20) formulation, "the press alone describes and interprets the events of public life that few citizens experience directly."[5] And in Neuman, Just, and Crigler's (1992:4) vivid account, "The majority of citizens operate in a world outside the rarefied realm of public discourse. It is a personal world, with an equally pressing set of career and family demands, economic and health problems, personal dreams and aspirations. For brief moments in a citizen's hurried day, there is an intersection of these worlds. Stepping out of the shower in the morning one might hear an interview with a former hostage on the 'Today show,' glance at the front page of the morning newspaper over coffee, hear the headlines on the car radio, or catch some evening news after dinner. The interconnection of public and private worlds is often unscheduled, incidental, and haphazard."

Note how utterly different these quotes are compared to those of Kaase and Newton (1995), Skocpol (1994), Soss (1999), and Rothstein (1991). It seems that we are left with a puzzling discrepancy: one group of distinguished scholars is convinced that personal welfare state experiences matter to political opinions. Another equally distinguished group doubts whether "the personal world" can generate much information relevant to opinion formation. On the contrary, politics is depicted as out of reach, out of sight, out of mind.

The Personal and the Political in Large Welfare States

Much of the influential work on public opinion and political behavior has been done in the United States. A basic suspicion in this study is that—from a European welfare state perspective—the idea that the personal and the political are separate is less convincing, and should not be taken as an a priori assumption. Because European welfare state arrangements are typically more pervasive than the American ones, reaching far into the personal realm of life, citizens typically possess a greater wealth of self-communicated information that is at least potentially relevant to many political choices. Most citizens are regularly in personal contact with the results of politics: health care, elderly care, child care, education, public transportation systems, public libraries, and so on. Saying that the interconnection of public and private worlds is unscheduled, incidental, and haphazard therefore seems exaggerated. After all, citizens both enter and leave the world under the aegis of public administration. Therefore, saying that they in fact have lifelong opportunities for direct observation of the biggest bone of political contention—the welfare state—appears a better abstract simplification.

A close relation between the personal and the political is a common ingredient in theoretical accounts of welfare state politics. One case in point is Swedish political scientist Jörgen Westerståhl's notion of *service democracy*.[6] In the pure version of this type of democracy, a great majority of voters want politicians to handle a number of societal problems by providing high-quality public services.[7] When inside the voting booth, people are driven by their perceptions of party competence in delivering public services, and retrospective evaluations of public service performance. Consequently, political parties compete on the basis of competence in providing such services. In short, a good politician in a service democracy is one who delivers public service to the people. In Holmberg's (1996:109) interpretation of the notion of service democracy, "citizens are consumers, politicians are producers; elections are marketplaces where service products are sold and accountability is achieved." In service democracies, then, political discourse is greatly concerned with the quality of public services and welfare state arrangements (Nilsson 1996a:184; see also Johansson, Nilsson, and Strömberg 2001). Welfare state experiences are important, not only in the sense that they are common in society, but also in the sense that they are a major political concern.

Moreover, because of the political attention given to welfare state experiences, one might suspect that they influence individuals politically. This point will be developed in greater detail later. For now, suffice it to say that an implicit premise in much opinion research—that citizens have few politically meaningful personal experiences in adult life—is not convincing in large welfare states. For sure, more theoretical and empirical work is needed to find out if, how, and when welfare state experiences affect attitudes. But such experiences cannot be a priori defined as nonexistent or politically irrelevant. In large welfare states, the political world is not necessarily out of reach, out of sight, out of mind.

The Personal and the Political in Past Empirical Research

These theoretical arguments about the relation between the personal and the political in large welfare states are just that: theoretical arguments. In fact, based on a large accumulation of empirical studies, the view that the personal is separate from the political has a lot to recommend it. Here, research on "economic voting" is especially important. This research program has been driven by the macro observation that incumbents do worse if the nation's economic situation has become worse recently. The task has been to uncover microprocesses underlying such aggregate correlations (see Norpoth 1996; Lewis-Beck and Paldam 2000).[8]

The literature has dealt with a number of subtopics. One of them is whether economic voting is driven by personal pocketbook experiences (or *egotropic* concerns), or by collective *sociotropic* perceptions of how the nation as a whole is doing economically. Sociotropic perceptions are perceptions of macroeconomic phenomena such as unemployment statistics, budget deficits, and inflation rates ("the economy has improved," "unemployment is rising"). With some exceptions, results show that sociotropic factors are more important than egotropic ones. Citizens' perceptions of the economy have political effects and these operate mainly, though not exclusively, at the collective, sociotropic level. In contrast to the impact of sociotropic economic perceptions, changes in people's private financial situations are relatively unimportant to political judgments.[9] As stated by Kinder and Sears (1985:690), "The political preferences of 'sociotropic voters' are shaped by the country's economic predicament, not their own. [...] voting seems to reflect more the assessment of national economic conditions than the economic circumstances of private life."

It has also been shown that economic judgments influence political trust variables like satisfaction with democracy, confidence in democratic institutions, and trust in politicians (Weatherford 1984; Monroe and Erickson 1986; Finkel, Muller, and Seligson 1989; Kornberg and Clarke 1992; Clarke, Dutt, and Kornberg 1993; Listhaug 1995; Hetherington 1998; Huseby 2000; Chanley, Rudolph, and Rahn 2000).[10] Again, personal experiences have less impact than perceptions of how the economy in the country as a whole is doing.[11] For instance, Huseby (2000:142) examined survey data from eight countries during the period 1982–1994 and concluded, "the influence of personal economy is weaker than the influence of national economy." Nye (1999:vi) summarizes the prevailing contention: "...loss of confidence is a social rather than a personal phenomenon. Few people report that their views of government derive from personal experience with it; rather, such attitudes are informed by the media and politicians."

The Sources of Sociotropic Perceptions

The results of the economic voting literature pertain to direct effects on political preferences. However, although personal experiences do not seem to have direct effects on attitudes under control for sociotropic perceptions, personal experiences may still exercise an indirect effect. That effect would arise if sociotropic perceptions were in turn significantly shaped by personal experiences. For instance, people who become unemployed or go through economic hardship could infer that many in the collective as a whole share these experiences. To the extent that sociotropic perceptions of collective experiences are affected by personal experiences, and given that sociotropic perceptions in turn matter for political attitudes, personal experiences will affect attitudes *indirectly*. The process would be one where people gather information themselves, perceive collective experience in ways that harmonize with what has been personally experienced, and finally adjust political attitudes accordingly.

But the link between personal experiences and sociotropic perceptions has proven to be weak. Experiences of violent crime, unemployment, personal financial problems, and the like, are at best weakly correlated with the extent to which one thinks these problems are shared by the population and society at large.[12] Summarizing her own and others' research, Mutz (1998:66) notes, "Despite the accessibility and obvious salience of personal experiences, they very seldom have a large or significant effect on judgments about collective-level reality."

Instead, sociotropic perceptions seem to be informed by elites in society. While there has been less research on this issue compared to economic voting, various reports indicate that the origins of sociotropic perceptions of the economy are to be found in mass media (Mutz 1998; Nadeau et al. 1999; Nadeau, Niemi, and Amato 2000), or among politicians and elite experts (MacKuen, Erickson, and Stimson 1992; Zaller 1992). Sociotropic perceptions of the economy are best described as responses to elite interpretations of collective economic reality. They do not seem to be the result of direct personal experiences with that reality.

In sum, the empirical literature suggests that citizens' personal experiences of politically relevant social phenomena do not move their political preferences. Personal experience is regarded as "depoliticised" (Mutz 1992), "morselized" (Lane 1962), or "cognitively compartmentalized" (Sears 1993).

Modeling Personal Experience Effects on Mass Preferences

Figure 1.1 summarizes how most researchers have modeled the problem (see Tyler 1980; Mutz 1992, 1998; Gilljam and Holmberg 1995).[13] The model also defines the playing field of this study. With this basic causal structure in mind we will later develop a theoretical framework about what kind of personal welfare state experiences might have what kinds of effects.

Previous research, conducted mainly in the economic field, has shown that effects represented by the "a" path are typically substantial, whereas "b" and "c" are relatively insignificant. It is sociotropic perceptions, not personal experiences that influence political attitudes. And sociotropic perceptions are more likely to be informed by the media than by personal experience.

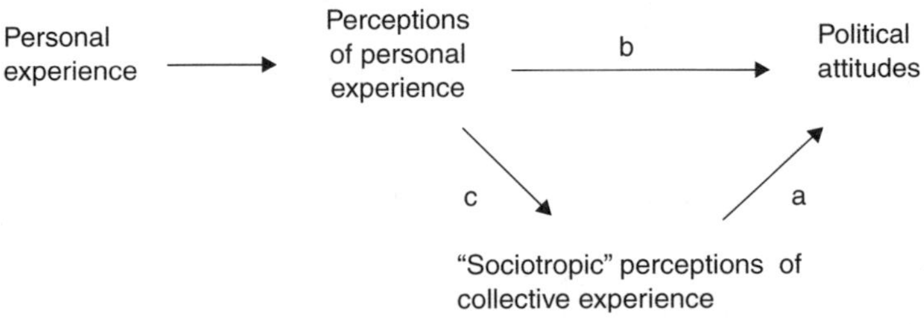

Figure 1.1   Personal experience, sociotropic perceptions, and political attitudes

The causal arrow connecting personal experience with perceptions of personal experiences has not been discussed so far. This path represents the fact that any experience has a number of objective qualities that must first be perceived by the individual. And if objective experiences are to affect attitudes, such perceptions must be used as political information in the opinion formation process. For example, objectively speaking, one may become unemployed, get richer, or be forced to wait a year for surgery. In order to affect attitudes, events must be perceived by the individual and then treated as political information forming a basis for political judgment. While this may seem an obvious point when made in the abstract, it will prove to be helpful in the concrete theoretical discussion.

Previous studies on personal experiences have concentrated heavily on only one policy area—the economy. For instance, the conclusion that personal experiences have weak effects on vote choice compared to those of sociotropic perceptions is derived mainly from experiences like changes in the private economy or personal unemployment (Mutz 1998:103). Similarly, most relevant studies on general political trust have concentrated on economics. To a curiously large extent, other potentially important aspects of government performance have been neglected. As McAllister (1999:188) notes, "almost no attention has been devoted to the impact of the broader policy outputs of government" (for similar arguments, see Miller and Listhaug 1999; Huseby 2000).

This study moves the model in figure 1.1 out of the economic realm and into welfare state territory. We now turn to the following questions. Why should we not automatically generalize findings from the economy to the welfare state? Why might personal experience effects grow when we move from the economy to the welfare state? I see two possible reasons. The first one has to do with the differing nature of *political responsibility* in the two policy realms. The second one has to do with the nature of *political information*. Let us consider these differences in turn.

The Welfare State and the Nature of Political Responsibility

Past research suggests that the political impact of both sociotropic perceptions and personal experiences depend on how people attribute political responsibility. People will rarely draw political conclusions on the basis of perceptions unless they see some sort of link between the perceived state of affairs and decisions taken by responsible politicians. In the absence of such a link, the perceptions are unlikely to stimulate political thinking and attitude formation (see Lewis-Beck 1988:156).

What is more, several studies indicate that citizens regard their personal economy as an area where most of the responsibility resides with the individual (Brody and Sniderman 1977; see Sniderman and Brody 1977). To a certain extent, this makes sense; while government policies are obviously not unrelated to citizens' private finances, politicians still have a rather indirect responsibility in this area. By and large, taking care of the personal pocketbook is chiefly, though not entirely, a personal responsibility. Rather, political responsibility for the economy, according to most observers, has to do mainly with *aggregate* phenomena such as unemployment level, inflation, budget deficits, and opportunities for investment and growth.

Indeed, several authors have found that the personal economy is an area where few people think that politicians have the main responsibility.[14] Brody and Sniderman (1977:339) discovered that few people regard personal finances as an area of government responsibility, as well as that "personal problems are likely to affect political choices to the extent that citizens hold government responsible for helping them cope with the problems they face."[15] Interestingly, among the minority who actually did attribute political responsibility for ups and downs in the personal pocketbook or for personal unemployment experiences, the correlation between experiences and political attitudes was clearly stronger than among the sample at large. Findings such as these have led researchers to conclude that an "ethic of self-reliance" in the economic field often prevents people from attributing political responsibility for personal economic experiences. Therefore, economic experiences will rarely affect political attitudes.

Personal welfare state experiences could function differently. The starting point here is that there is (or should be) a clearer political responsibility for what individual citizens experience in contacts with public agencies and programs. According to this argument, experiences of welfare state institutions are more immediate results of decisions taken by responsible politicians. After all, we are dealing with experiences with institutions that are supposed to implement public policy. This firmer link between personal welfare state experiences and responsible political actors might have a greater capacity to stimulate political attitude formation than the weaker link between personal economy and political actors.

These remarks received support in a study by Soss (1999). Based on both qualitative interviews and election study data, Soss (1999:369) found that his American respondents treated personal experiences with government services as political information. They were aware that services had been decided upon, and were ultimately controlled by, responsible politicians. Citizens "draw political lessons from their program experiences because welfare agencies are usually the most accessible and consequential government institution in their life. Welfare agencies are easily recognized as a part of government and have clear links to its other branches [...] they serve as the most direct source of information about how government works." Similar conclusions were reached by Möller (1996) on the basis of qualitative interviews with some 120 Swedish respondents with personal experiences from elderly care or child care.

These findings suggest that personal welfare state experiences are political in a way that personal economic experiences are not. As we move figure 1.1 out of the economy and into the welfare state, personal experience effects are not necessarily constrained by the "the ethic of self-reliance." The theoretical interpretation here is not just that there is a political responsibility for the public sector in the aggregate, just like there is a political responsibility for the aggregate economy. Rather, the argument is that the citizen has individual-level rights to expect certain things when encountering welfare state arrangements. Of course, the precise nature of these rights is a sensitive issue and depends on political conviction as well as on what kind of public service is up for discussion. This is, however, beside the point; while it is an ambiguous matter whether governments are responsible for our personal economies, there is a much more direct political responsibility for the products of welfare state institutions. The latter are public policies emanating directly from within the political system. Therefore, it would be interesting to investigate whether personal welfare state experiences are better at triggering political reasoning and political attitude formation compared to personal economic experiences.

The Welfare State and the Nature of Political Information

Tyler (1980) shows that the political effects of sociotropic perceptions depend on the *informativeness* and *memorability* of information. The more various facts are perceived to reveal about social trends and events, and the easier it is to remember them, the more likely they are to affect sociotropic perceptions and, in turn, political attitudes.[16] This finding leads us to the second reason that personal welfare state experiences may have a greater attitudinal impact than economic experiences. The sociotropic information available to citizens in the two policy domains differs with respect to both informativeness and memorability.[17] In the economic realm, citizens' economic perceptions have proven to be very responsive to a very small subset of macroeconomic indicators. Essentially, these factors are unemployment level, budget deficit, and inflation (Feld and Kirchgässner 2000; Paldam and Nannestad 2000). It could be argued that these indicators are relatively informative and memorable. They are informative as few, if any, would argue that such macro indicators are not highly relevant and important overall measures of the economic situation in a country. Also, such information is memorable as it can be parsimoniously summarized using just a few powerful quantifiable measures.

The high memorability and informativeness of macroeconomic information has consequences for both citizens and elites. For citizens it becomes a manageable task to form meaningful sociotropic perceptions to be used when forming attitudes. One does not have to be a political expert to form a reasonable impression of how the economy is doing. We all know roughly whether the economic situation is "good," "bad," "worse," or "better." In addition, the process discussed earlier by which sociotropic economic information trickles down to citizens from the media and economic experts becomes smoother. Journalists have access to relevant and not overly disputed macroeconomic information. This information can be parsimoniously presented in ways that make it easy for citizens to remember (e.g., using graphics). Sociotropic economic perceptions that are independent of our personal economies can be relatively easily formed.

It may be harder for citizens to form sociotropic perceptions of the welfare state. The key difference is that sociotropic welfare state information is more heterogeneous than economic information. First, the concept of the welfare state is by definition an aggregation of a large number of institutions. In order to form sociotropic perceptions of how the welfare state is doing one must simultaneously consider such diverse things as health care, public schools, social insurance systems, and so on. The institutional heterogeneity makes sociotropic welfare state information more complex and difficult to keep track of than aggregated, parsimonious macroeconomic statistics. It is therefore likely that welfare state perceptions are driven by the development within a subset of institutions. Hence, when survey respondents are asked to make overall evaluations of "public services," citizen A may have health care in mind whereas citizen B is talking about public libraries, and citizen C about primary-level education.

Furthermore, even forming a sociotropic perception of a single welfare state institution appears potentially more problematic than forming a macroeconomic sociotropic perception. This is because even for a single institution the measures of welfare state quality are numerous and disputed. While most people feel that unemployment, budget deficits, and inflation rates are valid indicators of macroeconomic health, there is no comparable parsimonious set of agreed-upon indicators for the welfare state. On the contrary, research on evaluation of public programs emphasizes the need to define the policy goals and the meaning of quality before sensible evaluation can begin (see Vedung 1998; Dahlberg and Vedung 2001). Does a welfare state institution seek to maximize some normative principle such as equal treatment or legal security? Or should various indicators of product quality be the focus, such as proportion of pupils who pass standardized tests, waiting time for surgery, or proportion of drug users returning to addiction? What weights ought to be attached to economic goals such as welfare state productivity? Also, regardless of which of these goals we personally prefer, we must still decide whether we are referring to the goals of politicians, voters, users, or public employees.

As the potential yardsticks become numerous and disputed, any single yardstick will become less informative, telling less and less of the full story. Also, memorability decreases as the number of reasonable quality indicators grows. Moreover, the probability that different indicators point in different directions increases. For example, the productivity in public health care might be impressive at the same time as employees are under great physical and mental pressure, treating citizens with less respect and care, and so on. As such ambiguity repeats itself across a number of welfare state institutions, sociotropic welfare state perceptions become harder to form.

Writing in the American context, Mutz (1998:116) nicely captures the importance of differences in political information and opinion formation across issue areas: "In the realm of economic issues, reliable statistics are readily available on a periodic basis, regularly distributed to the media, and then often thematically presented in news coverage [. . .] But for most issues, reporters do not have such a systematic means of monitoring change over time; thus their impressions of whether a given issue is becoming more or less problematic and whether it is improving or worsening will be based on educated guesses at best [. . .] The prospects for a sociotropic model [. . .] are considerably less when one considers issue areas in which national statistics are not regularly released and reported on. For example in areas such as education, health care, illegal drug use, racial inequality, and so forth, the idea that the aggregate public listens to, and moves in accord with, an informed elite analysis becomes far less tenable."

Finally, I do not suggest that the evaluation of macroeconomics is intrinsically less complex or sophisticated than the evaluation of the welfare state. Rather, the point is that elite discourse provides citizens with a memorable and informative set of macroeconomic indicators, which lends itself naturally to the formation of fairly accurate sociotropic perceptions. As a result, most of us know whether the country's economy is going up or down, and such views are easily separated from personal economic experiences. There is no comparable information about the welfare state. Therefore, saying whether welfare state institutions are improving or deteriorating is typically a more difficult question for citizens than saying something about the general state of the economy. Such information tends to be more ambiguous and more disputed so that no reasonably small set of indicators tells the full story of the well-being of the welfare state.

Maybe Personal Experience Comes into Play Again?

So what do citizens do if they find welfare state issues important but cannot access sociotropic information as easily as they do in the economic realm? One possibility is that they nevertheless rely more or less entirely on the information provided by elite actors and the mass media. Even lacking a parsimonious set of quantitative indicators, the media will often abound with reports about how the public sector is doing ("how long is the waiting time for bypass surgery?" "what are the costs of public child care?" "what is the situation for health care employees?"). And although this information is often less concisely informative and memorable than macroeconomic information, people may still try to synthesize many heterogeneous and perhaps conflicting reports into overall sociotropic perceptions of how various welfare state institutions are doing. However, because success and failure are such multifaceted concepts in these policy domains, the information becomes more heterogeneous and open to interpretation by politicians, by journalists, as well as by citizens themselves. Therefore, the bases and justifications for welfare state perceptions will probably vary more than what has proven to be the case for economic perceptions. Still, at a given point in time, a given individual could still hold sociotropic welfare state perceptions that may matter to attitude formation. What is more, this impact could still operate independently of personal experiences, and sociotropic perceptions could still be uncorrelated with personal experiences, thus keeping the personal separate from the political also in welfare state territory.

However, another possibility is that people to a greater extent resort to personally experienced welfare state information. In the economic realm, it makes little sense to anchor political orientations in personal economics, because the available macroeconomic information is highly informative and memorable. By contrast, because sociotropic welfare state information is heterogeneous and difficult to handle, citizens may make more extensive political use of their personal welfare state experiences. It is this possibility that is investigated in this study.

Actually, empirical studies of economic perceptions suggest that personal experience can even come into play in assessments of the economy, provided that good macro information is lacking. A number of studies have shown that the typically weak link between personal economic experiences and sociotropic perceptions of collective economic experience is considerably stronger among people who do not possess accurate information or sociotropic knowledge about for instance unemployment or inflation (Weatherford 1983; Conover, Feldman, and Knight 1986; Mutz 1998). This phenomenon goes by the name of the "default source" hypothesis. That is, in the absence of reliable macro information about the collective state of affairs, people tend to default back to personal experiences as the most basic source of information for the formation of sociotropic perceptions, and in turn for political attitudes.

There are reasons, then, to believe that the nature of the opinion formation process changes when we move out of the economic realm and into welfare state territory. Such increased reliance on personal experience in assessments of the welfare state would be understandable both from the perspective of political information, as well as from the perspective of political responsibility. Because welfare state arrangements offer heterogeneous and potentially conflicting sociotropic information, and because of the firmer link between welfare state products and responsible political actors, personal welfare state experiences might have a greater capacity to stimulate political reasoning and opinion formation than economic experiences. For these reasons, personal welfare state experiences could be a more important political information source than personal economic experiences.

Let us use the model in figure 1.1 to specify our expectations further. What could happen in terms of the various causal paths as we move the model out of the economic realm and into welfare state territory? There are two possibilities. The more obvious one is that the effect represented by the b path is strengthened. People find it so difficult to form sociotropic welfare state perceptions, and personal welfare state experiences appear so easy and relevant, that sociotropic perceptions become disconnected from politics altogether. We might still get people to answer survey questions about overall welfare state quality, but the answers will not be consequential in the sense of being related to political attitudes. Rather, controlling for sociotropic perceptions, differences in personal welfare state experiences would have a greater *direct* effect on attitudes, compared to the effect of personal economic experiences. If our empirical analyses would support this possibility, then the widespread image of voters as "sociotropic animals" would not seem to apply at all when it comes to welfare state politics.

The second and subtler possibility is that the *indirect* effects of personal experience increase. In statistical language the "c times a"-path increases in magnitude. In this case it is still sociotropic perceptions of collective experience that are of immediate attitudinal importance, and the notion of stronger experience effects in the welfare state is thus not necessarily incompatible with the notion of sociotropic animals. However, in this second case, sociotropic perceptions are in turn partly products of personal experience. Because of the more difficult sociotropic information and the greater political relevance of personal experience, sociotropic welfare state perceptions will be more tightly linked to personal experiences than what has proven to be the case in the economic realm. Personally collected welfare state facts then carry greater weight in the formation of overall welfare state judgments. As a result, the weak correlation between personal experience and sociotropic judgment found in economic voting research should become stronger. While citizens are still sociotropic animals, their sociotropic judgments are, to a greater extent than has proven to be the case in the economic realm, informed by personal experiences.

In conclusion, our model suggests two causal paths by which personal experiences might be generalized into political attitudes. This means there are also two ways in which personal welfare state experiences could be more politically influential than personal economic experiences. The extent to which this actually happens in reality will be investigated in chapter 6.

Nested Research Problems

This chapter has outlined the most basic research problem to which this study contributes. The question is to what extent people are driven politically by their own personal observations and experiences of politically relevant phenomena. Expressed differently, what is *the impact of the personal on the political* in different policy domains?

This overarching inquiry will lead us to several additional political science research problems. These are *nested research problems* in the sense that they will turn up in the theoretical chapters as consequences of the more basic research question whether personal experiences are *at all* important. In time, the concluding chapter 11 will return to all these nested research problems and discuss them generally in the light of the empirical findings.

In particular, soon after one has decided to study whether personal welfare state experiences matter to political orientations, one runs into the question of *how* they might matter. Chapters 2–4 approach this question from different angles. And as the reader will notice, one cannot deal with that question without addressing several nested political science problems. Here, a first nested problem concerns the relative impact of *self-interest versus social justice* concerns as factors behind public opinion formation. Based on previous research in this area, chapter 2 identifies three ways of conceptualizing personal welfare state experiences: self-interest, distributive justice, and procedural justice. We thus connect to a broad social science debate on the impact of economic self-interest versus social justice concerns in political reasoning and behavior (see Tyler et al. 1997). Also, the fact that we consider self-interest means that we contribute to the discussion on whether the welfare state produces a political cleavage between citizens relying heavily on welfare state services and citizens who do not (Dunleavy 1979, 1980c; Zetterberg 1985).

Chapter 3 takes a step back in the model and conceptualizes the actual objective properties of personal experiences. It thus runs across a second nested research problem: *the impact of institutional welfare state design on public preferences*. Using the concept of institutionalized citizen empowerment, hypotheses are developed as to how differently designed institutions in the same welfare state might generate different experiences and in turn different political orientations. In doing so, chapter 3 connects to a growing literature concerned with how different ways of designing welfare states affect the public (Svallfors 1997; Bean and Papadakis 1998; Lapinski et al. 1998; Soss 1999; Edlund 1999a). Here, a key concept is that of "path dependence." The idea is that institutional and policy choices made at one point in time affect popular preferences at the next point in time. In turn, these popular preferences will have a recursive impact on the institutional and policy choices made at a third point in time, and so on (see Pierson 1994, 2001; Rothstein and Steinmo 2002). As we shall see in the final chapter, some of the results throughout this study shed sharper light on how processes of path dependence might actually work in the realm of the welfare state: What types of welfare state designs have what type of effects on political orientations?

Chapter 4 is devoted to discussing the dependent variables identified in the title of the book. These are political trust (general attitudes toward politicians and the political system), and political ideology (left–right related orientations toward the size of the public sector and the level of state intervention in society). There are at least three main arguments for focusing especially on these dependent variables. First, as we will see in chapter 2, personal welfare state experiences can often generate information that has the potential to affect these orientations. In particular we will see that political trust and ideology are common in the research literatures on self-interest, distributive justice, and procedural justice. Second, as we will see in chapter 4, past research shows that political trust and ideology—by virtue of being very general tools for making sense of and evaluating political information—affect a wide range of political attitudes and behavior. It is thus valuable to contribute to the ongoing research program on what causes differences in political trust and ideology. This constitutes the final nested research problem. As will be discussed in more detail in the final chapter, we make a small contribution to straightening one of the bigger question marks in research on public opinion. That question mark relates to the fact that we know surprisingly little about *how and why citizens' general political orientations change in adult life.* A final argument for analyzing political trust and ideology is inspired by research in political psychology on how citizens translate political information into political preferences. As discussed in chapter 4, this research has implications for our understanding of how experience effects may arise, and which types of political attitudes may reasonably be affected by experiences.

Finally, it should be pointed out that while political trust and ideology constitute the main dependent variables in this study, they are not the only ones: Chapter 6 examines personal experience effects on support for the incumbent party and on "government approval." As discussed earlier, previous research on economic perceptions has concentrated on party preferences, and because chapter 6 explicitly wants to compare results in the economic realm with those obtained in the welfare state territory, it is meaningful to consider also such party-related variables for this particular purpose.

Theoretical Framework and Hypotheses

CHAPTER TWO

Self-Interest and Social Justice

"It was a miracle nobody was injured," said the director of the social welfare office to the journalist. It had been just an ordinary day in Härryda. Nobody in the peaceful little community had realized what was about to happen as a middle-aged man came driving up toward the social welfare office. Nobody would have thought that a few seconds later his car would blast through the entrance doors of the office at full speed. Why? The newspaper article reporting the incident did not contain any definitive clues, but the man had called earlier during the day and wanted to speak to a social worker. "In the past there have been few problems with disappointed clients," the director continued. "But I know that some employees feel bad at the moment. After this we might have to discuss how to improve safety and protection."

This story is about a unique event in the life of a unique human being. And while the story is certainly about "a personal welfare state experience," it seems to have little in common with most other people's experiences. The episode could easily have been complemented with less extreme stories that nevertheless have equally unique and personal qualities: a student applying for another semester on student aid, a woman delivering a baby in a public hospital, a visit to the demented father in an elder home. Because all such experiences have unique personal qualities, some may consider it a daunting task to use commonly defined concepts to formulate general hypotheses about welfare state experiences and their effects ("experiences of type X generally tend to produce effect Y"). The suspicion would be that such simplifications capture precious little of a complex and individualized welfare state reality.

On the other hand, one may just as well argue that the complex heterogeneity of personal welfare state experiences is exactly what creates a need for a simplifying theoretical framework. Such experiences, and their political effects, are difficult to discuss and investigate without a reasonably parsimonious set of general concepts and hypotheses. This is the line of reasoning that will be pursued here. Specifically, this chapter formulates a general and commonly defined theoretical framework addressing the question of what aspects of welfare state experiences affect political orientations.

Such a framework should meet at least two requirements. First, it should clearly allow for some complexity. Given the diversity in individuals' welfare state experiences, it may be unsatisfactory to characterize experiences along one single dimension. Second, as argued earlier, the framework should nevertheless be reasonably parsimonious. Exactly because welfare state experiences constitute a heterogeneous and bewildering reality, it would be helpful if we could arrive at a simplifying model. Such a model should have heuristic qualities while still capturing much of the essence of experiences and their political effects.

Unfortunately, the bulk of past research has not developed a conceptual framework that can be easily adopted and applied to the empirical material used in this study. Therefore, what is presented in this chapter is, to a great extent, a synthesis of relevant thought on how personal welfare state experiences could affect political orientations.

Immediately inspired by Tyler, Rasinski, and McGraw (1985), the outcome is a conceptual framework based on three explanatory perspectives: *the self-interest perspective, the distributive justice perspective*, and *the procedural justice perspective*.[1] Note from the outset that there is a kinship between the latter two: both the distributive justice perspective and the procedural justice perspective assume that people are attentive to whether experiences conform with normative expectations concerning what constitutes *social justice*. In contrast, the self-interest perspective is an application of rationalist public choice theory, which assumes that people are attentive to how much experiences contribute to their personal self-interest. This point will be developed in much greater detail later.

Admittedly, the theoretical trinity hardly exhausts all conceivable ideas that have been brought to bear on the subject. However, I believe that it captures most of the basic theoretical propositions that have been applied in previous empirical studies. Furthermore, most previous studies have, with some exceptions, tested only one or sometimes two of these perspectives in a single study or publication.

The convenient term "perspective" stands for a distinct set of theoretical assumptions about what aspects of personal welfare state experiences matter to citizens when drawing political conclusions. Expressed differently, the perspectives are three distinct families of independent variables that rest on different assumptions of what people pay attention to when they connect personal welfare state experiences to politics.

I have tried to strike a reasonable balance between complexity and parsimony. Beyond its moderate size, the framework is parsimonious also because it expects communality across individuals, institutions, and situations. By characterizing experiences along commonly defined dimensions, it assumes that the experience aspects that trigger political conclusions have something in common across different individuals, institutions, and situations. On the other hand, the framework allows for quite some complexity and heterogeneity: by identifying three perspectives, we consider seriously the possibility that no single "master variable" will suffice to capture all the politically relevant information generated by welfare state experiences.

The chapter begins by pondering at a more abstract level the notion of "a personal welfare state experience." It then goes on to discuss the three perspectives one by one, and finally closes by considering the relationships between them.

What is a Personal Welfare State Experience?

To explain what personal welfare state experiences are we must clarify both the meaning of "personal experience" as well as the meaning of "welfare state." As for the former, personal experiences refer to direct, personal, and unmediated contacts with an attitude object. Such experiences may be contrasted with other channels through which citizens acquire information about attitude objects (Asp 1986:64). One such channel is the *mass media*. Getting information about welfare state institutions through newspapers and television programs is an important information source, but it is different from personal experiences. Similarly, *interpersonal communication* with family members, neighbors, colleagues, and so on has proven to be politically influential (Katz and Lazarsfeld 1955; Huckfeldt and Sprague 1995). Still, listening to other peoples' accounts of welfare state institutions is a different process compared to personally and directly acquiring compatible information. Personal experiences thus refer to a more individualized mode of information gathering compared to the processes captured by a concept such as "socialization." Of course, the latter connotes—among other things—information exchange between people belonging to the same groups. In contrast, the personal welfare state experiences we are interested in occur when a citizen uses her five senses to see, hear, smell, feel, or taste welfare state institutions and their products.

Further, we concentrate on experiences with the "outputs" of the public sector, such as receiving services and benefits. Of course, many people have personal relations with the public sector beyond being consumers of services and benefits.[2] Most importantly, people can be said to have a personal relation with the public sector as *taxpayers*. That is, citizens do not just enjoy the outputs of the public sector. They also contribute to the financing of that output. And as pointed out by for instance Downs (1960), welfare state support should reasonably be the joint outcome of both experiences of welfare state outputs and experiences of taxpaying ("are the outputs worth the costs?"). The results of this study will fit well with such a contention in that the extent to which one contributes personally to the public budget (by necessity operationalized as family income) has an independent effect among people with comparable experiences of public sector outputs.[3]

In addition, many experience welfare state institutions as *public employees* (for a discussion, see Nilsson 1995, 1996b; Johansson, Nilsson, and Strömberg

2001). As discussed in greater depth later on in this chapter, Scandinavian public employees tend to display greater ideological support for the welfare state and they tend to stand further to the left than others (Knutsen 1998b). Our empirical estimates will lend further support also to this hypothesis.

Still, our empirical investigation deals largely with experiences on the output side. This is not because experiences related to public employment and taxpaying are deemed uninteresting. Rather, the reason is a more mundane need to limit the empirical task, coupled with the fact that the available data contain information mainly about output experiences. For these reasons, public employment and taxpaying appear only as control variables in our statistical models. What we are interested in theoretically is the effects of differences in output experiences, controlling for employment and taxpaying experiences.

What are "welfare state institutions"? While there is no exact agreed-upon meaning attached to the concept of the welfare state, its broad contours are clear enough for our purposes. We have in mind a broad spectrum of public transfers and services ranging from things like social assistance to unemployment insurance to public health care to public libraries.[4]

What welfare state concept ties this broad institutional spectrum together? Drawing on Flora and Heidenheimer (1981), we view the welfare state as a response to two major categories of demands, demands that are different both in terms of character and historical origin. The first set of demands relates to socioeconomic security. Here the starting point is that in modern societies, citizens are vulnerable to a great number of risks. Many of these risks are caused by capitalist market forces: people run the risk of becoming unemployed, injuring themselves at work, and so on. Other risks are related to particular parts of the life cycle and old age. Both market- and life-cycle related risks nurture demands for publicly guaranteed socioeconomic security. As Flora and Heidenheimer (1981:23) explain, "the welfare state is seen as an attempt to deal with specific problems of capitalist development, class conflict and recurring economic crises." The second set of demands relates to socioeconomic equality. The roots of such demands are typically traced back to the development of mass democracy and political equality (see Marshall 1950). As clarified by Roller (1995:167), "the demand for socio-economic equality is a consequence of the democratization process with its stress on political equality; effective political equality can be realized only under the condition of socio-economic equality." Needless to say, there is great disagreement as to exactly what kind of equality various welfare state institutions should try to establish. For instance, in one major discussion a Marxist "equality of results" is pitted against a liberal "equality of opportunity."

In conclusion, according to the above definition, "the welfare state is an integrative mechanism to neutralize the disruptive features of modernization, and its essence lies in a government responsibility for security and equality" (Alber 1988:456).

But what public institutions contribute to security and/or equality? Here, many authors have regarded transfer systems as the essential core of the welfare state (Wilensky 1975). In Sweden and elsewhere, one type of transfers ensures minimum-level security. Means-tested benefits such as social assistance and housing allowance are distributed to citizens who cannot support themselves or are otherwise deemed needy. Another type of transfers involves universal flat-rate benefits tied to citizenship; examples include basic old-age pensions and child allowances. A third transfer type includes earnings-related public social insurances related to unemployment, sick leave, old age, and so on. All these three transfer types are welfare state institutions as they try to satisfy demands for socioeconomic security and/or equality.

We also consider a range of public human services. These services are typically distributed by local and regional government and include activities like public education, health care, elder care, kindergartens, and so on. These policies belong to the welfare state because they redistribute wealth by being partly financed by progressive taxes, thus contributing to greater equality of results. Also, such services presumably equip citizens with basic capabilities and functions they will almost invariably need in order to get by in modern society, thus contributing to an equality of opportunity.

Furthermore, we take into account a variety of universally available services located on "the fringe" of the welfare state. Examples include publicly organized and subsidized services like cultural institutions and public libraries. While we rarely think of such services as "social policy" they are welfare state institutions as they are designed to foster equality of opportunity. Services like cultural institutions and public libraries provide information or "culture" that are useful for citizens in the pursuit of personal life projects. In this vein, Rothstein (1998:218) points out, "If citizens are to be able to act as autonomous individuals in the face of political, economic, and social structures, they must have the right to certain basic capabilities enabling them to make well-considered choices." So services like cultural institutions and public libraries belong to the welfare state as they contribute to "basic capabilities" that in turn foster equality of opportunity.

In summary, then, we consider a broad spectrum of public welfare state arrangements. This is a difference compared to much previous research on the welfare state: as authors like Cox (1998) and Smith (2002) point out, the comparative welfare state literature has in its attempts to classify and explain welfare state development in different countries often concentrated on central state transfer and insurance systems, whereas it has tended to neglect the "softer" human services that are often implemented at the local level (see also Clayton and Pontusson 1998).

Given our purposes, such a focus on centrally governed transfer systems would not be appropriate as local service experiences very often involve direct contacts, not only with welfare state outcomes, but also with public employees and the concrete physical environment of institutions. In fact, these features of public services should make them more salient and emotionally charged in citizens' memories (Eagly and Chaiken 1993). In contrast, experiences with insurances and transfer systems tend to involve less direct personal contact with public employees and actual physical institutions. Experiences are often reduced to the reception of an anticipated sum of money. Or as formulated by Nilsson (1997:131) "the Swedish welfare state is to a large degree synonymous with the local welfare state. It is mainly at the local level that citizens experience the welfare state."[5]

Now that we have pondered at a more abstract level the meaning of personal welfare state experiences, we may begin to consider different perspectives on what it is in such experiences that might affect citizens politically.

The Self-Interest Perspective

What we will label *the self-interest perspective* is probably the most common account of how contacts with welfare state institutions affect people politically. Its essence lies in the claim that people form attitudes toward political issues, institutions, and parties on the basis of their personal interests. The more issues, institutions, and parties satisfy interests, the more positive attitudes toward such objects become. As Lind and Tyler (1988:151–52) explain: "The [. . .] assumption is that the citizen will attempt to maximize his or her gain from the political system, just as a person would do in a financial marketplace transaction such as buying a car. This is the major assumption of public choice theory and provides the distinctiveness that sets that theory apart from other models of political behavior." Dunleavy (1991:3) formulates the same assumption like this: "people are basically egoistic, self-regarding and instrumental in their behavior, choosing [. . .] on the basis of the consequences for their personal welfare."

Defining self-interest, however, is a touchy business. Here, we shall rely on the self-interest definition that has been employed in most previous empirical research (Sears et al. 1980; Green 1988; Sears and Funk 1990, 1991). This literature has defined self-interest in terms of how political choices affect one's *personal, material, short-term* situation. A "self-interest effect" denotes the rational process by which a person becomes more likely to support a political alternative—an attitude, a party, an ideological point of view—because that alternative has the most positive implications for personal, material, short-term well-being. In the context of personal welfare state experiences, the prediction is that people make political choices on the basis of how much their personal, short-term, material interests are satisfied by various welfare state arrangements. The self-interest perspective thus conceptualizes experiences in terms of the varying "amount," "quantity," or "frequency" of personal reception of welfare state products. Such individual differences in "how much" one gets from the welfare state may explain individual differences in political attitudes and behavior. In chapter 7, we deal with two specific questions raised by the self-interest perspective: whether individuals who currently consume more welfare state services and benefits than others also tend to stand further to the left, and display more positive attitudes toward politicians and the political system.

Conceptual Pros and Cons

What are the pros and cons of this self-interest conceptualization? The major drawback is quite obvious: it does not capture all reasonable and potentially influential variants of interests. For instance, it excludes *group-interests*, at least to the extent that group-interest does not overlap with individual self-interest. In other words, the concept does not capture interests related to the well-being of some collective to which an individual belongs, without necessarily affecting the specific individual (see Sears and Funk 1991:16). Hence, the process by which rational working-class citizens choose to support extensive welfare state arrangements because they think such arrangements benefit workers as a collective is not a self-interest effect according to our definition. For purposes of clarity, we would rather refer to it as a group-interest effect. Moreover, the definition excludes *long-term* interests, such as a young woman being in favor of raised child allowance because she will probably some day have children of her own. Rather, the concept is concerned with more short-term reasoning such as "I want the child allowance to be raised because I'm currently getting it." Finally, the concept is concerned with material interests that can be more or less directly translated into economic terms. That is, it does not classify individuals in terms of how immaterial personal interests such as "life quality," "happiness," "justice," "social rewards," and the like, may be affected by different political alternatives.

While these are real limitations, the limited self-interest concept also offers two types of real payback. One payback is methodological in that a limited concept facilitates both falsifiable hypotheses and valid measurement. Consider for example the distinction between short-term and long-term interests. The problem with long-term interests is that almost anything can happen in our lives with at least a reasonable probability: most people *can* become unemployed, have children, become ill tomorrow, and so on, which means that most people can become beneficiaries of just about any welfare state service in the future. Such uncertainty has unfortunate consequences for empirical researchers. For instance, hypotheses about long-term interest become hard to falsify as almost any political preference or attitude could be rationally defended in terms of some long-term interest. More than this, the insecurity built into the notion of long-term self-interest makes it difficult for researchers to measure. In plain empirical language, it is notoriously difficult to decide individuals' values on the independent variable.[6]

Actually, this point can easily be directed also at the distinction between material and immaterial interests, and at the distinction between personal and group-based interests. Here, too, the problem is that the self-interest concept becomes terribly inclusive when we start to incorporate immaterial interests or group-based interests. Because there are so many conceivable groups that individuals belong to, and because there are so many potential immaterial values, hypotheses based on such an expanded concept would be difficult to operationalize. In addition, they would be hard to falsify as almost any attitude could be rationally defended in terms of some group-interest or some immaterial value.[7]

The second payback from the narrow self-interest concept is substantive. As we shall see, the notion of personal, short-term material self-interest has formed our understanding of welfare state politics. Moreover, as we shall also see, this definition of self-interest has been used in a large accumulation of empirical studies on political attitudes and behavior. I firmly believe that it becomes easier to contribute to these research programs if we use similar concepts.

But what, then, is the substantive reason for why previous research has focused on such a narrow notion of self-interest? The answer begins with the democratic postulate that citizens' political preferences should significantly affect public policies. Further, this crucial postulate carries an equally important amendment: "preferences" does not just mean any gut feeling or basic instinct that one may hold at a given point in time. Rather, it stands for the "enlightened choices" that (a majority of) citizens make when they have access to, and take their time to make sense of, greater quantities of information (Lupia 1994; Bartels 1996).

Naturally, different models of democracy have different answers to how enlightened political choices could be achieved. For instance, according to models of representative democracy, they can result from popular selection of a small political elite with sufficient skills and incentives to figure out what their voters would choose if they had access to as much information as the representatives (Manin 1997). And if representatives can make a case for why the current manifest public opinion does not correspond to such fully informed choices, they are allowed to enact policies at odds with the basic instinct of current public opinion (Pitkin 1967; Przeworski, Stokes, and Manin 1999).

Proponents of "participatory democracy" offer different solutions to the same problem. They suggest that citizens should be given more, rather than fewer, chances to participate directly in the decision-making process at different levels in the political system. This gives citizens both competence and a sense of responsibility, which makes them better equipped to make enlightened choices themselves (Barber 1984). Finally, proponents of "deliberative democracy" advocate yet a somewhat different strategy. Here enlightened opinions are presumably the results of open-minded debate, where different types of information, interests, and actors are allowed equal access (Fishkin 1995; Bohman and Rehg 1997).

In spite of their differences, these lines of democratic thought are united by the fear that people's manifest opinions do not correspond to what they would have chosen with more information, competence, and knowledge. Interestingly, while there are many potential sources of such a lack-of-fit between current opinions and "true interests," the perhaps most usual suspect is exactly personal, short-term, material self-interest. Such self-interest is seen as a default basis for political attitudes that will often drive choices in the absence of information concerning long-term, immaterial, and collective interests (Green 1988; Mansbridge 1990; Lewin 1988). Moreover, because preferences fueled by narrow personal, short-term, material interests are feared to deviate from what people would have chosen with more information, such preferences are believed to have a great potential for transformation through representation, deliberation, and participation. From this vantage point, the very narrowness of our self-interest definition becomes its greatest asset. Because narrow personal, short-term, material interests are feared to be perhaps the greatest threats to enlightened popular preferences, it becomes especially interesting to know more empirically about *this particular type of interest* (although other types of interest may be equally important determinants of attitudes). More precisely, two important empirical questions emerge from this discussion. First, is it true that citizens' preferences often change, for example, by becoming increasingly anchored in long-term, immaterial, and collective interests, as citizens get more political information and competence? Second, how true is it in the first place that short-term material interests explain citizens' political attitudes in the absence of extremely detailed information and debate? This study contributes to the ongoing research on the latter question, a literature to which we now turn.

The Self-Interest Perspective has Shaped
Our Understanding of Welfare State Politics

The self-interest perspective is no obscure product of researchers primarily interested in the oddities of the human mind. On the contrary, it lies at the very heart of our accumulated understanding of social development in general, and welfare state development in particular. In fact, respected theories about welfare state expansion and retrenchment assume that citizens take their personal welfare state self-interest into account when making political choices.

In particular, scholars tend to argue that leftist opinions and parties gain support where welfare state arrangements benefit, not just the worse-off working class, but also the well-educated and well-to-do middle classes. Short-term material self-interest is believed to be one important causal mechanism in this process. To put it harshly, the more voters that enjoy welfare state benefits and services, the more interest-based support will there be for such arrangements and the parties that protect them.

This view underlies Esping-Andersen's (1990:27–28) influential work on welfare state development. He argues that one secret behind popular support for welfare arrangements in Scandinavia is their ability to make middle-class citizens perceive that they gain from such arrangements: "Rather than tolerate a dualism between state and market, between working class and middle class, the Social Democrats pursued a welfare state that would promote an equality of the highest standards, not an equality of minimal needs as was pursued elsewhere. This implied [...] that services and benefits be upgraded to levels commensurate with even the most discriminating tastes of the new middle classes." Designing welfare state services in accordance with middle-class interests, Esping-Andersen argues, "constructs an essentially universal solidarity in favor of the welfare state. All benefit; all are dependent; and all will presumably feel obliged to pay." Rothstein (1998:153) has made the similar argument that "a universal welfare state can only exist if it enjoys support far up the social ladder. The 'poor,' the 'underprivileged,' the 'working class,' or any other such social group is simply too small to constitute a sufficient electoral base for a comprehensive universal welfare policy. And conversely, one can only reckon with support for this policy from white-collar groups and the middle class if it is so formulated as to serve their interests..."

These ideas were taken yet a step further in American historian Peter Baldwin's *The Politics of Social Solidarity* (1990).[8] Analysts of early welfare state development, Baldwin argued, have not sufficiently appreciated the weakness and inconsistency of the relationship between social class—as conceptualized in terms of relations to the means of production—and actual personal gain from welfare state arrangements. Baldwin therefore distinguishes between social classes and "risk categories," the latter tapping, in a nutshell, differences in individual welfare state interest. He concludes that European welfare state development was often shaped by somewhat surprising alliances between representatives of risk categories that rarely overlapped perfectly with the poorer working-class groups typically seen as the motor of social reform: "Solidaristic reform was the outcome of narrowly based battles between antagonistic interests, a change occasionally able to clothe itself in the vestments of high principle and lofty ideals [...] It succeeded only when sufficiently powerful elements within the bourgeoisie also stood to profit [...] Solidarity in the real world, after the veil of ignorance has been lifted, shifts burdens between identifiable groups of the disfavored and the fortunate" (Baldwin 1990:293–94).

Similar ideas have been applied to modern welfare state trends. A prominent example is Pierson's (1994) analysis of Reagan's and Thatcher's welfare state legacies. Interestingly, considering their neoconservative rhetoric, they managed surprisingly little welfare state retrenchment in practice.[9] According to Pierson, the previous welfare state expansion restructured the playing field of social policy so that many citizens now have a personal interest invested in one welfare state service or the other. And similar to Baldwin's argument, welfare state self-interest is not confined to traditional working-class groups or to the poorer segments of society. Therefore, "...efforts to dismantle the welfare state have exacted a high political price. The costs associated with cutbacks are concentrated and immediate, whereas benefits are likely to be diffuse and to appear only over time [...] The maturation of social programs has produced a new network of organized interests—the consumers and providers of social services—that are well placed to defend the welfare state" (Pierson 1994:180–81; see also Pierson 2001:411–13).

In sum, the self-interest perspective on personal welfare state experiences is embraced by respected macro accounts of welfare state development. Granted, self-interested political reasoning at the individual level is but one of several cornerstones of these theories, and nobody is suggesting that the sum of individuals' interests is driving welfare state development in any automatic fashion. On the contrary, authors like Esping-Andersen, Baldwin, Rothstein, and Pierson emphasize the varying ability of welfare-state oriented parties and interest organizations to form alliances at the elite level, as well as their varying abilities to make citizens "discover" their welfare-state related interests. Moreover, all interests are not considered to be personal in nature and scholars typically highlight group-interest mobilization, as well as perceived moral attractiveness (see especially Rothstein 1998) as explanations of why welfare state institutions receive support. Still, while keeping such theoretical amendments in mind, it is nevertheless evident that many successful macro theories of the welfare state to a significant degree build on the notion of self-interested political attitudes among the mass public. These theories have in turn shaped the way we think about politics in developed democracies.

The Self-Interest Perspective:
Previous Individual-Level Research

What does individual-level empirical research tell us about the viability of the self-interest perspective? It turns out that it has quite a lot to say about political ideology, but very little about political trust. As for the former, one accumulation of findings is offered by the literature on "sectoral cleavages" (see Dunleavy 1979, 1980a,b,c; Dunleavy and Husbands 1985; Taylor-Gooby 1986). This research, which was especially lively in Britain during the late 1970s and early 1980s, takes as its point of departure the declining impact of social class on political behavior noted all over the Western world (Dalton, Flanagan, and Beck 1984; Franklin, Mackie, and Valen et al. 1992; Oskarson 1994). Dunleavy's (1979) explanation of the decline was the emergence of "sectoral cleavages." The growth of public expenditure meant that significant portions of the population came to consume welfare state services. By the same token, a significant part of the workforce came to be employed in the public sector.

Dunleavy stressed that public consumption and employment were no longer confined to the industrial working classes or the poorer social segments. He identified a trend where more middle-class citizens became dependent on public services and argued that this produced a social cleavage between people who consume a lot of public services and those who consume less, and between those who are employed in the public sector and those who are not. The prediction was that heavy public service consumers and public employees are more likely to embrace leftist political attitudes and vote for leftist parties (as such parties presumably protect the public sector). The new sectoral cleavage was thought to "cut across" the older one between labor and capital in the sense that sectoral positions are not predicted well by positions in the old class cleavage.[10]

Similarly, Swedish sociologist Hans Zetterberg (1985) reported that the most important voter group for the Swedish Social Democrats is no longer the industrial working class.[11] Rather, the crucial target group is people employed in or otherwise dependent on public services and benefits. In Zetterberg's parlance, the Swedish electorate has become "an electorate in the grips of the welfare state." The metaphor implies that self-interested voters are almost forced to support the welfare state in the sense that there is no way they can resist its generous offers. In his analysis of the 1985 election Zetterberg argued that "An absolute majority of the 6.4 million enfranchised voters in this year's Swedish elections [...] consists of those who are employed in the public sector or belong to groups such as pensioners, the unemployed, the chronically disabled whose primary source of income are the funds in the public coffers. [...] The campaign and the outcome of the elections [...] will largely echo this structure" (Zetterberg 1985:1).

The employment hypothesis has fared quite well in empirical research. The public–private employment dichotomy is now routinely included in voting behavior analyses, especially in Scandinavia (Petersson 1977; Holmberg and Gilljam 1987; Knutsen 1998b; Borre and Andersen 1997; Oskarson 1990, 1994; Gilljam and Holmberg 1993, 1995; Aardal and Valen 1995).

But signals are mixed when it comes to the prediction that public service *consumers* are more inclined than others to vote left. Most relevant studies were conducted in Britain in the 1980s (Dunleavy 1979; Dunleavy and Husbands 1985). The data were usually from the late 1970s or early 1980s and indicated some impact, though perhaps of varying magnitude.

But sectoral cleavage theory was soon under attack. In Britain, Dunleavy's findings were criticized by for instance Franklin and Page (1984) who interpreted the uncovered effects as weak and unimpressive. In Sweden, Zetterberg's verdict was questioned by Hadenius (1986), Holmberg and Gilljam (1987), Oskarson (1990), and Svallfors (1996, 1999). Again, the political effects of public sector dependency were found to be marginal compared to those of variables such as traditional occupational class.

American researchers, too, have assessed the impact of welfare state self-interest. These studies—often referred to as the *symbolic politics* literature—have contrasted the impact of self-interest with that of so-called symbolic orientations (see Sears 1993; Kinder and Sears 1985; Listhaug and Miller 1985).[12] This literature offers a compelling explanation for the disconfirming findings in many European studies looking for sectoral cleavages. The explanation is that people do not calculate the personal benefits and costs implied by every new concrete political choice. Instead they use overarching predispositions—*symbolic orientations*—to arrive at an opinion. Such overarching orientations can be described as emotionally charged attitudes toward a group, a political party, or ideological abstract symbols like "welfare," "family," "market," "left," "right," and so on. Examples of symbolic orientations include party identification, left–right self-placement, and class identification. The idea is that people form their opinions in more concrete matters based on easily accessible cues or symbols telling them how the choice relates to their symbolic orientations. Few are cool enough to hold their horses and instrumentally ponder the impact of policies on their personal life situation. ("Can *I* use this welfare program? Will black children be bussed to *my* children's school?") In turn, symbolic orientations are presumably the result of preadult political socialization: They are regarded as very stable over time and charged with strong emotion and identity.

Sears et al. (1980:671) explain this alternative to the self-interest hypothesis: "The alternative point of view we wish to contrast with self-interest may be termed 'symbolic politics' [...] By this line of thinking, people acquire stable affective preferences through conditioning in their preadult years, with little calculation of the future costs and benefits of these attitudes. [...] When confronted with new policy issues later in life, people respond to these new attitude objects on the basis of cognitive consistency. The crucial variable would be the similarity of symbols posed by the policy issue to those of long-standing predispositions."

The empirical evidence includes strong effects of symbolic orientations on policy opinions, and weak and inconsistent effects of various self-interest measures (Sears, Hensler, and Speer 1979; Sears et al. 1980; Sears and Funk 1990, 1991; Green 1988). A typical finding is that opinions about a particular public social scheme are much better predicted by people's general symbolic orientations toward government intervention than by measures of short-term individual gain from that particular scheme, as typically measured by the extent to which one receives service from the scheme.[13]

For example, in his study of welfare state attitudes in Sweden, Hadenius (1986:121) concluded, "preferences with regard to public welfare arrangements, are thus largely a reflection of political symbolic beliefs [...] People appear to a very minor extent to assess the public sector from the viewpoint of personal utility." Sears and Funk (1991:76) reviewed a large number of such empirical studies and summarized the major findings like this: "The conclusion is quite clear: self-interest ordinarily does not have much effect upon the ordinary citizen's sociopolitical attitudes."

Most of the time, researchers have assumed that symbolic orientations are "symbolic": that is, stable, affectively driven, and mainly the result of preadult political socialization. However, some scholars have discussed the possibility that symbolic orientations themselves are in turn affected by self-interest (see Campbell et al. 1960:203–04). If this is true, symbolic predispositions are not entirely stable,[14] not entirely affective in nature, and not only the result of preadult socialization. Sears et al. (1980:676) opened up for this possibility by suggesting "Such predispositions may be constantly reformulated to capture and synopsize a variety of the voter's interests..." This is the empirical track followed in this study: we investigate the impact of self-interest on general "symbolic" orientations such as political ideology and political trust. Maybe such orientations reflect not just socialization, group identity, and gut-level affection but also short-term welfare-state related self-interest? If so, symbolic orientations would not appear as "symbolic" as the symbolic politics literature has assumed and supported with empirical evidence.

So far, this idea has not received support either. For instance, in their extensive study of the Californian "tax revolt" in the 1970s, Sears and Citrin (1982) found weak or insignificant effects of various indices of self-interest on symbolic orientations such as party identification or liberal–conservative ideology. Sears et al. (1980) reached similar conclusions using the American National Election Studies. And based on Swedish survey data, Svallfors (1996:109) and Hadenius (1986:101) have reported data indicating that general welfare state attitudes among frequent public service consumers do not differ much from those of other groups.[15] Goul Andersen (1993:43) concluded, "interests are almost irrelevant as determinants of welfare state support in Denmark" (see also Borre and Goul Andersen 1997). Finally, in recent years these country-specific findings have been sustained by comparative studies reporting weak correlations between the extent of welfare usage and the extent of general welfare state support (see Papadakis and Bean 1993; Bean and Papadakis 1998).

As for general political trust orientations, there is not much research to draw on. We know very little about whether people partly evaluate the political system and its politicians at large in the light of what the system does for one's short-term material well-being. One exception is Tyler, Rasinski, and McGraw (1985). Analyzing a sample of Chicago residents, they found that receiving services from public institutions correlated positively with displaying trust in government. In other words, those who personally consumed the products of the political system were also more likely than others to endorse it. Miller and Listhaug (1999:214) reached similar conclusions.

In summary, how should we judge the viability of the self-interest perspective? While macro theorists assume that self-interest matters, micro research has been tough on such assumptions: attitudes seem to be rather well explained by general symbolic orientations, but only rarely by short-term interests. And symbolic orientations do not seem to reflect self-interest either.

So why should we continue testing the self-interest perspective? Has it not been falsified already? Not quite yet! On a closer inspection, it turns out that most studies investigating the impact of self-interest on general orientations have used rather sparse information about welfare state interests. Chapter 7 develops this observation in greater detail and reassesses empirically the impact of welfare state self-interest using richer data on individual welfare state interests than many previous studies.

An Electorate in the Grips of the Welfare State?

The self-interest perspective has a weird and nonobvious implication. Given that welfare state experiences make at least some minimal contribution to one's short-term material situation, these experiences are bound to have positive effects on support for the welfare state and for the political system. Because political thinking is assumed to be driven by self-interest, and because most encounters with institutions to some extent increase people's material well-being, experiences will have positive effects. This deterministic view was clearly reflected in Zetterberg's (1985) paper *An Electorate in the Grips of the Welfare State.* The title implies that the welfare state had closed its trap around self-interested Swedish voters. The generosity of welfare state institutions coupled with the short-sighted egoism of individual citizens meant seriously antiwelfare parties and ideological viewpoints can no longer receive extensive support.

This sounds rigid. Surely, it is possible that personal encounters with public institutions communicate more than just facts about the extent to which one's self-interest is satisfied? Surely, our framework should allow the possibility that some welfare state experiences in fact undermine support for the welfare state and for the political system?

The point of departure for the next two sections is that people look for *social justice* just as much as they are trying to maximize their personal gain. People compare their experiences with some normative expectation about what they have "a right to experience." And if personal experiences fall short of social justice expectations, an experience may very well have negative effects on support for the welfare state and for the political system, even though it indeed made a substantial contribution to personal, short-term, self-interest.

In the coming sections, we develop two distinct versions of the social justice argument. First, we discuss the possibility that judgments of *distributive justice* in the encounter between citizens and the state are influential. Later, I develop the social justice argument with respect to *procedural justice.*

In the final section of this chapter, we consider different possible relations between self-interest and social justice judgments. We note that according to theories of social justice, judgments of experienced social justice are not supposed to be rationalizations of personal self-interest (or "self-interest in disguise"), but rather independent of the extent to which one's personal, material, short-term situation is improved by experiences.

The Distributive Justice Perspective

Trust in political actors and institutions continued to decrease in Sweden in the 1990s (Holmberg 1999). Svallfors traces part of the development back to deteriorating welfare state transfers and services (Svallfors 1996:17, 216). At first glance, this claim appears to belong in the discussion of self-interest. Discontent and declining support would then be explained by a declining ability of welfare state institutions to improve citizens' short-term material well-being.

However, Svallfors links outcome quality to *morally based expectations of what citizens have a right to.* Using the concept of "a moral economy" as a metaphor, he argues that as Swedes enjoyed the outcomes of one of the most generous welfare states, its institutions slowly generated morally charged conceptions of rights. For example, benefits such as receiving a certain percentage of your prior income in the case of unemployment were literally incorporated into the definition of citizenship. When outcome levels and service quality deteriorate many people will feel that the political elites have broken a tacit agreement with the people. Cynical attitudes toward the political system and its actors will develop.

Svallfors's account of the Swedish development builds on the same basic assumptions as *the distributive justice perspective.* First, citizens are assumed to have a strong drive for distributive fairness. Support for social and political institutions are therefore contingent on whether such institutions are perceived to distribute outcomes fairly. Just as "economic man" is assumed to be instrumental and selfish, "distributive justice man" is interested in the extent to which outcomes are consistent with normative distributive expectations. And whereas the self-interest perspective assumes that people pay attention to "the amount" they get, the distributive justice perspective assumes that citizens ask themselves if that amount can be regarded as fair.

A related assumption is that people have concrete beliefs about distributive justice. They have expectations as to what they have a right to in contacts with public services, and they use these distributive justice expectations to evaluate their actual outcomes. Welfare state experiences thus emerge as a "mix" of actually experienced services on one hand, and distributive justice expectations on the other. An implication of this mix—which I will refer to as experienced distributive justice—is that whether experiences are perceived as positive no longer depends entirely on their short-term material implications.

Previous research suggests considerable heterogeneity in distributive justice expectations. One source of heterogeneity is the multitude of potential distribution principles. Scholars typically distinguish between at least three broad categories of distributive ideals: "equality," which means everyone in a particular situation receives the same outcomes, "equity," where personal outcomes should match personal contributions, and "need," where outcomes vary according to personal need (Deutsch 1985). Which principle is applied in a given situation often depends on the goal that an individual attaches to a collective institution. In this vein, Lane (1986) suggested that equality is a more important ideal in the realm of the public sector than in the capitalist market (see also Hochchild 1981).[16] And as underscored by Tyler et al. (1997:57), "If people are pursuing economic productivity as a goal, they should use equity as a principle of justice. If they are trying to foster enjoyable and harmonious social relationships, they should use equality [...] Finally, to foster personal development and personal welfare, people should use need [...] In other words, the goals people are pursuing should determine the principles of justice they apply." In addition, which distributive justice principle is applied also depends on political values. For example, conservative and rightist people are usually more prone than others to favor equity, and less prone to favor equality (Rasinski 1987).

But perhaps the most important source of heterogeneity in distributive justice conceptions is the nature of the welfare state itself. After all, the welfare state comprises dozens of rather different institutions. Each distributes different services with different goals, and each has a distinct historical record. Distributive justice conceptions should therefore vary substantially depending on what service we are talking about. Abstract principles can only take us so far. For instance, the question of exactly what service is implied by "equality" in the context of, say, child care opens up a bewildering array of possible concrete distributive justice expectations.

The notion that distributive justice conceptions vary greatly across institutions received support in a Norwegian study by Ryghaug (1998). She analyzed distributive justice conceptions in concrete settings such as child care, hospitals, and job agencies, and found great variation across institutions and individuals. The same individuals tended to apply rather different distributive conceptions in different institutional settings. Similarly, Tyler et al. (1997:56) summarized previous research on the matter by noting, "principles of distributive justice are situationally based. People do not simply apply general principles of justice to all settings. Instead, they have situational frameworks that indicate that different principles of justice matter in different settings."

In short, citizens' views on what they have a right to expect in welfare state contacts are heterogeneous and complex. Therefore, the nature and origins of distributive justice expectations merit separate in-depth studies. Our concern, however, is not to investigate distributive justice expectations as such. Rather, our focus is on *the attitudinal effects* of variations in perceived experienced distributive justice. We investigate if those who personally experience distributive injustice also display lower levels of support for the political system, for public welfare state products, and for leftist ideology.

What would be the rationale for such patterns? One possibility is that people simply put a high moral value on distributive fairness (however defined by different individuals in different situations). Distributive justice is then an important moral currency in which "distributive justice man" assesses collective institutions. If so, he may develop negative attitudes toward public institutions that are perceived to undermine such fairness.

More rational lines of thought are also conceivable. Rothstein (1998, 2001) argues that the welfare state should not just be considered a redistributor of transfers and services; it is also a creator of various *public goods*. The defining feature of public goods is that everyone can enjoy them, regardless of whether they have contributed to their production. This typically stops such goods from being offered on profit-driven markets. Examples of public goods created by welfare state institutions range from the reduction of transaction and surveillance costs in otherwise inefficient insurance markets to the reduction of crime and social unrest. As Barr (1992:754) explains, "a welfare state is justified not simply by redistributive aims one may (or may not) have, but because it does things which private markets for technical reasons would either do inefficiently, or would not do at all."[17] According to this account, support for and development of welfare state institutions is not just driven by the usual explanations such as ideology or interests. As Levi (1993, 1997) and Rothstein (1998, 2001) argue, support is also contingent on the extent to which it actually manages to produce the public goods it promises.[18]

A prerequisite for the ability of a welfare state to create public goods is reasonably that services and transfers end up where they should. Therefore, people who experience distributive injustice in welfare state contacts may infer that the welfare state has problems. As a result, their feelings about large-scale government intervention and public arrangements may become hostile. Some may even come to think that the family or nonprofit organizations are better equipped to create the public goods in question. A parallel line of thought may reduce political trust. Experiences of distributive injustice are then taken as a sign that politicians and the political system are not performing well in controlling and steering the public services they are ultimately responsible for.

Previous empirical research has identified several factors that affect people's propensity to support shared institutions supplying public goods.[19] Consistent with the arguments above, one such factor is whether citizens perceive that institutions manage distributive justice. Building on his own and others' results within the field of social psychology, Wilke (1991) argued that distributive justice matters for cooperation and compliance in a great variety of different "social dilemmas" involving the production of public goods. Individuals' willingness to pay for, comply with, or otherwise support a common institution or resource tends to drop if it is not perceived to distribute its products fairly.

As for welfare state services, Eek (1999) analyzed the impact of distributive justice perceptions on Swedes' willingness to pay for public child care.[20] Drawing on both experiments and survey data, he found that a perceived discrepancy between personal distributive justice ideals and the actual perceived distribution of child care services, reduced willingness to support public child care.

A small number of studies have used broader political orientations as dependent variables. Tyler, Rasinski, and McGraw (1985:716) found that evaluations of Ronald Reagan were positively associated with perceptions of distributive justice. Those approving of the way benefits were distributed also tended to endorse the former Hollywood star. In contrast, such an effect was not apparent when "trust in government" constituted the dependent variable. However, drawing on American and Norwegian evidence, Miller and Listhaug (1999) concluded that distributive justice perceptions indeed affect political trust. This was true both for generalized "sociotropic" judgments of distributive justice and for personally experienced distributive justice.

Previous findings thus indicate that our hypotheses are not implausible. But more research is needed. Not even in social psychology—where empirical distributive justice research is most developed—have there been many studies on the effects of distributive justice perceptions on political attitudes (Eek 1999:28). Therefore, as noted by Miller and Listhaug (1999:213), further political science research is needed. Heeding their call, chapter 8 investigates whether social psychological findings related to more narrow and well-defined "social dilemmas" can be generalized to the broader political orientations at focus here. More precisely, we investigate whether people who have personally experienced distributive injustice display lower levels of political trust and lower levels of support for the welfare state and leftist ideology, compared to people who are personally content in this respect.

When it comes to effects on political ideology, chapter 8 will also discuss an alternative hypothesis. As several scholars have pointed out, it is not self-evident what ideological conclusions people should draw from negative distributive justice–related experiences. As noted above, social–psychology findings on social dilemmas suggest that distributive injustice generally results in weakened support for the common institutions that are supposed to resolve social dilemmas. However, exactly the opposite is also logically possible: that distributive injustice actually strengthens people's willingness to accept public spending and more leftist state intervention in order to come to terms with the problems. Moreover, this opposite effect could be especially common among people who already display a good amount of support for the welfare state. Among such people, the natural reaction to deficiencies such as distributive injustice may be an even greater willingness to protect and support welfare state arrangements (for similar points, see Kaase and Newton 1995; Huseby 1995; Pettersen 1995; Svallfors 2001; Johansson, Nilsson, and Strömberg 2001).

This alternative hypothesis poses a real threat to the empirical analysis. The problem is not just that the overall sign of the effect could be the opposite of what would be predicted by social psychology research on issues of social justice. The problem is also that the impact of experienced distributive justice could have a different sign depending on what ideological leanings a person had before experiences occurred. And if this is true, a zero overall effect could hide a great impact that has different signs in different subgroups.

In due time we will discuss the viability of these various possibilities. However, this is best done in the light of the actual empirical findings. And because the stage is not yet set for such a discussion, we postpone it to the end of chapter 8.

Procedural Justice

While the self-interest and distributive justice perspectives have readily apparent differences, they share the assumption that individuals are outcome-oriented. People are assumed to respond to personal experiences on the basis of end results. The self-interest perspective claims that people react to effects of outcomes on short-term material well-being. According to the distributive justice perspective citizens are sensitive to how fair outcomes are. In both cases, individuals evaluate and react politically to experiences on the basis of outcomes and results. As Lind and Tyler (1988:1) explain, "In social psychology, as in the behavioral and the social sciences more generally, people have often been viewed as evaluating social experiences, relationships, and institutions on the basis of the outcomes they receive. Theorists have differed in precisely how they think outcomes are linked to evaluations, but a general focus on outcomes characterizes some of the most widely accepted explanations of social behavior.[...] they all assume that people judge their [...] experiences in terms of the outcomes they receive and that attitudes and behavior can be explained by these outcome-based judgments."

But welfare state experiences may involve more than receiving and evaluating outcomes and results. They also involve an *interaction process* between citizen and institution. For example, people who receive social assistance have had face-to-face contact with a public employee before receiving benefits. Users of public libraries pay visits to a public building before borrowing books. Even Swedes receiving the universal child allowance—sent out automatically to mothers with children—experience some interaction with the public sector before the actual outcome is delivered: I am thinking of things like receiving information about child allowance, or even *waiting* for the child allowance to be sent out. Again, the common denominator is that these experiences occur during an interaction process leading up to an outcome. As we shall see, a frequent by-product of such processes is politically relevant information that might influence political orientations. Because of their focus on outcomes, however, neither the self-interest perspective nor the distributive justice perspective allows for the discovery of such effects.

Luckily, *the procedural justice perspective* directs our attention toward these processes (Thibaut and Walker 1975). This perspective assumes that citizens attach an independent value to procedural fairness in their dealings with the public sector. People assess their experiences by comparing the actually experienced interaction process with a normative expectation as to what constitutes a fair procedure in a given welfare state situation. As in the case of distributive justice, the nature and origins of procedural expectations are probably heterogeneous and complex. However, what we are interested in here is the impact of perceived procedural justice and injustice on political orientations.

A fair procedure is not the same thing as a fair outcome. It is perfectly possible to get a fair final "result," at the same time as the process that produced it was deeply unsatisfactory. Lind and Tyler (1988) exemplify this conceptual point by telling the story of a woman in Chicago who was charged with a minor traffic offence. The benevolent judge considered showing up in court and losing a day's work as a cruel enough penalty. He dismissed the case without hearing the woman. This meant that the woman, who was convinced of her own innocence, was not given the possibility to show photographs she had brought with her. In her mind they proved that a road sign had not been visible: "After her case was dismissed (a victory!) she was angry and expressed considerable dissatisfaction with the court (as well as making several unflattering remarks about the judge). Outcome-based models might find the woman's dissatisfaction difficult to explain, but process-based models would have little trouble in accounting for her reaction: the woman felt angry because the outcome she received was not arrived at using a procedure that met her standards" (Lind and Tyler 1988:2).

Previous research shows that perceived procedural justice is an important ingredient in individuals' evaluations of a wide range of situations (for an overview, see Tyler et al. 1997:chapter 4). These situations range from court experiences to work-life settings to interpersonal relations. People who perceive procedural aspects of allocation processes as fair are more inclined to express satisfaction, accept decisions, and comply with rules and restrictions. These effects are regarded as relatively independent of personal material gain and perceptions of distributive justice. Procedural justice perceptions thus influence attitudes even among people who receive comparable outcomes from a process, and who make similar distributive justice judgments of those outcomes.

A small number of studies have investigated how political attitudes are affected by perceptions of procedural justice in experiences with public institutions. For example, Tyler, Casper, and Fisher (1989) interviewed a sample of prisoners before and after their verdict. The authors found that even when controlling for attitudes toward government before the process, judgments as to whether the judicial process was fair strongly influenced attitudes toward government after the process. Notably, the severity of the sentence (in other words the outcome) had no impact on post-verdict assessments of authorities, when controlling for perceived procedural justice. The authors concluded, "the crucial feature from the citizen's perspective is not simply the distribution of burdens or benefits. Instead the political impact of the experiences we studied was driven by judgments of procedural fairness. We observed these strong procedural effects in one of the most threatening encounters that citizens can have with their government" (Tyler, Casper, and Fisher 1989:645). Similarly, in their pioneer study of "bureaucratic encounters," Katz et al. (1975:chapter 4) discovered that positive perceptions of procedures tended to generate positive generalized attitudes toward government and the political system. Finally, Tyler, Rasinski, and McGraw (1985) and Miller and Listhaug (1999) compared the effects of self-interest, distributive justice, and procedural justice perceptions respectively. Using political trust as the dependent variable, regression analyses suggested that procedures have stronger positive effects than either personal self-interest or distributive justice perceptions.

Overall, there seems to be some empirical merit to the claim that procedural fairness in contacts with public institutions affects political attitudes, controlling for outcome-based variables. However, we still know more about outcome-related factors (especially self-interest), compared to procedural effects. In particular, we know surprisingly little about whether procedural justice perceptions of personal welfare state experiences on political orientations can be generalized to other settings than the United States.

Voice Opportunities as Procedural Justice

What aspects of procedures are important? Previous research has highlighted a rather broad spectrum of possible variables. These include the efficiency and speed with which people get service outcomes (Wilke 1991), whether people are treated with dignity and respect (Rothstein 1998; Lane 1986), and whether there is consistency and predictability in procedures across time and people (Barrett-Howard and Tyler 1986).[21]

We will not analyze all possible aspects of procedural justice. Instead, we focus on the one that has probably received the most attention in academic as well as nonacademic welfare state discourse. Let us refer to this variable as *experienced voice opportunities*. The basic idea is that procedures will be regarded as more fair if people feel that they can exercise influence and communicate their views to public employees during the interaction process leading up to welfare state outcomes.

The concept of experienced voice opportunities has two intellectual sources. The first one can be traced back to Thibaut's and Walker's (1975) work on procedural justice in legal systems. One of their conclusions was that legal trials are perceived as more fair if they give disputants a greater amount of control over the presentation of information and evidence in the process. The more citizens control the facts and evidence that are put forward, the higher the amount of perceived procedural fairness. Further research in social psychology has largely confirmed that such voice opportunities constitute a crucial procedural aspect for citizens in a great variety of situations (ranging from court procedures to negotiating one's salary in employment settings). In addition, it has been shown that positive procedural justice judgments contribute to the legitimacy of the institutions and authorities in question even among people who receive comparable outcomes and who make similar distributive judgments of those outcomes, in other words controlling for factors related to self-interest and distributive justice (Lind, Kanfer, and Early 1990; van den Bos, Wilke, and Lind 1998).

Recent discussions on the future of the welfare state constitute the second intellectual origin. Such discussions often begin with alleged cognitive and value-oriented changes in developed nations. Increasing educational levels are said to produce greater cognitive capacities, political efficacy, and administrative self-confidence (Petersson, Westholm, and Blomberg 1989). Individualist or even "postmaterialist" values are becoming more widespread (Inglehart 1990). These trends are believed to have consequences for what citizens want out of their welfare state contacts. It is argued that knowledgeable, self-confident, and individualistic citizens will no longer be content with being passive service recipients. They also want to make their voices and opinions heard in the process. At the same time, several studies have shown that many citizens feel they have rather poor opportunities to influence experienced public service institutions, as well as the personal life situation (Petersson, Westholm, and Blomberg 1989; Petersson et al. 1998).

Arguments like these have had practical repercussions on the relations between citizens and the welfare state (see Hoff 1993; Sørensen 1997; Lindbom 1995). One increasingly popular reform is that users of an institution (a school, a day care center, or a home for the elderly) are given the opportunity to collectively elect representatives to a user board. This board is given real decision-making power, or in some cases an advisory function, in various local matters that are of varying importance to users (see Sørensen 1997; Goul Andersen, Torpe, and Andersen 2000; Jarl 2001). Such institutional arrangements for collective influence have been widely implemented in Denmark and are under way in for instance the Swedish school system.

In addition to these increasingly popular collective resources for voice, there is a trend in public services in the direction of market-like organizational solutions, which among other things are designed to promote exit-options and freedom-of-choice for citizens in their individual service contacts. These organizational solutions are inspired by the so-called "new public management," and include competition among different providers of comparable services, contracts between the political "demand side" and service providers, as well as publicly financed and regulated "vouchers" that follow citizens in their choices of service providers (see Blomqvist and Rothstein 2000). Such organizational solutions are thought to promote voice opportunities because the market-like competition forces service providers to be more responsive to the preferences of citizens who personally experience the services in question.

The Impact of Experienced Voice Opportunities

Both social psychological research on procedural justice as well as the institutional welfare state development raise questions about the actual effects of experienced voice opportunities. Here, the theoretical literature has identified a rather large number of potential effects.[22] One category of alleged consequences has to do with the quality of public services; quality is often believed to improve if institutions take into account the opinions and points of view of those who directly experience a service. According to this argument, patients, parents of schoolchildren, users of libraries, and so on, have wishes and knowledge that are useful if welfare institutions are to deliver appropriate services.

Another possible effect is found in arguments used to buttress the case for improved collective voice opportunities. Inspired by participatory and deliberative democratic ideals (see Pateman 1970; Barber 1984; Elster 1998), proponents of collective voice opportunities typically claim that such opportunities have positive democratic effects on citizens. For example, service users who participate in discussions and meetings with politicians, employees, and other users are believed to develop an increased understanding for the constraints and dilemmas of the political process. Also, their general interest and engagement in politics is thought to be boosted, especially when user boards are given real decision-making power in important local issues.

How realistic are such predictions? The best answer is that we do not really know. As Jarl (2001) and others have emphasized, there is a dire need for further research. A smaller number of studies have investigated the impact of participation in collective and institutionalized user influence resources such as user boards (see Duit and Möller 1997; Kristensen 1998; Goul Andersen and Hoff 2001). In an overview of these and other studies, Jarl (2001:134–43) notes that while such participation may stimulate political knowledge and engagement, the uncovered effects so far appear confined to the institution in question. They have rarely been shown to "spill over" to general political engagement and knowledge.

Further, from the perspective of this study, it is especially interesting to note that experienced voice opportunities are often believed to affect general political attitudes such as political trust and ideology (see Möller 1996; Rothstein 1998; Dahlberg and Vedung 2001). Attitudes toward both the current political system as well as toward the welfare state are believed to grow more positive if people feel that they can directly exercise influence during their interaction with system outputs and services. In fact, this was a main reason that the Swedish Social Democratic government initiated the development toward increased user influence in the early 1980s (Strandberg 1998:327–29). Indeed, "By giving users improved opportunities to influence the public services one uses personally, the Social Democrats hoped to avoid that citizens seek private alternatives" (Jarl 2001:61).[23] Similar concerns have been raised about a negative impact of poor voice opportunities on political trust. There is a widespread worry that citizens in large welfare states end up in "the black hole of democracy" (Rothstein 1998). In this dark place, people depend greatly on public service and welfare production for everyday life to function. At the same time, there is too little opportunity to influence those services. The power to determine both one's own life project, and to influence public policies is limited. Such limited opportunities are often believed to foster negative attitudes toward the democratic system as it functions in practice.

The underlying assumption here is that citizens regard voice opportunities as an important procedural value during contacts with welfare state services. People do not just want to be passive recipients of satisfactory public services; they also want to "have a voice." Moreover, to the extent that this assumption is correct, it becomes conceivable that good experienced voice opportunities increase both the popularity of a large welfare state as well as the legitimacy of the existing democratic process. Given that people value voice, the legitimacy of both welfare state arrangements and democratic institutions may increase when citizens notice that the system and its employees are interested in and responsive to people's opinions. In contrast, those who experience a public sector that does not seem to pay attention to citizens' views may take this as a sign that welfare state institutions and the political system are not performing its democratic tasks very well. This may result in negative attitudes toward the welfare state, and toward the political system and its politicians.

These hypotheses are not terribly well researched either. However, they have indeed received some empirical support when it comes to effects on political trust. Möller (1996) provided qualitative interview evidence of a link between experienced voice opportunities and broader political trust: people who perceived good opportunities to exercise influence in their contacts with child care and elder care tended to use this as arguments in their reasoning about the responsiveness of the political system at large. Using Swedish survey data from the end of the 1980s, Assarson (1995) came to similar conclusions.

Chapter 9 discusses the concept of experienced voice opportunities further and continues the empirical research program on the link between experienced voice opportunities and political orientations. In doing this, chapter 9 tries to make a contribution to both the more general research on procedural justice, as well as to the scholarly debate on voice opportunities and the future organizational look of the welfare state.[24]

Social Justice as Self-Interest in Disguise
(or is Social Justice Really Social?)

So far I have discussed the three theoretical perspectives one by one. Little has been said about their interrelations. This conveys the impression that self-interest, distributive justice, and procedural justice have little to do with each other beyond providing potential explanations of political attitudes. To relax this exaggeration, I close the chapter by considering the relations between variables representing the three perspectives.

The notion of three unrelated families of independent variables is rooted in the two social justice perspectives. They build on the assumption that people put great value on experiencing social justice, as well as on the assumption that people tend to develop expectations as to what outcomes and procedures people rightly deserve in a given welfare state situation. Assessments of experienced justice reflect independent and intellectually honest comparisons between normative expectations and actual experiences. These independent and intellectually honest comparisons are not biased by each other or by self-interest concerns.

If this is correct, we have no reason to expect strong correlations between variables representing the three different perspectives. There is for instance no reason that those satisfied with the distributive aspect of experiences should also be satisfied with procedures. By the same token there is no reason why those whose material well-being is greatly improved by the welfare state should perceive procedures and distribution more favorably than others. Self-interest, distributive justice, and procedural justice simply constitute independent dimensions of welfare state experiences.

In particular the self-interest perspective challenges these ideas. Self-interested citizens are not believed to hold meaningful normative expectations that they subsequently compare with actual experiences in an intellectually honest and independent way. Rather, judgments of experienced social justice reflect strongly the degree to which experiences have actually served short-term material self-interest. As Tyler (1990:173) puts it, "Economic analysts have suggested that ethical judgments are no more than socially appropriate justifications for evaluations and behavior actually governed by concerns of self-interest. If this is true, then empirical research will not be able to separate concerns about justice from judgments of personal gain and loss. If fairness judgments are only rationalizations for judgments based on outcome favorability, we should be able to predict individuals' fairness judgments by knowing whether or not they benefited from the outcome."

According to this account, it is more socially acceptable for self-interested citizens to assess welfare state institutions using arguments of social justice than arguments relating to one's own economic interests. Because people are essentially driven by self-interest, and because they usually seek a politically and socially correct disguise for that interest, citizens who gain a lot from the welfare state in general or from a particular institution will typically tell you they have experienced distributive and procedural justice. Conversely, people who gain less for themselves will tend to judge justice aspects of experiences unfavorably, thus rationalizing their poor outcomes and resulting dissatisfaction. Social judgments are not particularly social at all, but rather function as a disguise for strictly personal interests.

In contrast to theories of social justice, then, the self-interest perspective predicts that levels of personal economic gain from public services strongly predict perceptions of experienced justice. Therefore, in addition to investigating attitudinal effects of experiences, we must consider empirically the internal relations between variables representing the three theoretical perspectives. To what extent are social justice judgments nothing but self-interest variables in disguise? This question is answered particularly throughout chapters 8 and 9.

CHAPTER THREE

The Institutional Interface

Up until now we have thought about personal welfare state experiences in an individualist fashion. We have made a case for why personal welfare state experiences may have greater attitudinal effects than personal economic experiences. Moreover, individual welfare state experiences were conceptualized in terms of self-interest, distributive justice, and voice opportunities. Hypotheses were developed as to how such experiences may affect political trust and ideology.

In this chapter, however, we begin to think about the collective structures behind individuals' experiences. More to the point, we consider institutional explanations for differences in experiences, and in their political effects. We note that different people in the same country experience radically different kinds of welfare state institutions. The hunch to be developed is that some types of institutions are better than others at generating positive experiences and, in turn, support for the welfare state and the political system.

How does this task fit into the greater purpose of the study? Consider figure 1.1—our causal playing field. One feature of this model is that personal experiences and "perceptions" of the same experiences are conceptually distinct: the experience effect is the result of a process where "actual" experiences give rise to perceptions of experiences, perceptions from which some political conclusion is drawn (either directly or through "sociotropic" generalization). Thus, an implication of the model is that we should find empirical correlations between actual personal experiences on the one hand, and experience perceptions and political orientations on the other.

Unfortunately, testing such implications is difficult: it presupposes external observations of actual personal experiences that are independent of the individual's own perceptions. Such independent information could be used to create measures of actual experiences in terms of self-interest ("how much did experiences contribute to material well-being"), distributive justice ("did the person actually get the service she deserved?"), and voice ("did someone actually listen to her views?"). Unfortunately, such information is extremely difficult and expensive to collect for analyses of survey data comprising thousands of respondents.[1] It is easier to measure perceptions of experiences as obtained through subjective survey questions to respondents themselves.

For at least two reasons, however, it is not very satisfying just to consider subjective perceptions of experiences. First, from a substantive point of view, such measures would only offer tests of a rather amputated version of the model represented in figure 1.1. The research problem covers the full causal chain specified in this model, and we therefore want information about whether actual experiences affect political orientations, not just about the effects of subjective perceptions. Second, from a methodological point of view, it is easy to become suspicious of survey measures of personal experience perceptions. As will be discussed at greater length in chapter 5, one risk is that subjective accounts of experiences are mainly projections of already existing political predispositions, rather than true reflections of actually experienced events. Of course, this suspicion becomes somewhat less problematic if it can be verified that subjective perceptions do correlate with measures of actual experiences.

This study attempts to deal with "actual" personal experiences in two ways. First, chapter 7 will develop measures of both the "objective" extent to which welfare state arrangements satisfy a respondent's self-interest, as well as subjective perceptions of interests. The theory behind the second attempt is outlined in this chapter. By conceptualizing differences in which types of welfare state institutions people have actually experienced, the following discussion develops a framework for thinking about and measuring objective differences in actual personal experiences, and not just perceptions thereof.

The New Institutionalism in Political Science

The theory in this chapter is inspired by "the new institutionalism" in political science. This research program suspects that the organization of various political institutions systematically structures individuals' political preferences and behavior (see March and Olsen 1984, 1989; Skocpol 1994; Steinmo, Thelen, and Longstreth 1992; Ostrom 1995; Rothstein 1996; Immergut 1998; Thelen 1999; Peters 1999; Rothstein and Steinmo 2002). March and Olsen (1984:734) explained the point of departure like this: "a new institutionalism has appeared in political science [...] The resurgence of concern with institutions is a cumulative consequence of the modern transformation of social institutions and persistent commentary from observers of them. Social, political, and economic institutions have become larger, considerably more complex and resourceful, and [...] more important to collective life."

The research agenda of the new institutionalism is broad and heterogeneous. It theorizes the nature, the causes, and the political effects of a great variety of institutions. These institutions involve for example, party systems, government structure, electoral systems, court systems, and so on (see

Rothstein 1996; Peters 1999).[2] From our perspective, it is interesting to note that several scholars see welfare state institutions as causal factors influencing orientations toward welfare state arrangements and the political system. Such arrangements, it is argued, are not just endogenous results of political preferences and interests among the population. They are also seen as independent variables in their own right, with a potential capacity to exercise a reciprocal influence on citizens' preferences. In Cox's (1998:2) formulation, "the attention of scholars has shifted. Until the 1980s, researchers sought to define and explain the development of the welfare state. In the current period, scholars take it as a given that the welfare state exists and seek to discover what effects it has [...] the welfare state was once the dependent variable, and now it is employed as the independent variable."

The literature abounds with variants of this basic idea. Rothstein (1998:135) argues that "Opinions, interests, values, ideology [...] all influence institutions and policy. But policies and institutions also influence opinions, etc." Welfare state arrangements are said to "generate their own conceptions of justice, morality, and distribution"[3] (Svallfors 1996:18), and to affect "the way individuals define what is rational and what their preferences should be" (Jacobs and Shapiro 1994:13; see also Korpi 1980; Skocpol 1994; Pierson 1994).

These scholars identify an interesting direction for public opinion research. However, most claims in this vein are too general to contain falsifiable propositions, and we need to shed more theoretical and empirical light on the problem. It is no coincidence that statements like the ones above almost always lack references to empirical studies. We have surprisingly little empirical knowledge about *which* welfare state institutions have *which* political effects on citizens.

For sure, there is no shortage of theorizing. Typically, the idea that welfare state institutions affect public opinion comes in either of two versions. First, it has long been argued that the sheer size and generosity of welfare state institutions influence how people in different social groups perceive their political interests. For instance, according to a common hypothesis, welfare states that extend services to the well-off middle classes build self-interested support for themselves also among these groups (see Dunleavy 1979; Taylor-Gooby 1986; Zetterberg 1985; Esping-Andersen 1990; Baldwin 1990; Pierson 1994; Svensson 1994). Essentially, this hypothesis is a macro version of the self-interest perspective discussed in chapter 2.

Second, it has been suggested that not only size, but also design, matters (see Schneider and Ingram 1997; Rothstein 1998; Soss 1999). Here, welfare state design refers to the structure of the direct encounter between citizens and welfare state institutions. From this perspective, the focus is not so much on what people eventually get from an institution. Rather, similar to the social justice perspectives, the emphasis is on institutional characteristics that affect what people see, hear, and feel when experiencing institutions. Different ways of structuring the encounter between the individual and the organization teach people different lessons about the welfare state

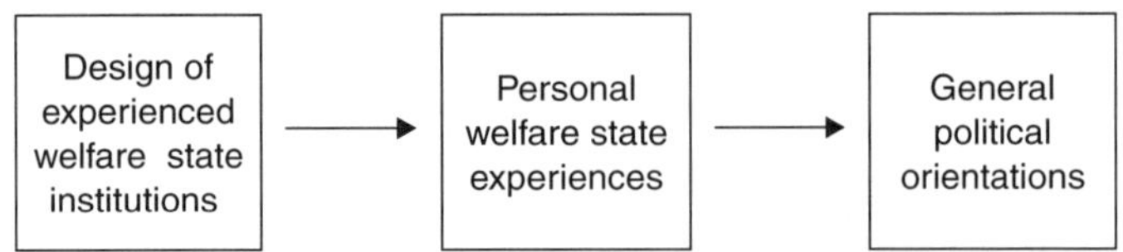

Figure 3.1 Welfare state design affects experiences, experiences affect orientations

and the political system. It has been suggested that such differences in "the institutional interfaces" seen by citizens during experiences can give rise to systematic differences in experiences and, in turn, political attitudes. In this spirit, Rothstein (1998:222) argues that in designing welfare state institutions "we also in large part determine the normative attitudes citizens hold about welfare policy." Similarly, Schneider and Ingram (1997:200) contend that welfare state design "is an important independent variable that shapes citizens' orientations."

The idea that welfare state design affects public opinion is founded on two important assumptions, displayed in figure 3.1. First, welfare state design is believed to affect citizens' personal experiences with welfare state institutions. Second, citizens are believed to generalize their personal experiences when forming broader political orientations (see Soss 1999). Very specific experienced facts thus "spill over" into very general political orientations.

The three boxes and two arrows in figure 3.1 constitute five intriguing theoretical problems to be addressed before empirical analysis of the problem can begin. We have the three questions of how to conceptualize institutions, experiences, and orientations respectively. Also, we are in need of testable hypotheses representing the two causal arrows.

Fortunately, chapter 2 has already conceptualized experiences, and chapter 4 will explain why political trust and ideology constitute our dependent variables. The work to be done in this chapter is to explain what welfare state design means in this study, and to present hypotheses about how experiences with different types of institutions may produce different effects on political orientations. Chapter 10 undertakes empirical tests of these hypotheses. In a nutshell, the question is whether the extent to which institutional interfaces *empower* citizens matters for how citizens' perceive experiences, and in turn for political trust and ideology.

Conceptualizing Institutions

There is still a discrepancy between the frequency with which neo-institutionalist arguments about popular preferences have been put forward, and the amount of individual-level evidence there is to support them (see Svallfors 1996; Edlund 1999b). In fact, the discussion has only recently begun to influence empirical public opinion research. Let us, however, take a look at some of the empirical studies that *do* exist. In particular, we are interested in how these studies have conceptualized differences across welfare state institutions.

Most studies to date have drawn on Gøsta Esping-Andersen's (1990) welfare state regime typology. Building on Titmuss (1974), Esping-Andersen argued that the nature and development of welfare states fall into three qualitatively distinct categories, or "worlds of welfare."[4] In brief, he discerned one "liberal" welfare state regime where the capitalist market is the main provider of welfare for most citizens. Public welfare consists of not particularly generous flat-rate benefits, which are distributed on the basis of economic means-testing, and cater largely to the poor or otherwise needy segments of society. Archetypal countries in the liberal world of welfare are for instance the United States and Australia. A second welfare state regime category is the "conservative" one, containing Germany, France, and various southern European countries. Here, benefits are both more encompassing and generous than in the liberal regime. However, benefits are typically related to past income, and are often differentiated according to occupational affiliation. Moreover, conservative welfare state arrangements encourage the traditional role of the family as welfare providers; a principle of "subsidiarity" prescribes that the public sector intervene mainly where the family can no longer adequately care for its members. The third regime type is labeled "social democratic." Here, most public benefits are both generous and universal in that they are connected to citizenship, rather than to occupational status as in the conservative regime, or means-tested as in the liberal regime. Still, most benefits are income-related. As Esping-Andersen (1990:28) explains, "all strata are incorporated under one universal insurance system, yet benefits are graduated according to accustomed earnings." Finally, social democratic welfare state arrangements do not try to promote the traditional social role of the family, but rather seek to develop universal services such as child care and elder care. The Scandinavian countries together with the Netherlands are typically seen as social democratic welfare states.

A series of comparative studies have tested the predictions that the regime framework makes about cross-country differences in political attitudes and conflict patterns. For instance, it has been investigated whether citizens in liberal welfare states display more ideological resistance to public welfare, and whether people in "social democratic" regimes endorse such policies. A second hypothesis derived from the regime framework is that the effect of social class on welfare state support is stronger in liberal welfare regimes and weaker in social democratic regimes. The causal mechanism would be that in social democratic regimes public services are heavily used also by the middle classes. Where differences in the degree of public service usage is less correlated with traditional social structure, the impact of social structure on welfare state support might be diluted (Dunleavy 1979; Esping-Andersen 1990).

Recent empirical findings have not been entirely kind to these hypotheses (Papadakis and Bean 1993; Svallfors 1993, 1997; Papadakis 1993; Bean and Papadakis 1998; Lapinski et al. 1998; Edlund 1999a,b). It seems to be a stable result that the effect of social class does not vary much across welfare regimes. When it comes to the overall level of welfare state support, there is more uncertainty. Bean and Papadakis (1993, 1998) and Svallfors (1993) analyzed cross-national variations and found only weak support for the prediction that welfare support is lower in liberal regimes. On the other hand, Svallfors (1997) and Edlund (1999b) discerned cross-country differences consistent with the regime framework. Svallfors (1997), however, still concluded that the differences in the strength of class effects predicted by the regime framework were not to be found.

The status of the regime framework in the conceptual toolbox of opinion research will be decided by future findings. However, several scholars have suspected that this conceptualization is not ideal for uncovering institutional impact on opinion. Bean and Papadakis (1998:231) argue, "the [...] approach represents a fairly blunt instrument for trying to identify the influence of politics on opinion." Similarly, Lapinski et al. (1998:21) contend that "Esping-Andersen and others have constructed elaborate theories of welfare state development. Our analysis raises questions about the microfoundations of these theories. What are needed are institutional and political analyses [...] anchored in accurate models of public perceptions, attitudes and behavior."

Shifting the Attention toward Individuals' Experiences of Welfare State Design

From the viewpoint of individual-level opinion formation, there are at least two problems with the regime framework. First, this otherwise useful typology is a macro concept whose natural unit of analysis is the state. In other words, the typology hovers quite far above the experiential and informational factors that influence individuals politically. As a consequence of this conceptual characteristic, many studies have used comparative datasets from the World Values Studies or the International Social Survey Program. In addition to its many strengths, this strategy involves measuring crucial factors such as "interaction with welfare institutions" with rough proxy variables such as whether or not respondents live in a social democratic, conservative, or liberal welfare state.

Second, the regime framework focuses on welfare state size. People are thought to be affected by welfare state relations through group- or self-interest. Other types of experienced information such as perceived distributive and procedural justice are largely absent as causal factors. The focus on welfare state size and interests has left other hypotheses about experience effects of welfare relatively neglected. Particularly variations in the institutional interfaces that citizens see during processes leading up to welfare outcomes are underconceptualized.

In contrast to much previous research, this study investigates how different welfare state designs *within one country* structure individuals' experiences, and which effects these experiences have on broader political orientations. Hence, we do not bundle diverse micro-level experiences together into single macro-level welfare regimes. Also, rather than probing mainly interests and outcomes, it offers an analysis of institutional differences as to how contacts between citizens and the state are designed.

Empirically, chapter 10 will utilize a sample drawn from the Swedish population. Interestingly, although all respondents obviously live in the same welfare regime, there is nevertheless great variation within this regime as to the number and nature of individually experienced welfare state institutions. A central argument is that if such within-regime institutional variation is conceptualized and measured, we gain important insights about the impact of welfare state design on opinion formation. A similar approach was used by Soss (1999) who compared Americans with experiences of the AFDC (Aid to Families with Dependent Children) and the SSDI (Social Security Disability Insurance) respectively. Drawing on both in-depth interviews and the American National Election Studies, Soss found that AFDC experiences had negative effects on electoral participation and beliefs about the responsiveness of government whereas SSDI experiences did not. This difference could not be attributed to socioeconomic differences that existed prior to welfare interaction. Rather, the differences were attributed to the AFDC having more power over its clients than the SSDI, and to the AFDC being worse at considering clients' views and preferences. By giving citizens the feeling of being underdogs in relation to the state, AFDC experiences generated negative attitudes toward public institutions and the political system. Very similar conclusions were reached by Möller (1996) in his in-depth interview study of Swedes with experiences from either child care or elder care.

I extend previous studies using the described strategy by simultaneously considering a large number of institutions (rather than just two), and by using survey data (rather than mainly in-depth interviews). Before that, however, I will outline the crucial concept to be used in formulating hypotheses about which institutional designs have which effects on political orientations.

The Concept of Institutionalized Citizen Empowerment

The concept of *institutionalized citizen empowerment* is a tool for thinking about differences in how the institutional interface between citizen and organization is structured. The concept emphasizes welfare state design rather than welfare state size and generosity of outcomes. Although the concept can be traced back in the literature some 30 years (see Katz and Danet 1973; Katz et al. 1975; Lipsky 1980; Goodsell 1981, 1983; Petersson, Westholm, and Blomberg 1989; Nilsson 1996a; Schneider and Ingram 1997; Sørensen 1997, 1998; Goul Andersen, Torpe, and Andersen 2000; Peters and Pierre 2000), it has only recently inspired empirical research into the link between welfare design and political preferences (Hoff 1993; Möller 1996; Soss 1999). Outside of public opinion research, however, the concept of empowerment has been increasingly discussed. For instance, we noted in chapter 2 the worry that citizens in large welfare states can end up in "the black hole of democracy" (Rothstein 1998), and that this worry has resulted in various institutional changes in the direction of more user influence.

The concept of institutionalized citizen empowerment can be thought of in terms of a power balance, which can weigh over to either the citizen or the public institution. In abstract parlance, the citizen becomes more powerful (or "empowered") the more she can influence circumstances that the public agency or the citizen herself values. The citizen becomes less powerful, the greater control the agency has over circumstances that the agency or the citizen values (Hoff 1993:78–79).

An important assumption is that the degree of citizen empowerment is partly affected by how an encountered institution is designed and organized. To use the concept of empowerment in empirical analysis, we must thus identify institutional factors that in reality determine the power balance in the encounter between the citizen and the public agency. The abstract definition above gives few hints. Its wide and vague nature opens up an, in principle, endless list of relevant variables. Empirically, this study emphasizes the two most important institutional factors highlighted in the literature: (1) the presence/absence of bureaucratic discretion, and (2) the extent of realistic exit-options. The next section considers these two factors, after which I discuss additional institutional traits that are theoretically relevant.

Bureaucratic Discretion and Exit-Options

Bureaucratic discretion refers to the degree of decision-making power that public service institutions and their officials have in determining whether or not an individual shall be granted access to the services that the institution distributes (Lipsky 1980; Vinzant and Crothers 1998; Schierenbeck 2003).[5] In some public services the amount of discretion is low. A Swedish example is the child allowance, which is an installment that is automatically sent to all mothers with children between 0 and 16 years of age. Here, the bureaucratic allocation decision is reduced to an unambiguous registration of objective facts. Given the availability of appropriate official records, the decision is easy enough for computers to handle (Rothstein 1998). Other public schemes are allocated in accordance with less objective policy guidelines that are subject to interpretation. Potential beneficiaries have to make credible that they fulfill linguistically constructed entitlement conditions. Decision-making of this kind cannot be made by computers. On the contrary, it presupposes human interpretation and application of more or less ambiguous and vague rules to each individual case.

An important assumption—elaborated by Michael Lipsky (1980) in his studies of "street-level bureaucracies"—is that the citizen usually becomes less powerful the larger the discretionary power bureaucrats have. Conversely, citizens are empowered when discretionary power is decreased. Lipsky argued that street-level bureaucrats must often compensate the vagueness inherent in centrally decided allocation principles by developing further principles of an informal, subjective, and less explicit character. Such an informal praxis is often developed in the face of a considerable workload, and serves to make the difficult decisions manageable to solve without an unrealistic effort.

From the perspective of the citizen, the existence of informal rules and praxis means that there is always a risk that civil servants to some extent use "prejudice, stereotype, and ignorance as a basis for determination" (Lipsky 1980:69). Hence, the bureaucrat exercises great influence over something that is highly valued by the citizen: the service that she wants to access. Since services do not have the character of social rights, but rather that of negotiable and interpretable goods, it is more difficult for the citizen to "be tough" in the interaction with the agency. At the same time, bureaucrats have incentives to signal that the informal praxis around which their work is partly built is not open for discussion or influence. Discretion thus gives rise to an asymmetric power relation in which the citizen is well advised not to "rock the boat" with too much persistence.

In addition to discretion, exit-options are important power resources for citizens. The possibilities for people to turn their backs on a public agency in the case of discontent influences the degree of empowerment (Hirschman 1970). Exit-options come in two major versions. First, there may be one or several other organizations—private or public—offering a comparable service. Second, citizens may sometimes exit a public service without reentering another comparable service at all.

A theoretical assumption is that public agencies and their bureaucrats usually perceive an incentive to "keep its customers." For instance, librarians would not prefer it if people would use private bookstores instead of libraries. Public schools do not desire an exodus in the direction of private education. Thus, as exit-options improve, bureaucrats and public employees become more likely to listen to citizens' complaints, adjust to their preferences, treat them with respect, and so on. In sum, exit-options make the power balance lean over to the citizen.

In order for exit-options to have an influence on the degree of empowerment, an important requirement must be met: options must be realistic. While in principle it is true that citizens are almost always free to leave public services, they are often tied down by economic considerations. When it comes to services such as social assistance, unemployment benefits, and so on, there are rarely real exit-options. Even when they exist, emotional costs might make them unrealistic (as in the case of moving your child from a public kindergarten to a private alternative). To the extent that options are not realistic, and as long as bureaucrats are aware of it, options cannot be expected to increase the degree of empowerment.

Finally, one may add the requirement that exit-options must be potentially costly to the public agency. Lipsky (1980:55) points out that the demand for certain public services sometimes greatly exceeds the supply. In such instances, the fact that some citizens choose an exit-alternative might serve as a relief rather than as an incentive for responsiveness. Therefore, theoretically speaking, it is not obvious whether there is a positive net effect of larger exit-opportunities on the degree of empowerment. Empirically, however, several studies have yielded results that highlight the difference that exit-options make. For example, Möller (1996) concludes that citizens who encounter service institutions where there are real exit-opportunities seem to exercise more influence over their public agency. When exit-opportunities are low or nonexistent, influence decreases. Furthermore, Petersson et al. (1998) examined survey data over time and discovered that Swedish reforms designed to improve exit-options and freedom of choice in the areas of health care and primary education seem to have increased opportunities to affect services, as perceived by respondents.

Other Factors Affecting the Degree of Empowerment

Discretion and exit-options are not the only institutional aspects that contribute to the level of citizen empowerment (see Hoff 1993). For instance, as discussed in chapter 2, it has been increasingly debated whether public service institutions should be designed so that they allow opportunities to *directly influence* services. As previously mentioned, in Danish public schools parents have the right to elect a representative board with a significant amount of decision-making power in matters concerning the school (Sørensen 1998; Lindbom 1998; Goul Andersen, Torpe, and Andersen 2000; Jarl 2001). A somewhat different type of user influence has to do with the extent to which citizens' opinions are registered as an inherent part in policy evaluation of public services (see Dahlberg and Vedung 2001).

Moreover, the extent of citizen empowerment may be affected by the extent to which service entitlement and quality are "individually enforceable." To what extent do citizens have specified, detailed, and legally binding rights to a certain kind of service, in a certain kind of situation, within a certain time frame? Interestingly, the degree to which public service rights are individually enforceable varies substantially. For instance, Karlsson (2003) shows that British citizens have more specified rights in relation to the National Health Service through the so-called Patient's Charter, than do Swedes in contacts with their health care system.

A further institutional empowerment factor suggested in the literature is the extent to which citizens are isolated from each other in contacts with an institution (Lipsky 1980). In some public services citizens do not meet, see, communicate with, or otherwise encounter other people who interact with the agency. The middle-aged home-owner who experiences an unfriendly voice on the phone when trying to get through to the tax authorities cannot determine whether the unfriendliness is a general pattern or simply the result of a single public employee having a bad day. However, when the same home-owner—who desperately needs a book on brick-laying—has to wait forever for help in the public library, he has much better odds of discovering that he is not the only one in the same situation.

As stated more generally by Lipsky (1980:118), "Isolated clients are more likely to think of themselves as responsible for their situations. They are unlikely to see their condition as a reflection of social structure and their treatment as unacceptable." When viewed from this angle, increased citizen interaction means enhanced citizen power. To see or hear of other people experiencing the same problems as oneself makes individuals more inclined to regard problems as something that the agency—not the citizen—should solve. Citizens become more confident and persistent in their interaction with bureaucrats. Complaints become more common and intense. Hence, the agency is more likely to solve problems in manners consistent with citizens' preferences.

Yet another institutional empowerment factor is the extent to which institutions demonstrate power using physical and architectural symbols. For instance, Goodsell (1977) used direct observation to measure occurrences of for example symbols indicating responsiveness and service-mindedness, such as soft and comfortable waiting room furniture, name badges or plates giving the receptionist's name, decorative pictures or calendars, informative signs or instructions ("walk in," "apply here"), plants or flowers visible to visiting citizens, and so on. Conversely, Goodsell also registered symbols indicating authority, such as flags, counters with risers or barriers between citizens and employees, emblems, certificates, diplomas, and so on (see also Fernlund 1988).

Finally, while these additional factors are inherent parts of the theoretical concept that could enrich future empirical research on the issue, they cannot be explicitly considered in our particular empirical analysis. First, although discussions and experimentation concerning institutionalized voice opportunities and citizen charters are currently going on in Sweden (Karlsson 2003; Jarl 2001), they are at present too unusual to contribute empirically to this study. In contrast, the extent of citizen interaction, the use of citizen-oriented program evaluation, and the use of physical power symbols are institutional factors that offer a real-world variation that can already be exploited in empirical analysis. However, to measure these aspects, one would probably want to consider qualitative approaches that deal more intensely with a smaller number of citizens and institutions than is the case in this study. It is likely that these aspects vary substantially across different offices, hospitals, public schools, and so on. Direct observation and in-depth interviews are methods that seem better equipped than survey analysis to register such variation (see e.g., Goodsell 1977). Here, it should be kept in mind that most previous research on the effects of institutionalized empowerment has used qualitative approaches to deal with a small number of institutions, and one advantage of this study is that it simultaneously analyzes experiences with a large number of institutions among a large representative sample of citizens. However, the price to be paid is that we cannot consider all conceivable theoretical aspects built into the concept of citizen empowerment. Instead, our classification of institutions will be based on two major institutional factors highlighted in previous work—discretion and exit-options. These aspects are more manageable in the context of our research strategy because they give rise to a relatively clear-cut classification as to how much different institutional interfaces generally empower citizens. This is the task to which we now turn.

Classifying Institutions with Respect to the Degree of Empowerment

Ultimately, we are interested in making predictions about attitudinal effects of experiences with institutions with different levels of citizen empowerment. A step toward formulating such hypotheses is to classify real-world institutions according to how much their institutional designs empower citizens. Following Hoff (1993) and Möller (1996), the adopted approach involves coding different service institutions along an ordinal empowerment variable with three categories, as introduced in table 3.1. The categories are labeled *customer institutions, user institutions,* and *client institutions,* respectively.

In the left-hand column we find the customer institutions. The label is indicative of the fairly high amount of power and influence that citizens enjoy in their contacts with these public agencies. Customer institutions rarely make discretionary decisions as to whether one shall get service access. Moreover, experiences are structured by the fact that exit-options are frequent and realistic. Citizens can usually choose either some kind of private alternative, or do without the service altogether. In customer institutions, therefore, the power balance leans more to the citizens' side than otherwise.

It should be pointed out that Hoff (1993) and Möller (1996) use the word *consumer* to denote a high degree of empowerment.[6] I have chosen the term *customer* instead because I think it captures the market similarities better: All citizens who use a public service are—strictly speaking—consumers of that service, regardless of the characteristics of the institution in question.

Table 3.1　Swedish public service institutions categorized according to degree of institutionalized citizen empowerment

Customer institutions (higher degree of empowerment)	*User institutions (medium degree of empowerment)*	*Client institutions (lower degree of empowerment)*
Public transportation	Kindergartens	Elder care
Public sports facilities	Child health care	Social assistance
Public libraries	Local health care	Housing allowance
Public culture activities	Hospitals	Public transportation subsidies
Public leisure time activities		Public job agencies
Public dental care		Handicap care

The right-hand column contains client institutions. The term signals that citizens enjoy a low degree of empowerment in relation to the public institution. For instance, clients are usually dependent on a discretionary decision. Also, to the extent that exit-options exist, they are often less realistic or easily exploited in that they are associated with economic costs. In addition, there are often emotional and physical costs involved in exiting from these institutions: Elderly people, for instance, are in all likelihood fairly reluctant to move (see Möller 1996).

In the middle column, we find institutions that can be regarded as compromises between the customer and the client extremes. Consequently, a term that is relatively neutral—*user institutions*—has been chosen. The word bears with it little in the way of market connotations as does the word customer. This indicates that citizens cannot be regarded as free-to-leave autonomous actors. Neither does it conjure up the underdog picture of a client with little influence over what his representative does on his behalf. Typically, there are few or no alternatives to user institutions; exit-opportunities are scarce, thereby reducing the degree of institutionalized empowerment. Again, to the extent that exit-opportunities exist, there are emotional costs involved that reduce their effectiveness (most people would hesitate before sending their child to a different, perhaps private, kindergarten). As a counterweight to this, however, users are not in the hands of a street-level bureaucrat making ultimately subjective interpretations in order to reach a discretionary allocation decision. Who shall be granted access to user institutions is usually relatively unambiguous. Entitlement is connected to citizenship, which enhances the degree of institutionalized empowerment.

Hypotheses

It is now time to put the conceptual building blocs together into concrete hypotheses. An important prediction is that higher degrees of institutionalized citizen empowerment tend to yield more positive welfare state experiences in terms of perceived distributive and procedural justice. Here, one causal mechanism is that empowering institutional interfaces signal that it is a legitimate role for the citizen to voice opinions and criticism (Schneider and Ingram 1997). When citizens do not feel like powerless clients but rather like empowered customers, they may be more likely to communicate preferences concerning procedural and distributive aspects to employees. At the same time, enhanced empowerment often increases an institution's incentives to adjust to citizens' expectations. In particular, the existence of exit-options means that a public institution runs a certain risk of losing its customers unless it is responsive. In summary, if citizens are more likely to voice expectations about outcomes and procedures, and if public institutions and employees are more likely to be interested in them, experienced distributive and procedural justice might reasonably grow more positive (for similar arguments, see Lipsky 1980; Goodsell 1981; Möller 1996; Rothstein 1998; Soss 1999).

Moreover, bureaucratic discretion may produce negative distributive judgments through an additional mechanism. Since discretion is usually associated with more or less ambiguous, vague, or otherwise difficult policy guidelines interpreted by a powerful bureaucrat, things are bound to "go wrong" more often than in universal public services (for similar arguments see Lipsky 1980; Goodsell 1981; Rothstein 1998). Some of those who, according to guidelines, are actually among "the deserving" will occasionally be denied access, and less deserving applicants will occasionally be granted access. A related problem is that some citizens may make problems worse by exploiting the difficulties created by bureaucratic discretion. This involves misusing public services by cheating, lying, or otherwise trying to be perceived as a deserving recipient. Even the honest majority of citizens who have no such intentions may notice that such possibilities exist for others.

Discretion might also complicate procedural aspects of experiences. This is a possibility both when it comes to experienced voice opportunities, as well as when it comes to other procedural aspects like being treated politely and respectfully, and receiving service swiftly and efficiently. Again, the point of departure is that client experiences involve a more asymmetric and perhaps less pleasant relation between the citizen and the state, compared to other experiences. As a consequence, the confidence and opportunities to communicate opinions to the agency often decrease (Möller 1996). In fact, the discretionary powers of client institutions can even mean that the citizen sees a greater incentive "not to cause problems" by complaining (Lipsky 1980). Experienced voice perceptions may thus grow negative. Also, the absence of exit-opportunities in client experiences may reduce employees' incentives to appear interested in and responsive to citizens' views and preferences.

In contrast, think about customer experiences. The relatively high degree of power that customers exercise could give the citizen confidence and opportunity to voice discontent with distributive and procedural aspects of service provision. At the same time, bureaucrats no longer have the same incentives to appear tough and unresponsive to guard against criticism of an informal discretionary praxis. Also, exit-options are an additional resource for welfare state customers. This resource should often give institutions incentives to be responsive to procedural and distributive preferences among citizens. For instance, incentives may increase to "keep customers" by means of swift and polite service delivery than would otherwise be the case.

Finally, as elsewhere in this study, we are interested in the extent to which citizens generalize experiences into more overarching political orientations. To what extent do people draw general inferences from specific and personally experienced facts when forming broader political orientations? Do experiences with different types of institutions affect, not only perceptions of experienced distributive and procedural justice, but also general political orientations?

Specifically, we will investigate whether experiences have a more positive impact on support for state intervention, satisfaction with democracy, and trust in politicians, the more empowering institutional interfaces are. This hypothesis is basically an extension of the hypotheses presented in the sections on social justice in chapter 2. Experienced distributive and procedural justice judgments are seen as information relevant to the formation of political orientations. For instance, experienced distributive justice may inform people about the extent to which the welfare state functions in practice ("do service and help end up where they should?"), and about how well the political system is managing the welfare state. Likewise, procedural aspects such as efficiency, politeness, and the quality of voice opportunities say something about how the public sector and the political system treats citizens, and how responsive to popular preferences the political system and its implementing institutions are.

But experienced distributive and procedural justice are not the only mechanisms through which these effects may work. In particular it is possible that especially discretion structures views, not only of what one has personally experienced, but also one's view of other citizens. We have opened for the possibility that discretionary services have a higher probability than other institutions to raise suspicion concerning cheating and abuse. It is therefore conceivable that personal exposure to discretionary services tend to stimulate negative views on other people's morality and trustworthiness (Rothstein 2001). Indeed, based on one of the datasets used in this study, it has been demonstrated that the greater the number of discretionary public services individuals have recently experienced, the lower the level of generalized trust in other people they tend to display. This effect is present also after controlling for political ideology, personal life satisfaction, and a range of socioeconomic and demographic variables (Kumlin and Rothstein 2003). These findings are interesting as generalized trust in other people in turn has a certain tendency to increase both political trust as well as support for leftist ideology and state intervention (see Newton 1999). Hence, in addition to experienced distributive and procedural justice, generalized trust might be an additional causal mechanism through which the hypothesized institutional effects might operate.

In conclusion, these hypotheses build on the theoretical contention that the design of experienced welfare state institutions affects political orientations. As underscored by Schneider and Ingram (1997:200–01): "The theory of design presented here contends that attitudes and participation are influenced by public policy [...] Public policy is an important independent variable that shapes citizens' orientations and perpetuates certain views of citizenship." Chapter 10 will tell us something about whether this theoretical line of reasoning is empirically fruitful.

C H A P T E R F O U R

Political Trust and Ideology

In chapters 1–3, we thought mainly about the explanatory side of our research problem—how personal welfare state experiences affect political orientations. We have discussed potentially influential aspects of welfare state experiences, and how different sorts of welfare state institutions may systematically affect these aspects. However, while chapter 1 gave away the basic information that the dependent variables will be political trust and ideology, little has actually been said about these political orientations and the processes through which they may be affected by personal welfare state experiences.

We have proceeded like this with good reason. The main research puzzle outlined in chapter 1 has to do with a will to learn more about political effects of personal welfare state experiences, rather than an aim to explain a maximum amount of variation in any given dependent variable. Nevertheless, we are left with a theoretical gap and the purpose of this chapter is to fill it.

It begins by discussing different possible mental processes underlying experience effects, a discussion that is structured by a distinction between "memory-based" opinion formation and "on-line" opinion formation respectively. This discussion leads to the two major groups of dependent variables: political trust and ideology. After having pondered definitions of, and alternative explanations for, these political orientations, we consider the possibility that the ingredients of the experience effect vary across trust and ideology. Specifically, we raise the suspicion that the relative importance of self-interest and social justice varies depending on whether political trust or political ideology constitutes the dependent variable.

The Experience Effect: Memory-Based or On-Line?

A fundamental assumption of the new institutionalism is that individuals have limited cognitive capacity. In a complicated and volatile world, individuals look to stable institutions and standard operating procedures for guidance as to what attitudes and behavior are appropriate (see March and Olsen 1989; Steinmo, Thelen, and Longstreth 1992; Rothstein 1996). Interestingly, while explicitly acknowledging limited cognitive capacity, the literature often implicitly promotes overoptimistic views on how politically sophisticated and motivated citizens are. Individuals are assumed to keep track of a large number of sociopolitical orientations, including values, norms, identities, opinions, attitudes, and ideologies. Also, people are assumed to be motivated enough to update these orientations in the light of new relevant information emanating from institutions. As expressed by March and Olsen (1996:249), "Institutions organize hopes and dreams, and fears as well as purposeful actions [...] emotions and expressions of emotions [...] sentiments of love, loyalty, devotion, respect, friendship, as well as hate, anger, fear, envy, and guilt." Likewise, Rothstein (1998:135) argues, "Opinions, interests, values, ideology [...] all influence institutions and policy. But policies and institutions also influence opinions, etc."

The implicit assumption that people hold and update a large number of political preferences is problematic. It has long been known that citizens' political belief systems typically fall short of the classical ideal when it comes to scope and crystallization (Converse 1964; Luskin 1987; Delli Carpini and Keeter 1996). People simply do not walk around with a great number of preexisting political attitudes that are all changed in the light of new information. Therefore, we want to specify in more detail what type of political attitudes might reasonably be affected by experiences with welfare state institutions.

A first step in the search for realistic dependent variables is to distinguish between two broad categories of opinion formation models: memory-based opinion formation and on-line opinion formation respectively. It should be pointed out right from the start that the intention is not to explicitly test the empirical viability of these models. This would be a task for many separate studies. Instead, we take advantage of the research that has accumulated around them. This discourse will eventually help us in selecting dependent variables that are meaningful when looking for political effects of welfare state experiences. In fact, as we will eventually see, the choice of dependent variables is based on the idea that on-line opinion formation is often the more realistic model for such effects.

Memory-Based Opinion Formation

According to memory-based models, the immediate cause of an attitude is the information about the object in question that can be remembered at the time of forming the attitude. An attitude is the outcome of the particular mix of "pros and cons" or "likes and dislikes" one can recall at the time of forming the attitude. Memory-based explanations of political attitudes and behavior are common. For example, according to Kelley's and Mirer's (1974:574) theory of "the simple act of voting," "the voter canvasses his likes and dislikes of the leading candidates and major parties involved in an election [...] he votes for the candidate toward whom he has the greatest number of net favorable attitudes."[1]

An important category of memory-based models builds on the notion of *agenda-setting* (McCombs and Shaw 1972). As in the case of other memory-based models, one of the assumptions made by agenda-setting–based models is that politically unmotivated citizens do not consider a great amount of information. Rather, they draw on the facts that are immediately available in memory, in which there is just space for a limited number of considerations at a given time. Because of such limited cognitive capacity and motivation, people do not form attitudes on the basis of all potentially relevant issue areas, but mainly those that are easily accessible in memory. Models building on the notion of agenda-setting include those of "priming" (Iyengar and Kinder 1987; Miller and Krosnick 1996) and of "party competence" (Schmitt 2001). According to these models, citizens evaluate parties and candidates based on perceived performance and future competence in salient issue areas (that is, issues that are high on the agenda and readily available in memory).

Yet another example of a memory-based model is Zaller's (1992:49) model of opinion formation. According to this model, opinions are usually not formed before the survey researcher asks for them. If prompted for an opinion, the respondent forms it "on the spot" aided by the information that happens to be immediately available in memory: "persons who have been asked a survey question [...] answer the question on the basis of whatever considerations are accessible 'off the top of the head.' In some cases, only a single consideration may be readily accessible, in which case people answer on the basis of that consideration; in other cases, two or more considerations may come quickly to mind, in which case people answer by averaging across accessible considerations."

Memory-driven opinion formation is somewhat problematic in the context of personal welfare state experiences. Such effects would presuppose that a person memorizes a personal experience and recalls it as a political argument when at some later point it is time to make a political choice. This is an extremely demanding psychological foundation for experience effects. The problem is that the subsequent political choice—perhaps casting a vote or answering a survey question—typically lies far away in the future. And we know that most people are not greatly motivated to remember political information for future opinion formation. Rather, citizens are prone to forget political information, facts, and arguments rather quickly (Lodge, Steenbergen, and Brau 1995). Specifically, it has proven empirically unlikely that political arguments drawn from "the top of the head" are products of personal experiences. Rather, as demonstrated by Zaller (1992) and others, immediately available pros and cons in salient issues are likely to be the result of recent media attention to partisan and expert elites. Such elite messages are often more readily available in memory as arguments than personally collected information.

Of course, some welfare state experiences are not just discrete, isolated events that people forget easily. Contacts with institutions like kindergartens, schools, public transportation, and so on, often entail regular repetition of more or less the same experience. Memory-based experience effects seem more plausible if people are repeatedly reminded of for instance a deficiency in a service that is important to them. Such repeated experiences could carry a rather stable salience weight that survives shifts in the elite discourse. On the other hand, many welfare state experiences are in fact not repetitive processes. Visiting an emergency room, applying for housing allowance, borrowing books in the library, and many other types of experiences, are often best depicted as rather discrete events; it may take a long time before one has a comparable experience again.

Sometimes political choices are made soon after personal experiences have occurred. At the time of an election or opinion poll, many citizens have had some recent contact with one welfare state institution or the other. These experiences can reasonably stay available in memory for a number of days or weeks, so as to automatically pop up as a pro or contra argument when it is time to form the preference. But then again, such memory-based experience effects clearly denote a rather short-term impact: only very recent experiences matter, whereas past experiences are inconsequential as they are no longer readily available in memory.

Here, it should be pointed out that elite discourse and the mass media may remind us of the political relevance of past everyday experiences. Mutz (1998:147) launched the hypothesis that the mass media has the power to "contextualize" and "politicize" personal experiences: "By weaving discrete events into a continuing story, media may enable people to see their problems and concerns as part of a broader social pattern [. . .] mass media contribute to the politicisation of personal experience by exposing people to the similar experiences of others. It is through media coverage that the unemployed worker learns she is one of many thousands nationwide and that the crime victim learns his robbery was not an isolated incident, but rather part of a pattern of increasing drug-related crime." Empirically, Mutz examined the impact of personal unemployment concerns on ratings of U.S. presidential performance. She found that under a period of heavy unemployment coverage in the media, the causal link between personal unemployment concerns and presidential ratings was strengthened by increased media usage. In a similar vein, Johansson (1998) discovered that the agenda-setting power of local mass media in the health care area was greater among Swedes with recent personal health care experiences. Taken together, these studies suggest mutually strengthening interaction effects between the political impact of personal experiences and that of mass media coverage: both personal welfare state experiences as well as mass-mediated welfare state information become more influential when the two are similar to each other (see also Iyengar and Kinder 1987).

Memory-based accounts of personal experience effects appear more realistic if the media remind people of an otherwise forgotten political relevance of personal experiences. However, the prerequisites are tough. In fact, Mutz (1998) found that mutually strengthening interaction effects only happened when personal experience perceptions and media coverage were similar to each other, that is when the media were depicting unemployment in ways that "matched" or "fitted with" many people's personal situation. Mutz (1998:151–52) concluded, "it is only when media coverage of the impersonal world coincides with personal experience that these experiences appear to take on additional political significance." More than this, the data even indicated that when personal experience perceptions and sociotropic perceptions did *not* match, personal media usage even had a weakening, depoliticizing influence on the link between personal experiences and political attitudes.[2]

The conclusion to be drawn from this discussion is that memory-based accounts of personal experience effects are problematic. While memory-based experience effects certainly occur, the memory limitations on which the model is founded also seem to disarm the political force of a dismayingly large number of welfare state experiences. In fact, if we were to base personal experience effects exclusively on memory-based assumptions, many politically relevant personal experiences could in fact not play a great causal role. Rather, such impact would be reserved for recent or reoccurring experiences. Alternatively, impact would be reserved for experiences that fit with current extensive media reports about welfare state institutions. Clearly, this group of experiences only makes up a small portion of the total amount of personal welfare state contacts.

On-line Opinion Formation

The on-line model tells a different story about how people transform incoming political information into political attitudes (see Hastie and Park 1986; Lodge, McGraw, and Stroh 1989; Lodge and Stroh 1993). The point of departure of this model is that people often have an easier time telling you their opinion on some issue or party than they have giving an accurate account of the information and facts behind their stand. Affective elements such as values, opinions, and evaluations are thus believed to stick in memory with more persistence than the facts and information that once created them, especially when individuals lack motivation.

Moreover, in contrast to the assumption that only information that sticks in memory matters, the on-line model states that incoming information is more or less immediately translated into a new attitude (or, more commonly, into an updated version of an already existing attitude). After this operation, the information that caused the update of the attitude is forgotten. However, while the information itself is forgotten, the attitudinal result of that forgotten information lingers on. In this way, the on-line model explains why years later we may still know perfectly well whether we liked, say, a movie, at the same time as we have long forgotten the data that created our evaluation: scenes, actors, plots, or even how it all ended.

The on-line model thus predicts a difficult time for citizens in answering accurately questions about the facts, events, and information behind their evaluations and attitudes. Of course, that people do not give accurate answers does not mean they cannot provide some kind of answer. But as formulated by Lodge, Steenbergen, and Brau (1995:311), "At best, citizens' recollections will represent a biased sampling of the actual causal determinants of the [...] evaluation." Or as Rahn, Krosnick, and Breuning (1994:585) argued in the context of a study of U.S. congressional candidate evaluation "voters do not necessarily store all of those specific pieces of information in memory, and they are likely to forget some of those they do store as time passes [...] Therefore, they are likely to remember only a subset of this knowledge on election day, and that subset may well be unrepresentative of the larger pool of information on which their overall candidate evaluations were based." More than this, such recollections might be nothing but rationalizations that do precious little to reveal the real informational basis of attitudes. Indeed, "a great number of studies have now shown that people are unaware of many of the most important causes of their preferences [...] when asked to explain their preferences, people are biased toward mentioning reasons that sound rational and systematic" (Rahn, Krosnick, and Breuning 1994:584).

The on-line model facilitates a realistic way for personal welfare state experiences to bring about political effects. According to the on-line model, citizens do not need to store experienced facts for some distant point in time when it might be needed for opinion formation, voting, or for making some other political decision. They only have to update an attitude at the time of the experience, after which they can safely forget all its political connotations. When the researcher after some time asks why a person holds a certain opinion, she will hardly come to think of the experience as a prominent reason. Still, although its political connotation is not remembered, the experience may have played a causal role. If this is the case, we should find a correlation between experience measures and attitudes.

The on-line model opens for a more long-term political impact of experiences, as the attitudinal update brought about by an experience can linger on after its political relevance has been long lost. This also means that a greater number of experiences can play a political role, compared to memory-based opinion formation: experiences that did not occur recently, as well as those that are not of the reoccurring kind, can indeed matter for political attitudes. Likewise, political impact is no longer reserved mainly for experiences that fit with current and intensive media reports that remind citizens of a forgotten personal–political connection that would otherwise not be remembered.[3]

Preconditions for On-Line Opinion Formation

Based on the discussion earlier, it seems sensible for this study to use dependent variables that could reasonably be affected, not just by information immediately available in memory, but also through on-line opinion formation. Here we must be cautious: while memory-based effects could occur for just about any opinion, attitude, or orientation, on-line processes are realistic for a rather limited number of potential dependent variables.

We may discern a number of preconditions for on-line opinion formation (see Feldman 1995; Huckfeldt et al. 1999; Lavine 2002). First, in contrast to the implicit but unrealistic assumptions in the neo-institutionalist literature, the number of continuously updated attitudes must be quite limited. We thus subscribe to Zaller's (1992:50) observation that "Although a fair amount of evidence supports the on-line model, there are strong reasons for doubting that it holds generally within the domain of political attitudes [...] it is wildly unrealistic to expect citizens to use each piece of incoming information to update all of the 'attitudes' to which it might be relevant. Thus, for example, a news story about the suffering of homeless people would, in the idealized world of on-line processing, require updates of attitudes toward the welfare system, the value of big government, the efficiency of capitalism, the president's attempts to trim welfare spending, voluntary charity, the American way of life, among others—which is to say many more subjects than a person could possibly rethink at the moment of encountering each new piece of political information." This quote, then, illustrates that the notion of limited political cognitive capacity and motivation among citizens is clearly violated if we begin to assume that people apply the on-line strategy to each and every political judgment for which there might be survey data.

Second, on-line opinion formation becomes more realistic when people see it as a useful exercise for the future. For instance, based on experimental data, Hastie and Park (1986) found that on-line opinion formation was more common if subjects were instructed beforehand that they would later be asked for the particular evaluation in question, whereas memory-based processes dominated when subjects were not supplied with this information. It thus appears as if keeping track of an attitude, and updating it in an on-line manner in the light of new information, becomes a more meaningful and common exercise if people expect to make some use of the attitude in the future.

From this one may deduce that on-line opinion formation becomes more realistic if an attitude is of a general and overarching character, so that it will be relevant for many political choices in the future. Many studies emphasize that although most citizens do not walk around with firm, pre-existing opinions on a large number of concrete issues, they often have a small set of general political orientations or values. These orientations can be described as "shortcuts" to concrete opinions, or as "ideological schemas" that are used for interpretation of new incoming information. They are affective/moral orientations toward large classes of political objects and issues, but are not necessarily accompanied by a great amount of knowledge, information, and facts that could serve as rational arguments for such basic political stands (Lau and Sears 1986; Popkin 1991; Sniderman, Brody, and Tetlock 1991; van Deth and Scarbrough 1995).

Furthermore, frequent use of an attitude has two additional consequences that both facilitate on-line processes. One is that frequently used attitudes have a tendency to grow emotionally stronger and are held with more intensity than "newborn" opinions formed "on the spot." And because emotionally strong attitudes typically have an easier time staying accessible in memory, they are also more likely to be subject to on-line updating. Another facilitating condition created by frequent use is related to "evaluative repetition," that is, the number of times an individual recalls, uses, and updates an attitude. The idea is that people gradually learn to notice the implications of new information for the attitude in question, thus gradually getting better at updating it in an on-line fashion (Lavine 2002).

Finally, there is an empirical rule-of-thumb for identifying attitudes to be potentially affected by on-line processes. More specifically, such attitudes should be much more stable over time than memory-based attitudes made "on the spot" based only on immediately available information drawn from off "the top of the head." This is because in the on-line case the respondent reports a firm preexisting score along the measured dimension, one that only changes gradually due to new information. In contrast, in the pure world of memory-based political choice, attitudes are dependent on whatever considerations that are currently available in memory. Because the mix of such immediate considerations is typically very unstable over time, and because it is recalled from memory in a highly probabilistic fashion, memory-based opinion formation fosters attitude instability to an extent that on-line processes do not (Feldman 1995).

This discussion has implications for which dependent variables should be chosen in a study of personal welfare state experiences and political attitudes. More exactly, as hinted at the end of chapter 1, this study analyzes mainly two categories of political orientations. These are political trust (general attitudes toward politicians and the political system), and political ideology (left–right related orientations toward the size of the public sector and the level of state intervention in society).

Chapter 2 showed that these political orientations are common in theoretical accounts of political effects of personal welfare state experiences. To this we may now add an additional argument for why we focus on these particular dependent variables. It is argued that these orientations are suitable candidates for on-line opinion formation: First, they are few in number, which means we do not make unrealistic assumptions about citizens' motivation for opinion formation. Second, as we will see later, these orientations have a general relevance for a very large number of political situations, facts, issues, actors, parties, and debates. This time-persistent and general relevance are reasons to believe that they function as basic "schemas," "shortcuts" or "heuristic devices" for handling and evaluating information about the political world. And of course, a high probability that an orientation will often be of use should increase citizens' motivation and ability to remember and continuously update the orientation in the light of new-experienced facts. Third, analyses of panel data have shown that these orientations exhibit a rather high individual-level stability among the Swedish population, thus indicating that on-line updating is not unrealistic (Granberg and Holmberg 1988, 1996; Bennulf 1994; Oscarsson 1998; Holmberg 1999).

In the coming sections I discuss political trust and ideology in more detail. This involves conceptual discussions as well as a brief presentation of some of the most important alternative explanatory perspectives previously investigated. I start by discussing political trust orientations and later move on to ideological orientations.

Political Trust

Just like most past research on what we refer to as political trust,[4] we draw on David Easton's (1965, 1975) typology of "political support." The starting point of this conceptualization is that orientations toward the democratic system have several conceptually and empirically distinct aspects. Indeed, "the concept of political support is multidimensional. Rather than talking about 'political trust' in every case we need to specify its object. Just as 'social trust' can refer to trust towards one's family and friends, one's neighbors and community, or to citizens in different countries, so political trust depends upon the object" (Norris 1999:1).

In this spirit, Easton distinguished between political support for three basic groups of objects in the political system. First, and most basically, people may to various degrees endorse their "political community." That is, they may or may not feel that a particular geographical area and its population constitute appropriate units for common democratic decision-making. The second and third objects of political support are "the political regime," and "political authorities." Borrowing Klingemann's (1999:33) explanation, "The regime is constituted of those principles, processes and formal institutions that persist and transcend particular incumbents. And the political authorities are those officials occupying governmental posts at a particular time."

Recently, Norris (1999) expanded the Easton framework by delineating three sub-aspects of regime support: First, support for "regime principles" denotes support for basic democratic principles such as political equality and freedom of speech, as well as one's rating of democracy compared to authoritarian systems. Second, support for "regime performance" refers to how people think the democratic system actually functions; to what extent are regime principles actually realized in practice? The third type of regime support entails attitudes toward "regime institutions," such as the parliament, the executive, or the civil service.

The conceptual expansion has proven fruitful. Based on global comparative survey data, one major conclusion drawn by the contributors to Norris (1999) was that support for democratic governance depends greatly on which of the five levels is analyzed. In fact, citizens in modern democracies increasingly resemble a notion of "critical citizens." Such citizens strongly support the idea of democratic governance in their country, as well as basic democratic principles. But they are skeptical or at times even cynical about how the beautiful principles are being realized in practice.

The notion of critical citizens underscores the importance of distinguishing different types of political trust. Unfortunately, Norris laments, "These distinctions are often blurred in practice, when popular discussions about declining confidence in legislatures, trust in politicians, and support for democratic values are treated as though interchangeable. This practice has led to considerable confusion about claims and counter-claims in the literature" (Norris 1999:1).

In sum, the expanded concept of political support specifies a hierarchy of five objects in the political system that citizens orient themselves toward. At the top of the hierarchy, the question is whether people on an abstract level are willing to cooperate politically with other people living in an area. At the bottom of the hierarchy, the question is to what extent citizens trust politicians in general or particular incumbent representatives and officials. Hence, as clarified by Dalton (1999:58), "in reality this is a continuous dimension from evaluations of the immediate actions of government officials to identifying with the nation state."

Government Performance Should Affect Mainly
Concrete Objects of Political Trust

On which levels of political support should we look for effects of personal welfare state experiences? The answer starts with yet another conceptual distinction: In addition to identifying the various objects of political support, Easton also separated between "specific" and "diffuse" *kinds* of political support. There are several defining differences between the two. For instance, whereas diffuse support takes the shape of a durable and emotionally or morally based identification, specific support is instrumental and cognitive in nature.

A related difference is that they are subject to different causal forces. More exactly, "the uniqueness of specific support lies in its relationships to the satisfactions that members of a system feel they obtain from the perceived outputs and performance of the political authorities" (Easton 1975:437). In contrast, diffuse political support "refers to an evaluation of what an object is or represents [...] not of what it does. It consists of a reservoir of favorable attitudes or good will that helps members to accept or tolerate outputs to which they are opposed [...] Outputs and beneficial performance may rise and fall while this support in the form of a generalized attachment, continues. The obverse is equally true. Where [diffuse] support is negative, it represents a reservoir of ill-will that may not easily be reduced by outputs and performance" (Easton 1975:444).

While the type of support is conceptually distinct from the object of support, most authors suspect that they covary empirically. Support for abstract objects such as the community and regime principles are typically believed to be of the diffuse kind (long-term, affective identifications). Conversely, support for more concrete aspects of the political system such as regime performance, regime institutions, and trust in politicians are thought to be specific in nature (short-term, instrumental, cognitive).

This is to say that support for the community and the abstract principles of democracy are hardly affected by poor short-term policy performance, at least not in reasonably established democracies. Many years of democratic government, the argument goes, slowly create an affective reservoir of diffuse support for the ideas and principles of democracy (Almond and Verba 1963; McAllister 1999). This reservoir is not easily drained by short-term hardship. Decades of both good and bad times teach citizens to distinguish between, on the one hand, the democratic system as a set of abstract principles, and, on the other hand, democratic institutions and political actors as they function in practice. Thus, short-term performance such as economic trends, unemployment, or welfare state performance affect mainly trust in current political actors, parties, or the democratic system as it functions in practice. At the same time, such dissatisfaction does not undermine support for the more basic aspects of political support, such as identification with the community or basic beliefs in democratic principles.

Empirical research largely supports the suspicion.[5] For instance, in her extensive eight-country study of government performance and political support, Huseby (2000:245) found that short-term government performance "first, and foremost, influenced less general objects of political support [...] While support for political authorities and regime processes were strongly influenced by performance evaluations, there was little evidence of a relationship between evaluations of government performance and priority between democracy and dictatorship." Similarly, based on the 1987 German Socio-Economic Panel, I reported elsewhere that both economic evaluations and evaluations of social security clearly affected the extent to which West Germans were satisfied with the way democracy works in practice in their country. In contrast, evaluations were not related to how respondents felt "about democracy, not an existing democracy, but rather the idea of democracy" (Kumlin 2002; see also Listhaug 1995).

Consistent with these results, what we have in mind when wondering whether "welfare state experiences affect political trust," is impact on trust in the practical functioning of the current democratic system and its actors, rather than on basic support for democratic principles or for the political community. Therefore, we will use as dependent variables measures of "trust in politicians" and the extent to which respondents are "satisfied with the way democracy works." These indicators will be presented further in chapter 6.

Causes of Political Trust: Government Performance

Let us look at some of the most important explanations of variation in political trust investigated in past research. Needless to say, the discussion will not be able to exhaust the available theories and results (for more complete introductions, see Fuchs and Klingemann 1995; Borre and Scarbrough 1995; Kaase and Newton 1995; Nye, Zelikov, and King 1997; Norris 1999; Pharr and Putnam 2000). Instead, the purpose is to give a very brief introduction. In doing this, we learn more about political trust, and lay a foundation for the selection of control variables to be included in subsequent multivariate models.

Personal welfare state experiences belong to a larger category of independent variables that are labeled government performance. Such explanations build on the idea that citizens' attitudes toward their political system partly hinge on the extent to which that system is able to produce satisfactory policy outcomes in issue areas that citizens deem important. As explained by Huseby (2000:10), the major hypothesis is that "poor government performance in salient political issues leads to negative evaluations of government performance, which in turn influences the citizens' support for the political system."

Government performance explanations are rooted in a particular model of representative democracy. According to this model, a functioning representative system is characterized by independent political leadership and retrospective accountability (see Schumpeter 1942; Held 1987). While political outcomes and results are rarely considered democratic values as such, poor performance is nevertheless problematic to the extent that political accountability is at all difficult to manage. Such difficulties have many sources, including frequent power shifts, fractionalized coalitions, and government attempts to cloud performance failures or blame them on someone else. Yet another source is the multilevel structure of political systems in which several levels share political responsibility for the same policy areas. Of course, political systems vary greatly along these variables across space and time. However, because political accountability is hardly ever perfect in these and other respects, there is always a risk that poor government performance translates into negative attitudes toward the democratic system. As the lines of political responsibility become unclear, it also becomes harder for citizens to express their dissatisfaction through the vote or through other types of participation aimed at responsible political actors. Dissatisfied voters who want to "throw the rascals out," but cannot because of fuzzy political responsibility, are seen as particularly prone to develop negative attitudes toward the democratic system, not just toward incumbents (see Powell and Whitten 1993; Huseby 1999; Taylor 2000).

Chapter 1 discussed the impact of citizens' perceptions of economic performance and welfare state performance in the context of the debate on sociotropic perceptions versus personal experience. As for political trust, we noted that past research has found a moderate but consistent influence of sociotropic economic perceptions on political trust variables. Recently, it has been shown that policy areas other than the economy are of importance. Using comparative survey data, Huseby (2000) examined the impact of government performance in three policy areas—the economy, basic social welfare, and the environment—and found that all three were of clear relevance for political support variables. Also, while the author concluded that economic performance was slightly more influential than welfare state performance, she pointed out the need for further research using data designed especially for these purposes (Huseby 2000:chapters 8 and 10; Miller and Listhaug 1999).

The conclusion that evaluations of public services matter has also received support in the Swedish context. For instance, Nilsson (1997) reports a rather strong correlation between Swedes' overall satisfaction with public services in the municipality and satisfaction with how democracy works in practice in the municipality (see also Johansson, Nilsson, and Strömberg 2001; Kumlin and Oskarson 2000). In a similar vein, Holmberg (1999:122) investigated political trust at the national level and concluded, "without a doubt the most important political explanation has to do with government performance—with people's evaluations of what they get from government and their assessments of what the government does. Government performance, and people's perceptions of that performance, are the central factors."

In sum, we have good reason to suspect from the outset that evaluations of both economic and welfare state performance affect political trust. Moreover, to reiterate the major points of previous chapters, the distinct contribution made by this study to the literature on government performance and political trust is that we explicitly consider the distinction between personal experience and sociotropic judgment, that we distinguish different aspects of experiences (self-interest, distributive justice, voice), and that we analyze institutional variation that might structure experiences and, in turn, political trust.

Causes of Political Trust: Other Perspectives

Government performance is certainly not the only explanatory factor emphasized in past studies. One major alternative explanation is the "policy distance hypothesis" (Miller 1974). According to this hypothesis, people compare personal political opinions and policy preferences in salient issues with the actual policies that are perceived to be implemented by incumbents. The assumption is that the closer the match between personal preferences and actual policies, the more favorable the attitudes toward the political system. The policy distance hypothesis thus predicts that a political system will enjoy greater support when policies in salient issues to a greater extent resemble those of many citizens. This hypothesis has been refined by for instance Petersson (1977), who argued that what matters is not so much policy distance to the policies of the incumbent. Rather, the crucial distance is that between the citizen and the particular party she votes for. According to this hypothesis, a political system will enjoy greater support the better the parties are at advocating policies in salient issues that lie close to the average preferences of its particular voter group. Finally, several empirical studies support these hypotheses. Not least in Scandinavian countries, individuals' policy distance to responsible political actors seems to affect political trust (see Borre 1995; Borre and Goul Andersen 1997; Aardal 1999; Holmberg 1999).

A different category of explanations for political trust highlights, not so much what politicians and parties do, but rather the way journalists and the mass media portray them. It has been suggested that highly negative, dramatic, and critical modes of reports about politics and politicians have a tendency to undermine citizens' trust in politicians and faith in the functioning of the democratic system. For example, by spending a disproportionate amount of time and space on depicting politics as a game between strategic actors (so-called game frames), rather than on the actual political substance ("issue frames"), the mass media is believed to activate and strengthen images of crooked, egoistic, and dishonest politicians (Cappella and Jamieson 1997). Moreover, such assumptions are typically linked to the idea that things have become worse over time. Here, the development of more independent and professionalized journalists, as well as the emergence of television as a main source of political information, are among the important underlying trends (Sabato 1991).

Empirically, several studies indicate that journalists have become more critical, independent, and perhaps also more negative in their political coverage (Westerståhl and Johansson 1981; Patterson 1993; Esaiasson and Håkansson 2002; Djerf-Pierre and Weibull 2001).[6] However, it is less certain whether the effects on political trust are really negative. Several studies have found a rather weak impact of various measures of media usage on political trust (Holmberg 1999; Strömbäck 2001). Moreover, in contrast to the view that the media breed cynicism, several researchers argue that the media can have a mobilizing impact on citizens. There are indications that media negativity is correlated with a good deal of real political conflict and polarization, something that may counterbalance or even outweigh a negative impact of media usage on political trust (Brants and van Kempen 2002).

Explanations of trust have also been sought outside the political system altogether. First, it has been suggested that socioeconomic status variables like social class, education, and income, may play a causal part. Well-educated middle-class citizens, the argument goes, have more resources and political confidence. They therefore also tend to see more of the bright side of the political system and thus evaluate its performance more positively. Empirical results, however, have not been overly kind to such predictions. The effects of variables such as class, income, and education are typically moderate at best. Using Holmberg's (2000:35) summary of the findings, "a sociological model is not very useful when it comes to explaining political trust." Still, this should not be taken as a sign that socioeconomic factors are irrelevant. Differences between groups along any single socioeconomic status variable are "often very small but taken together the results form a pattern. Dissatisfaction is greater in certain vulnerable groups compared to more established and well-to-do groups"[7] (see also Aardal 1999). This observation is underscored by the fact that subjective personal assessments of the extent to which individuals are satisfied with the lives they lead have proven to be relatively strongly related to political trust (Kornberg and Clarke 1992). Happy people are often happy with the political system.

Another category of nonpolitical explanations is related to Inglehart's (1977, 1990, 1997) work on post-materialism and postmodernization. Societal trends such as economic development and increasing educational levels are believed to produce fundamental value changes as generations are replaced. These value changes include an increased focus on personal well-being and intellectual stimulation as opposed to material issues and economic security. Moreover, as mentioned earlier, the process of postmodernization is believed to create "critical citizens." On the one hand postmodern citizens are deeply committed to the basic principles of democracy. On the other hand they have less respect for authorities than previous generations, and they are skeptical about the traditional hierarchical institutions of representative democracy as these do not leave enough room for more direct individual forms of political participation and post-materialist self-expression. Or as Inglehart (1999:236) explains, "The post modern phase of development leads to declining respect for authority [...] but at the same time, it gives rise to growing support for democracy [...] the same publics that are becoming increasingly critical of hierarchical authority, are also becoming increasingly resistant to authoritarian government, more interested in political life, and more apt to play an active part in politics." (See also Petersson, Westholm, and Blomberg 1989:chapter 10.)

Political Ideology: State-Intervention Orientations and Left–Right Self-Identification

We now move to the second category of political orientations to be potentially explained by personal welfare state experiences—political ideology. More exactly, we are interested in orientations related to the classic political conflict between the Left and the Right. Such orientations mirror what has for more than half a century been the most important substantive political struggle in the Swedish party system. This struggle, as we will see, has close links to the question of how generous, ambitious, and encompassing welfare state arrangements should be.

Past research emphasizes that left–right related attitudes and beliefs offer a widely used mental framework for Swedes to understand and evaluate the political world (see Särlvik 1974; Petersson 1977; Gilljam and Holmberg 1993; Bennulf 1994; Holmberg 2000). For instance, Oscarsson (1998:308) analyzed extensively the dimensionality in citizens' party evaluations during 40 years and concluded, "Undoubtedly, throughout the period 1956–1996, the left–right dimension has been Swedish voters' most important tool for handling and evaluating information about the ideological conflicts between the parties."

These findings are in line with Granberg and Holmberg's (1988) and Niemi and Westholm's (1984) comparisons of Swedish and U.S. voters. Their results indicated that whereas left–right related ideological belief systems are not particularly stable or internally coherent among Americans (Converse 1964),[8] they are so to a much greater extent among Swedes. Moreover, measures of left–right related ideology are powerful predictors of party choice (Gilljam and Holmberg 1995), as well as specific issue opinions (Gilljam 1988; Kumlin 2001b), and there are no immediate signs that they will lose their prominence in this respect (Holmberg 2000).

All these findings are important for this study as we regard personal experience effects operating through on-line opinion formation as more realistic if the orientation in question is frequently used in political reasoning and choice. As discussed earlier, frequent usage increases the likelihood that people will call to mind and update an orientation in the light of a new personal welfare state experience. Given this prerequisite, and given the research referred to earlier, left–right related ideological orientations seem to be a good place to look for effects of personal welfare state experiences in Sweden.

Based on past research, we separate between two somewhat different approaches to conceptualizing and measuring left–right related ideological orientations: (1) "state-intervention orientations," and (2) "left–right self-identification." Let us consider each in turn.[9]

State-Intervention Orientations

State-intervention orientations can be defined as a general attitude toward the extent to which public schemes, policies, and regulation should intervene in the market economy. This classic ideological conflict is intimately related to the industrial age class-based conflict between workers and capitalists (see Lipset and Rokkan 1967; Franklin, Mackie, and Valen 1992; Oskarson 1994). Thus, a sensible alternative label could have been "economic" or "materialist" left–right orientations. As explained by Knutsen (1995:65), "In industrial society the left-right division was related to the materialist struggle which emerged from the labor market conflicts between workers and the owners of the means of production. The political values underlying the industrial 'left'–'right' polarisation were conflicts related to economic inequalities, differences in ownership to the means of production, and conflict over the desirability of a market economy."

There is a conceptual kinship between orientations on state intervention and the welfare state. This kinship is constituted by the fact that the size and nature of welfare state arrangements strongly affect the degrees of "market economy," "inequality," "redistribution," and "public ownership of the means of production," in a society. Consequently, state-intervention orientations are often measured in surveys by asking questions concerning the preferred general size, generosity, or form of welfare state arrangements. Such questions include suggestions about "reducing the size of the public sector," or about the extent of "privatization," and "redistribution." And as will be evident, this is also the type of indicators that we will use. In this study, then, state-intervention orientations stand for general attitudes toward the size and generosity of welfare state arrangements in society.

Having said this, we know that not all reasonable measures of state-intervention orientations are necessarily related to measures of general support for welfare state arrangements. For instance, based on comparative data from nine Western European countries, Borre and Viegas (1995) examined attitudes toward how much the government should intervene in the economy using a number of strategies, many of which were not directly related to welfare state policies. Their data included opinion items on "wage control," "price control," "government management of the economy," and "government ownership of industry," and showed that such items rarely correlate very strongly with welfare-related state-intervention responses such as "cut government spending."[10]

It seems unsafe, then, to assume that attitudes toward all types of "state-intervention" form one single dimension. This study focuses on measures of state-intervention orientations that have a clear connection to general support for the welfare state, believing that this orientation is more likely to be affected by personal welfare state experiences. Hence, when we speak about state-intervention orientations we mean support for intervention in the sense of general attitudes toward the size of the welfare state and the public sector.

Left–Right Self-identification

The second approach to conceptualizing and measuring ideological orientations is "Left–Right self-identification." This concept is widely used in past research and has proven to be important for understanding opinion formation and voting behavior in a large number of Western democracies (see e.g., Inglehart and Klingemann 1976; Granberg and Holmberg 1988; Holmberg and Gilljam 1987; Fuchs and Klingemann 1989; van der Eijk, Franklin, and Oppenhuis 1996; Oscarsson 1998; Borre and Andersen 1997; Aardal and Valen 1995; Knutsen 1998a). The concept is typically measured by asking respondents to place themselves on a scale ranging from, for instance, zero (labeled "far to the left") to ten ("far to the right").

Left–right self-identification is conceptually distinct from state-intervention orientations. This is because, taken on their own, left and right are substantively undefined political categories, and strictly speaking left–right identification refers to nothing but individuals' tendency to identify politically with the spatial metaphors of left and right. Indeed, as emphasized by Knutsen (1998a:294), these metaphors "can be considered as empty containers ready to be filled with political content." In contrast, state-intervention orientations are political values with inherent political substance and implications. And it is an empirical, not conceptual, question whether subjective left–right self-identification is correlated with various substantive political values. In fact, nothing prevents left and right from having different substantive meaning at different points in time, in different countries, or among different groups of citizens.

What political content do citizens attach to the left–right semantics? There are two major answers. A first possibility is that answers to questions about left–right self-identification reflect respondents' party preferences. This interpretation is typically referred to as the "partisan component" of left–right self-identification (Inglehart and Klingemann 1976; Granberg and Holmberg 1988; Knutsen 1998c). According to this interpretation, people who say that they stand "far to the left" have inferred their position from their party preference, or mean that they support a leftist party. However, this partisan component does not necessarily reveal much about policy-related values or attitudes.

The second major possibility is that left–right identification reflects "real" values that have policy implications. In fact, past research suggests several possible value-based interpretations of the left–right semantics (see van Deth and Scarbrough 1995), three of which have been especially successful in empirical studies. The first one has to do with state-intervention orientations as defined earlier, where left means a stronger support for a larger intervening public sector. A second possible interpretation has to do with "Christian traditionalism." According to this interpretation, Christian traditionalists, who hold positive attitudes toward "Christian values," "the family," "law and order," and "national traditions" define themselves as further to the right than others. The third important interpretation is rooted in theories of "new politics" (Inglehart 1977, 1990; Minkenberg and Inglehart 1989). Such politics is driven by a value conflict between "materialists" on "the new right" (who value economic consumption standard and physical protection) and "post-materialists" on "the new left" (who emphasize nonmaterial values such as quality of life, democratic principles, and a healthy environment). This new value conflict would structure not only the meaning attached to left–right semantics, but also attitudes toward a wide range of topics such as ecology issues, democratic principles, decentralization, political activism and so on.

How widespread are the various value-based interpretations of left–right semantics among ordinary citizens? Knutsen (1995) studied eight Western European countries and found that state-market orientations, Christian traditionalism, and post-materialist orientations all affect citizens' subjective left–right identification (see also Inglehart 1990). Notably, in recent years there has been a tendency in many countries for post-materialist orientations to become more strongly associated with left–right identification. These results demonstrate that "the left–right semantics have an impressive absorptive power. This is an overarching spatial dimension capable of incorporating many types of conflict lines, and with different meanings to different people" (Knutsen 1995:86–87).

In comparison to other West European electorates, Swedes appear more one-dimensional and stable in their understanding of left–right semantics. In particular, Oscarsson (1998:308) found that "The substance of the left–right dimension has not changed during the last thirty years." His results showed that left and right continuously seem to be defined in terms of industrial age questions concerning the extent of state intervention, the size of the public sector, and the extent of privatization. In addition, past Swedish research contends that new post-materialist politics does by no means form Swedish political conflict with the same strength as old materialist politics (Bennulf 1994; Bennulf and Holmberg 1990).

We may conclude from the discussion that both state-intervention orientations and left–right self-identification can to some extent be seen as two somewhat different indicators of generalized welfare state support. State-intervention orientations denote support for intervention in the sense of general attitudes toward the size of the welfare state and the public sector. Left–right self-identification reflects (among other things) both such state-intervention orientations, as well as an inclination to vote for and otherwise support leftist parties. And of course, in Sweden it is the leftist parties (most notably the Social Democrats) who have been and continue to be the primary political forces behind a large public sector and welfare state (Esping-Andersen 1985). Conversely, to the extent that there has been resistance in this respect, it has come from the right (most notably the Moderate Party).

Causes of Ideology: Other Perspectives

In order to learn more about state-intervention orientations and left–right self-identification, let us take a brief look at some of the alternative explanatory perspectives (for more complete introductions, see Coughlin 1980; Taylor-Gooby 1985; Borre and Scarbrough 1995). Several of these explanatory factors will be represented by control variables in later multivariate analyses.

We noted earlier that left–right related ideological orientations are regarded as emanating from the cleavage between people with different professional and social relations to the means of production (Lipset and Rokkan 1967). Consequently, the most emphasized explanations for variation in such orientations are variables related to socioeconomic status and class. Empirically, it has often been shown that working-class affiliation, lower income, and lower education strongly increase individuals' propensity to both define themselves as standing further to the left as well as display support for greater state intervention (see Särlvik 1974; Petersson 1982; Svallfors 1997; Oscarsson 1998). Moreover, while there has been a reduction in the extent of class-based voting in Western countries during much of the second half of the twentieth century (Franklin, Mackie, and Valen 1992; Oskarson 1994), the link between class and ideological welfare-state related orientations remains surprisingly strong. For instance, drawing on data spanning three decades and a large number of West European countries, Pettersen (1995:230) concluded that "theories of class formation provide a superior explanation for people's public spending preferences over the entire time period analyzed."

The link between socioeconomic status and welfare state support is brought about by several causal processes. For example, it is typically assumed that those with lower socioeconomic status perceive that their interests are better served by leftist and state interventionist policies (Lipset and Rokkan 1967). Further, it has been emphasized that individuals in different socioeconomic groups live in very different informational environments. By this logic, it is usually easier for, say, upper-class citizens to adopt antiwelfare and rightist preferences for the simple reason that so many people in their vicinity communicate mostly information that foster such preferences (Katz and

Lazarsfeld 1955; Huckfeldt and Sprague 1995). Also, the link between socio-economic status and political orientations seems to operate through early family socialization mechanisms, where parents' political orientations are adopted by their children. With regard to ideological orientations in Sweden, Westholm (1991) found that among a sample of early adolescents and their parents, both left–right self-identification and attitudes toward "social welfare" were strongly affected by such family socialization. Such findings, taken together with the fact that socioeconomic status is also often inherited as well as with the observation that ideological orientations are quite stable, help explain why we often find a correlation between an individual's socioeconomic status and her ideological orientations.

A very different group of theories are concerned with explaining, not so much differences between individuals, but rather with aggregate opinion differences across time and across countries. For instance, the theory of "government overload" predicts that as welfare states expand, citizens will gradually come to expect that it is the state's responsibility to solve new problems that appear on the political agenda by means of public schemes. The initial implication of this is that welfare state attitudes will gradually become even more expansionist as welfare states themselves expand. At some point, however, the demands on the government become so high that, for fiscal and other economic reasons, many of them can no longer be met. When the performance of the welfare state falls short of the public's expectations, the result will be widespread dissatisfaction which undermines the public's belief in the welfare state as a social problem solver (Crozier, Huntingdon, and Watanuki 1975). According to overload theory, then, "the revolution of rising expectations makes today's luxuries tomorrow's necessities [. . .] Politicians promise more and more at election time, but the more demands they recognize [. . .] the less likely they are to deliver [. . .] Government becomes overloaded and society becomes ungovernable. As a result, public opinion becomes increasingly cynical and disillusioned. Ultimately, it withdraws its support from the state, so undermining the system of government" (Kaase and Newton 1995:71–72).

Overload theory has not always survived confrontations with data. For instance, comparative Western European surveys do not reveal a spiral of rising demands on governments, nor systematically declining levels of support for welfare state institutions during the 1970s and the 1980s. Instead, public endorsement of welfare state arrangements and leftist ideology seems to move in a more cyclical fashion (Pettersen 1995). Moreover, in stark contrast to what is predicted by overload theory, demands for state expansion has proven to be higher in countries with less developed welfare states and a higher level of socioeconomic inequality (Roller 1995; Borre and Viegas 1995). This research suggests that "public opinion is not irreversible," but rather that "demands for government spending on some services seem to level off in wealthier nations compared with poorer ones. In short, the spiral of rising expectations of the public sector has been replaced—to some extent at any rate—by a spiral of falling expectations"

(Kaase and Newton 1995:73). Similarly, within Sweden, Johansson, Nilsson, and Strömberg (2001:chapter 6) found that demands for increased public efforts in different public service areas have typically *decreased* over time as actual services have expanded.[11]

In retrospect, then, overload theory seems to have been a rather time-specific product of the early 1970s. While it fitted well with the emerging neoliberal criticism of the welfare state, its predictions about public opinion have rarely been confirmed in empirical studies. So for mundane empirical reasons, overload theories "seem to have gone the way of bell-bottoms, Afghan coats and patchouli oil" (Norris 1999:5).

The failure to detect long-term linear developments in welfare state opinion has pointed toward more short-term factors. These factors include both economic trends and opinion formation by political elites. In Borre's (1995:385–86) formulation, "On the one hand, policy demands are not to be considered autonomous phenomena but malleable by government and opposition parties as well as the mass media. On the other hand, policy demands are clearly related to objective needs."

As far as "objective needs" are concerned, welfare state attitudes are not only more expansionist in poorer countries with more socioeconomic inequality. Also within countries over time, they have a tendency to become more expansionist in times of recession and unemployment. Such economic hardship appears to fuel demands for state intervention and increased welfare state spending, because it highlights a number of social problems and inequalities. This factor was clearly at play in Sweden during the economic malaise of the early 1990s. After a decade of neoliberal ideological trends in public opinion[12] (Gilljam and Holmberg 1993), a couple of years of rising unemployment and poor growth seem to have shifted attitudes back in the direction of increased general support for public sector spending and greater suspicion toward privatization of central welfare state institutions (see Nilsson 1996b, 1997; Johansson, Nilsson, and Strömberg 2001).

The Ingredients of the Experience Effect
May Vary Across Trust and Ideology

We have discussed at some length the two categories of dependent variables—political trust and political ideology. The next step is to consider differences between political trust and ideology with respect to how they are affected by personal welfare state experiences. Do the ingredients of the experience effect vary between trust and ideology?

We take as our starting point the three perspectives that were introduced in chapter 2—self-interest, distributive justice, and voice. Our question is whether the relative importance of these aspects can be expected to vary depending on whether political trust or political ideology constitutes the dependent variable. The answer is yes. As the discussion that follows will explain, we have reasons to expect that the relative impact of self-interest versus distributive justice and voice is greater for ideological orientations than for political trust.

Chapter 2 explained that self-interest variables have usually been shown to bear a weak relationship to public opinion (Sears and Funk 1991). This generalization notwithstanding, it is not that difficult to find exceptions in this large literature (see e.g., Sears and Citrin 1982; Dunleavy and Husbands 1985: Nilsson 1996b; Sannerstedt 1981; Pettersen 2001; Winter and Mouritzen 2001). It appears as if citizens *sometimes* align in the patterns suggested by the self-interest perspective. One wonders whether we are dealing with trifling randomness, or whether we have systematic variation at hand.

Past research comes down in favor of the latter possibility. In the most extensive study on the topic, *Self-Interest, Public Opinion and Political Behavior,* Donald Green (1988) discovered that there are several factors that systematically increase the impact of self-interest on public opinion. In fact, "the contention that self-interest has little influence on public opinion is overstated. The point is not merely that there are exceptions. Our objection is rather that the class of exceptions constitutes an important subset of those political issues that are submitted before the court of public opinion" (Green 1988:334).

Green found that the impact of self-interest depends on the extent to which several conditions are fulfilled. For example, the individual must recognize the sources of differences in self-interest. Self-interest cannot affect attitudes toward, say, housing benefits unless people know whether they are potential beneficiaries. In other words, people must know whether their objective life circumstances imply entitlement to housing benefits. Those who do not have knowledge about such conditions are not in a position to calculate benefits and costs in a very meaningful way. Another precondition is that the individual pays attention to self-interest. When citizens are not attentive to self-interest considerations, the impact of variables measuring actual self-interest will decrease. Moreover, it is necessary to have accurate information about the costs and benefits implied by different political positions. To the extent that people do not possess cost–benefit information, they cannot make accurate self-interest calculations, and self-interest variables will explain less. Finally, although people might recognize the sources of self-interest, be attentive to self-interest considerations, and possess accurate cost/benefit information, self-interest might still fail to influence political decisions. This occurs if a person regards self-interest concerns as inappropriate or immoral in the political sphere. Green's (1988:29) results suggested that "One person's conscience may not permit him to shrug off his obligation to the public good in pursuit of private gain; another person may feel no remorse at all." Only among the latter type of citizens did self-interest variables display a sizeable impact.

The Level of Abstraction and the Nature of the Stakes

Green's results implied that the degree to which these conditions are fulfilled varies across individuals, across sociopolitical contexts, and across different types of political choices (Green 1988:chapter1). Because our present concern is potential differences across political trust and ideology, the following discussion focuses on choice-related variables.[13] More precisely, we will now in turn consider two important variables that could govern the extent to which conditions of self-interest effects are fulfilled. We refer to these governing variables as "the level of abstraction" and the "nature of the stakes," respectively.

First, a distinction between concrete and abstract choices has proven useful (Green 1988; Sears and Citrin 1982; Sears and Funk 1991). Several scholars argue that the more concrete an issue is the more likely one is to recognize its potential relevance for objective living conditions giving rise to different interests. Moreover, concreteness means that the potentially relevant information about costs and benefits of different alternatives becomes more limited and manageable.

If we take as an example the rather concrete proposal to "raise the unemployment benefits," it is immediately clear that there is a distinct group of people—the unemployed—that have a particular interest in the enactment of that policy. And it is not a daunting task to figure out approximately how much they have to win or lose in the personal, material, short-term sense. Conversely, when I make the abstract suggestions to "increase the size of the public sector," or "introduce more market economy" it is not equally clear who gains, and how much. Because the amount of potentially relevant information is large, and involves complicated trade-offs between the impact of many specific policies, it would take quite some effort to figure it out. And probably the result would easily be open for discussion.

Consistent with these remarks, chapter 2 showed that past research doubts whether more abstract political orientations are affected by self-interest (a doubt that will be put to further tests in chapter 7). To this we may now add that several studies show that, when it comes to really concrete opinions on specific public services, attitudes are indeed influenced by self-interest. For instance, in a detailed study of attitudes toward a great variety of local public services, Sannerstedt (1981) found that personal usage of a given public service is a crucial variable in explaining whether individuals want more spending on that service. Similarly, Nilsson (1996b, 1997; see also Johansson, Nilsson, and Strömberg 2001) has demonstrated that personal usage of a public service greatly increases the propensity to express satisfaction with, and support for, that particular service. Also, drawing on data from several European countries, Pettersen (1995; 2001) has found that self-interest structures people's acceptance for increased spending on various specific welfare state programs.

Sannerstedt's (1981:163)[14] conclusions nicely illustrate that concrete welfare state opinions may be aptly explained by self-interest:"factors related to citizens' personal demands, wishes, and actual usage of services matter. Those living in multi-family houses have greater demands when it comes to housing policy. Those who live outside the urban centre have greater demands for public transportation, roads, schools, water, and sewage. [...]

Those with schoolchildren have higher demands for schools. Those with pre-school children have higher demands for child care, especially if they do not have place in a kindergarten, but desire one. The old have higher demands for elder care, the young for child care, sport facilities and leisure time activities. Low-income groups have higher demands for social welfare. The highly educated have higher demands for libraries and culture. Those who visit libraries have higher demands for that service area than those who do not, and so on" (see also Johansson, Nilsson, and Strömberg 2001:137–45).

The second choice-related factor regulating the impact of self-interest is "the nature of the stakes." This concept may be further divided into the *size* of stakes and the *visibility* of stakes. As far as size is concerned, the straight-forward assumption is that individuals will be more motivated to evaluate different political stands in terms of economic self-interest if different alter-natives have larger implications for one's short-term material situation (Sears and Citrin 1982). Moreover, in addition to rising motivation, such large costs and benefits might make it easier to shrug off one's obligation to the common good.

Visibility of stakes refers to the extent to which benefits and costs are concealed from citizens. Hence, the focus is not so much on whether self-interest is moderated by morality and motivation. Instead, the concern is whether the information at hand permits and stimulates people to make political cost–benefit analyses. In a series of experiments, Green (1988:chapter 4) demonstrated that the impact of self-interest on concrete policy opinions was increased so as to match that of general ideological orientations, if respondents were provided with clear information about costs and benefits (see also Hadenius 1986; Sears and Funk 1991). This suggests, "the influence of self-interest hinges on the degree to which people think about material costs and benefits when evaluating a particular policy. When people are reminded of their material interests or confronted with a policy choice that lays out the costs and benefits in an explicit fashion, material considerations exert a sizeable influence on policy preferences. In the absence of such cues, mass political decision making is for the most part unaffected by personal interests" (Green 1988:212).

Political Trust and Ideology Compared

What does this discussion reveal about how the ingredients of the experience effect vary across political trust and ideology? It suggests that the relative impact of self-interest, versus distributive justice and voice, will be stronger on political ideology than on political trust.

Think first about state-intervention orientations and left–right self-identification. As an earlier section in this chapter explained, the defining elements of these ideological conflicts concern issues of redistribution, and the generosity and size of welfare state arrangements. One must not have a vivid imagination to come up with the idea that some lose and some win depending on which course of political action is taken in these overarching conflicts. This is to say that the defining elements of ideological orientations are intimately intertwined with significant economic stakes. Because interests and ideology are conceptually intertwined, people may indeed update these orientations based on self-interest related aspects of welfare state experiences. Of course, it is likely that more concrete opinions on specific programs and services are even more sensitive to personal costs and benefits, by virtue of making stakes more visible and cost–benefit information more tractable. Nevertheless, because ideological orientations are conceptually intertwined with economic stakes, the self-interest perspective has some credibility in the context of political ideology.

In contrast, think now about political trust. Chapter 2 introduced the theoretical possibility that the political system is evaluated in terms of whether its policies satisfy personal interests. This possibility notwithstanding, we must admit that political trust judgments are not conceptually intertwined with large or visible stakes. While thinking about state intervention and left–right almost by definition forces us to start thinking about politics of redistribution and welfare state generosity, thinking in general terms about the democratic system seems less likely to stimulate such thoughts. This becomes clear when one considers the indicators typically used to gauge political trust, for instance, questions about how satisfied respondents are with the current democratic system, or how much faith they have in politicians and parliament. Compared to state-intervention orientations and left–right identification, these "political choices" are further removed conceptually from interest-related politics, and so they are less likely to draw one's attention to policies involving large or visible stakes. In terms of personal welfare state experiences, it should therefore be easier to start thinking about self-interest related ingredients of experiences if one is updating ideological orientations, compared to if experiences inform political trust orientations.

These remarks pertain to the nature of stakes. But what about the level of abstraction? It is readily apparent that this factor does not vary all that much across political trust and ideology. Both are overarching orientations that can be used by citizens to understand and evaluate many types of political information and situations. More than this, it is the general and abstract qualities of these orientations that make them suitable candidates for on-line opinion formation.

However, while the variance in the level of abstraction across political choices could be greater, it is probably not a constant. In fact, it may be argued that political trust orientations are slightly less concrete than ideological orientations. While political trust refers to citizens' attitudes toward the totality of the political system, its performance, or its actors, ideological orientations refer to somewhat more concrete evaluations of policies and actors within that system. Left–right related orientations would therefore have a more concrete connection to everyday politics than political trust.

And as we saw earlier, concrete political choices seem more susceptible to self-interest.

In conclusion, we expect that the ingredients of the experience effect vary across political trust and ideology. More exactly, we expect a stronger relative impact of self-interest on political ideology compared to political trust. Moreover, given that people have limited cognitive capacity, as well as limited motivation for carefully extracting the political relevance of experiences, experience aspects pertaining to distributive justice and experienced voice may be partly "crowded out" as the importance of self-interest rises, thus producing a weaker impact of those experience aspects.

$$\star\ \star\ \star$$

The theoretical stage is set. The empirical action can begin. In chapter 5 the reader is invited to take a sneak preview at the data and the case. After that we begin to use the data in order to test the hypotheses presented in chapters 1–4. These tests will tell us more about how, and how strongly, personal welfare state experiences affect political trust and ideology.

Findings

The Data and the Case

The theoretical framework laid out in previous chapters will be tested using Swedish cross-sectional survey data. The purpose of this chapter is to present these data and to think about their strengths and weaknesses. We begin by discussing Sweden as a laboratory for studying political effects of personal welfare state experiences. The chapter then proceeds to a brief presentation of the primary and secondary data sources. It closes with a discussion on potential perils of cross-sectional data: in particular, we consider how political orientations held prior to experiences may affect or interact with the impact of experiences.

Sweden as a Laboratory for Observing Political Effects of Welfare State Experiences

Most of the empirical analyses will build on survey data that were collected in Sweden during 1999. This choice of empirical setting is by no means the result of a carefully crafted research design. Rather, it followed naturally from the fact that I have worked in a research environment specialized in collecting such data in Sweden. As the reader will notice, the opportunity to influence primary data collection in a cumulative research environment has been important, not least as measuring personal welfare state experiences rarely has been a major concern for primary investigators of public opinion surveys. The obvious drawback, on the other hand, is that the hypotheses will be tested in just one particular country during a limited period of time. Because Sweden is a choice of convenience rather than of research design, the empirical results of this study cannot tell us much about whether results can be generalized to other countries and contexts. By and large, this is something that will have to be sorted out by future studies.

Nevertheless, to the extent that the framework receives support in the present study, at least two circumstances suggest that future tests may bear some empirical fruit as well. First, the most basic proposition put forward in this study—that welfare state experiences could be more politically important than personal economic experiences—should be at least logically valid elsewhere too. The supply of parsimonious and not overly disputed sociotropic information should, in many countries and contexts, be better in the economic realm. Likewise, many people in many places should reasonably perceive a clearer political responsibility for welfare state services compared to the fuzzy link between the personal pocketbook and political decisions.

Second, some hypotheses have already undergone partial tests in other countries (though they have not necessarily been part of encompassing studies of welfare state experiences). For example, the contention that people manage to draw general political conclusions from specific personal welfare state experiences, and the hypothesis that these conclusions vary systematically with the level of empowerment built into institutional designs, have been put forward most convincingly by an American scholar (Soss 1999) based on American data (both qualitative interviews and the American National Election Studies). Likewise, the self-interest based hypothesis that state intervention support is higher among those who personally consume public services received at least some support in Britain in the 1970s (Dunleavy 1979; 1980a,b), even though those studies typically drew on rather sparse data on welfare state consumption. To this one may add that theories of distributive and procedural justice have to a large degree been developed and tested in the United States. Some of these tests, though far from all, have involved studies of personal encounters with various public authorities (Tyler et al. 1997).

Having pointed out these indications of generality, an important indication of specificity must now be acknowledged. It starts with the straightforward observation that the *salience* of welfare-state related political issues varies across countries and contexts. Much of the time in advanced industrial democracies, topics such as health care, public education, and social benefits, are rather high on the agendas of parties and the media. Yet, some of the time such topics are crowded out altogether by completely different concerns. What is more, we know from research on the agenda-setting capacities of political elites and the mass media that in the latter situation, welfare-state related issues will be perceived as less important by citizens than when such issues are extensively emphasized by politicians and journalists (see Asp 1986; Iyengar and Kinder 1987; Johansson 1998).

The impact of such salience variation on the processes under study here is not immediately self-evident. As discussed in chapter 4, the on-line model of opinion formation does not presuppose that a personally experienced welfare state institution is salient at the time of reporting an attitude or otherwise making a political choice. It is enough that the experience—which may have occurred a long time ago—made an attitudinal imprint at the time, after which the information that created that imprint may well be forgotten. For example, in order for health care experiences to affect political trust or ideology, it is not necessary that a person is still thinking about health care issues and experiences at the time of expressing the attitude. It is enough that health care issues were seen as important at the time of the experience, and that the experience triggered a political conclusion.

However, salience could affect the extent to which another precondition for personal experience effects is fulfilled. The likelihood that experiences stimulate opinion formation should increase if—at the time of the experience—people perceive that the experienced institution belongs to a politically important issue. To put it simply, if people feel that their personal experiences tie in to an area or problem that is politically important, the greater the chance that their experiences will stimulate political thinking and perhaps an update of political orientations.

Of course, such salience does not hinge exclusively on media and elite coverage. Rather, past research shows that the personal experience itself greatly enhances the probability that an experienced welfare state institution is thought of as an important political topic (Johansson 1998; McCombs 1999). People who have personal experiences with, say, health care are more likely than others to regard health care issues as politically important. Nevertheless, if on top of a direct experience, a person is also exposed to heavier health care coverage and debate at about the time of the health care experience, it becomes even more likely that the experience will trigger political thinking.[1]

In conclusion, the political emphasis and coverage devoted to various parts of the welfare state can be expected to vary across space and time. In turn, such variation may affect the magnitude of experience effects. This is interesting as past research suggests that the last years of the 1990s in Sweden was a context where many of the policy areas under study were heavily emphasized by political parties and by the mass media (Holmberg and Weibull 2000; Johansson 2000). Also, the top priorities of voters in the 1998 election campaign had to do with issues such as health care, education, child care, and elder care (Holmberg 2000). It seems, then, that "Sweden 1999" is hardly an environment that is hostile to political effects of personal welfare state experiences. This means that our hypotheses are probably not exposed to the hardest conceivable tests. On the other hand, one could argue that we test them in something like a typical context, at least if one agrees that, in the long run, welfare state issues are almost always among the most salient political topics in developed welfare states.

Finally, these informed speculations shall not overshadow the main message in this section: "Sweden 1999" was not chosen by design, but because it made primary data collection possible. Therefore, we need studies that test similar hypotheses in other contexts and countries. They will tell us more about the extent to which the results are possible to generalize.

The Data

The main data source of this study is *The 1999 West Sweden SOM Survey*.[2] It was conducted by *The SOM Institute*, which is managed jointly by the Institute for Journalism and Mass Communication, the Department of Political Science, and the School of Public Administration at Göteborg University. Since 1986, the SOM Institute has conducted interdisciplinary survey research in Sweden on the topics of Society, Opinion, and Media, hence the name SOM.[3]

Ever since 1986, a main activity has been the administration of an annual nationwide mail survey (see Holmberg and Weibull 2002). Since 1992, the SOM institute has also conducted a number of local and regional surveys, including an annual survey in West Sweden. In the early West Sweden SOM surveys, the sampling area covered Göteborg and a smaller number of municipalities near the city. In 1998, the survey was expanded so as to cover the entire Västra Götaland region. This region contains 1.5 of the 8.9 million Swedish inhabitants. Göteborg, the second largest city in Sweden, is located in the region.

Financed by the Swedish Council for Social Research, this project collected primary data under the auspices of the 1999 Västra Götaland SOM survey (referred to below as the 1999 West Sweden SOM Survey). Questionnaires and return envelopes were sent to a random sample of 5,900 individuals between 15 and 80 years of age, living in the Västra Götaland region, out of which 3,760 completed and returned the questionnaires by mail. The net response rate was 68 percent. The data were collected between October 1999 and January 2000 (for more information, see Nilsson 2000a; Nilsson and Olsson 2000).

Collaborating with the West Sweden SOM survey was fortunate as one of its main research topics has always been the usage of and satisfaction with welfare state services (see Nilsson 1996b, 1997; Johansson, Nilsson, and Strömberg 2001). By adding survey items particular to the present study—related to for instance self-interest, distributive justice, and procedural justice—alongside items routinely included in the survey, a dataset was created that is extremely useful for studying the political impact of personal welfare state experiences. The various items will be presented as we go along through chapters 6–10.

The fact that the data are collected in only a part of the country does not seem to pose much of a problem. Many previous analyses suggest that parameter estimates yielded by unweighted West Sweden SOM data are typically very similar to those generated by the nationwide SOM studies or by national election studies (see Johansson and Nilsson 2002). In fact, this contention will receive further support in chapter 6 where in some instances we can compare West Sweden SOM estimates with those for the whole country. It is thus unlikely that any major conclusions would have been different had the data been collected in the country as a whole.

Apart from the 1999 West Sweden SOM survey, we will occasionally draw on two auxiliary data sources. One is *The 1999 European Parliament Election Study*, which was conducted by the *Swedish Election Studies Program* in cooperation with Statistics Sweden (SCB). The Swedish Election Studies Program is located at the Department of Political Science, Göteborg University, and is currently directed by Sören Holmberg. Its activities—which were initiated by Jörgen Westerståhl and Bo Särlvik in the early 1950s—include voter surveys at the time of each national parliamentary election and national referendum, surveys with members of Parliament, and media content analyses.[4]

The 1999 European Parliament Election Study is a post-election survey involving face-to-face interviews. The sample is drawn from a population of Swedish citizens between 18 and 80 years of age, and the interviews were carried out by trained SCB interviewers between June 14 and September 27, 1999 (the election was held on June 13). The number of interviewed respondents was 2,022, which means the net response rate was 75 percent (for more information, see Hedberg 2000). As I participated in the main report of this study (Holmberg et al. 2001), I was given the opportunity to include some questions on both personally experienced public services as well as on "sociotropic" evaluations of public services. These items will be put to use in chapter 6.

A second auxiliary data source is provided by *The 1992 Swedish Living Standard Survey*.[5] The principal investigator of this survey was Björn Halleröd, Department of Sociology, Umeå University (see Halleröd et al. 1993; Halleröd 1994). The data were collected in spring 1992 by means of face-to-face interviews, again carried out by trained SCB interviewers. The sample was drawn from individuals in the Swedish population between 20 and 75 years of age. Out of a total sample of 1,075 people, 793 were interviewed, which makes for a response rate of 74 percent. An interesting feature of this study is that information from public records about benefits from transfer systems and social insurances have been added to the dataset. This information will be useful in chapter 7 when it comes to constructing measures of welfare state self-interest.

Selecting, Projecting, Resisting, and Constructing Experiences?

Let us close this chapter by considering potential perils of cross-sectional data. The point of departure is the basic causal model illustrated in figure 1.1. This causal scheme is a parsimonious account of a complicated process. It does not incorporate the rather obvious fact that citizens do not enter experiences as newborn babies (except in maternity hospitals). Rather, people take with them preexisting values, beliefs, and attitudes into their experiences. Such *predispositions* may in various ways affect the extent to which people get in contact with welfare state institutions, and how they perceive and react politically to their experiences. As Zaller (1992:6) puts it, "Every opinion is a marriage of information and predisposition." From this perspective, figure 1.1 is simplified as it only models political effects of an information source (personal experiences), while being silent about how predispositions may affect the process.

Adjusting as best as we can for these deficiencies, the final task in this chapter is to think about four possible versions of the suspicion that predispositions affect, and interact with the impact of, welfare state experiences. In turn, we will discuss the possibilities that, depending on their predispositions, people *select, project, resist*, and *construct* personal welfare state experiences. I first describe the intellectual origins of these four possibilities, after which I explain why this study unfortunately cannot consider them in any great empirical depth.

A first possibility is that people "select" experiences. This means that predispositions affect the extent to which people actually get in contact with various welfare state institutions. Individuals with certain attitudes are to a greater extent than others drawn to (certain) public services, regardless of their "objective needs"—income, health, age, number of children, and so on. In statistical language, selection effects operate directly, controlling for objective needs.

Theoretically, selection effects lie outside the scope of this study. Our substantive interest is effects of, not explanations for, personal experiences. Empirically, however, some of the attitudinal predispositions that drive the selection of experiences may be (earlier versions of) the dependent variables of political trust and ideology. And because the empirical analysis will be based on cross-sectional data, we might not always be able to sort out what affects what.

Especially preexisting ideological orientations might play a role here. For example, those who already hold rightist and antistate orientations might be less likely than others to seek out public help and services of various sorts. They are more prone to regard nonpublic entities such as the individual, the family, or nonprofit organizations as the appropriate locus of welfare production. It is thus possible that such attitudes make them more likely to refrain from using public services if they can, and opt for some form of nonpublic alternative.

The notion of selection effects has consequences for the empirical analysis. Consider the hypothesis that more frequent personal usage of welfare state products produces greater self-interested support for state intervention and leftist ideology. Chapter 7 tests this prediction by examining the cross-sectional relation between ideology measures and variables counting the number of welfare state institutions from which respondents are currently receiving service. If there is such a correlation, it may be interpreted in at least two ways. First, in line with the self-interest perspective, the correlation could reflect a real causal impact of differences in welfare state consumption. Second, in line with the notion of selection effects, it may be that those who already support state intervention are more prone to seek out organizations that they already like.

Consider in a similar fashion the hypothesis that experiences have a more positive impact on ideology, the more empowering institutional interfaces are. As discussed in chapter 3, one mechanism would be that institutionalized empowerment improves judgments of experienced social justice. But again the perspective of selection effects offers an alternative interpretation. It starts with the observation that more empowering experiences involve more exit-options. And it is possible that empowering experiences correlate more strongly with leftist ideology, not because of improved judgments of experienced social justice, but because this is the part of the welfare state where selection effects are allowed to operate freely. User institutions like libraries and sports facilities are open for selection effects in a way that client institutions like social assistance and elder care are not. This could explain why experiences of user institutions have a stronger positive relation with ideology.

A second risk is that people "project" experiences (see Krosnick 2002). This could occur for instance, when we ask them to subjectively describe or evaluate their experiences in terms of distributive justice or voice opportunities. The risk is that answers to such questions are, not so much judgments of actual experiences, but rather rationalizations of preexisting political attitudes. Take as example a cross-sectional correlation between perceived distributive justice and state-intervention support. According to the "projection" hypothesis, the explanation is not that negative welfare state experiences lead people to question the practical utility or the legitimacy of big government. Instead, the argument goes, it is people who already endorse antistate attitudes who tend to bring their answers to experience questions in line with their political orientations.

Though selection and projection denote different processes, they lead to similar methodological problems in the context of this study. More precisely, the problem is the theoretical possibility of reciprocal causation, coupled with the empirical analysis of cross-sectional data. It is not self-evident how we should interpret a cross-sectional correlation between experiences and political orientations. There are logically reasonable interpretations of a causal impact in both directions, and the data could be consistent with both.

A third possibility is that people "resist" experiences. The point of departure is the well-known tendency that individuals are more susceptible to political information that is perceived to fit with their preexisting orientations. In fact, virtually all successful theories of mass political preferences have, in some form, and to some extent, incorporated the notion of resistance (or "selective perception").[6] For instance, in the classic Michigan model of voting behavior, "Identification with a party raises a perceptual screen through which the individual tends to see what is favorable to his partisan orientation" (Campbell et al. 1960:1333). Likewise, more recent models subscribe to the axiom that "People tend to resist arguments that are inconsistent with their political predispositions" (Zaller 1992:44; see also Berelson, Lazarsfeld, and McPhee 1954; Klapper 1960; McGuire 1985; Eagly and Chaiken 1993). As for welfare state experiences, the resistance axiom implies that people might very well notice some positive or negative aspect of an experience, but they may not accept the information as "valid," "fair," "representative," or the like, because the observation does not jibe well with preexisting political orientations. And such resisted observations should exercise a smaller impact.

Such processes pose a potential threat to our general hypotheses. These hypotheses all build on the idea that negative and positive experiences—conceptualized in terms of self-interest, distributive justice, or voice—have a general impact on political trust and ideology. This impact is general in the sense that it operates with the same strength and direction, regardless of what political orientations and leanings a person subscribed to before experiences occurred. However, if resistance processes were widespread, one would expect a pattern where people who are already skeptical about the welfare state and the political system are more susceptible to negative experiences. Conversely, one would expect citizens with preexisting positive feelings about these entities to give greater political weight to positive experiences.

Here, it should be pointed out that we are talking about tendencies. People *tend* to resist inconsistent information, and predispositions are thus never perfect information filters. People are almost never motivated or sophisticated enough, and the evaluative implications of predispositions are rarely clear enough, so as to allow for perfect resistance to uncongenial information. Most people, therefore, will typically reject some information that is reasonably consistent with preexisting orientations, and accept some information that is reasonably inconsistent with those orientations (Gerber and Green 1999). This means that the notion of resistance draws our attention to a gradual interaction effect: the impact of experiences on subsequent political orientations gradually increases, the greater the consistency between experiences and preexisting orientations. However, because preexisting orientations are no perfect information filters, there should usually be a certain small effect of a particular type of experiences even among people where experiences do not fit predispositions.

Moreover, two objections can be made against the notion of resisting incompatible information in the context of personal welfare state experiences. These objections somewhat diminish the threat posed to our general hypotheses. First, the idea of resistance stems from research on opinion persuasion, for instance, persuasion by political elites through the mass media. It has been shown that people often use their preexisting political orientations to selectively sort and evaluate this type of information. Moreover, many people do this because they are not motivated to examine in detail, or carefully deliberate on, political elite information. Instead, they use predispositions toward the political world as informational shortcuts (Popkin 1991; Sniderman, Brody, and Tetlock 1991; McGraw and Hubbard 1996). As an example imagine a leftist pro-welfare person who hears a conservative politician arguing that a public service should be privatized. This person will typically not examine in detail the logical coherence or factual accuracy of the message. Rather, he or she may opt for the convenient informational shortcut that "I know that I don't like that sort of politics and politicians," thus resisting the information based on political predispositions.

Of course, this can only occur to the extent that there are easily available cues that make it clear how a piece of information fits with predispositions. And this assumption is probably more fulfilled in the context of elite messages than in the context of personal welfare state experiences. In the former context, messages often come with information about how different politicians, parties, and interest organizations describe reality. Based on such cues, and based on how the individual is predisposed toward these actors and their ideologies, a person can take convenient shortcuts in the information jungle. In contrast, personal welfare experiences generate a more raw and less prepackaged type of information that does not contain equally self-evident cues to what one "ought to" think about it. Moreover, because "The key to resistance [. . .] is information concerning the relationship between arguments and predispositions" (Zaller 1992:44), resistance processes may be less widespread for personal experiences than they have proven to be in the case of persuasive communication with political elites.[7]

Second, resistance processes could be less widespread when personal involvement rises. Normally, citizens are not sufficiently motivated and involved in order to carefully examine political arguments and information. Because most citizens follow politics with, at best, one eye open, they have a need to make swift predisposition-based judgments of new incoming information (Popkin 1991). In the absence of motivation and involvement, careful examination of the logical and empirical relevance of such elite-level information would be unbearably tedious and time-consuming. Indeed, "people process information superficially and minimally unless they are motivated to do otherwise [. . .] people must have sufficient motivation to turn to more effortful, systematic forms of processing" (Eagly and Chaiken 1993:674).

This study, however, investigates a type of information that may be able to arouse considerably more involvement and motivation than the average news story. After all, we are talking about direct, personal, and potentially important events, not just any distant and obscure political issue or debate that one may notice from the corner of the eye. It seems plausible that people are more interested in carefully thinking about such political information, compared to the average day-to-day politics reported in the mass media (Fiske 1986:51). If so, people no longer have the same chronic need to use simplifying predispositions as shortcuts to swift decisions on what information should be resisted and endorsed respectively.

Past research lends some credibility to these remarks. Especially Petty and Cacioppo (1986) have, based on a series of experiments, found that individuals with no personal involvement with an issue are more likely to be lazy and rely on easily accessible cues concerning information source ("who says it"). They are also less likely to be affected by the actual nature and quality of the information. Conversely, subjects with greater personal involvement are less concerned with easily accessible cues and informational shortcuts, and are prone to examine in more detail the information at hand. Resistance to arguments based on source cues is thus less widespread among the personally involved and motivated (see Eagly and Chaiken 1993:287–89).

Finally, let us think about the possibility that people "construct" experiences. We start by observing that our hypotheses more or less take for granted what political conclusions should be drawn from negative and positive experiences respectively. More precisely, our hypotheses suggest that a positive experience (in terms of self-interest, distributive justice, or voice) is information that should typically produce positive effects on political trust, and leftist effects on ideological orientations. The assumption is thus that everyone draws more or less the same political conclusions of such experiences. Expressed differently, the political meaning of negative and positive experiences respectively is regarded as self-evident and invariant.

This assumption is not only embraced by our hypotheses, but also by the notion of "resisting" experiences: Predispositions serve to detect whether one should reject or endorse political information. However, the actual political meaning of the information—what conclusions it should logically lead to—is seen as unproblematic. It is assumed to be more or less self-evident what political response a given piece of information should stimulate if it is accepted. Of course, some may reject the information whereas others may endorse it. But the information means the same political thing to everyone.

This somewhat rigid assumption is relaxed by the notion of "constructed experiences." The basic idea is that there are not always definitive answers to the question of what political conclusions should "logically" follow from a given piece of accepted information (see Neuman, Just, and Crigler 1992; Gamson 1992; McQuail 1994). Rather, political meaning must often be "constructed." It must be figured out by the individual, based on his or her preexisting political attitudes and knowledge. More than this, depending on predispositions, very similar information may be interpreted differently, and hence produce very different "effects" among different people. In other words, construction processes draw our attention to an interaction effect of predispositions into the relationship between experiences and subsequent political orientations.

Actually, chapter 2 identified a specific version of the general idea. We observed that the literature on distributive justice assumes that poor assessments of distributive justice reduce support for common institutions. However, it was also noted that the opposite effect is conceivable, especially among individuals who already strongly supported such institutions before experiences occurred. Specifically, among pro-welfare state citizens, the natural response to, say, strongly inadequate health care experiences might not be an increased negativity toward public sector arrangements. On the contrary, they may draw the conclusion that such arrangements have too little resources and must receive even *more* resources and support in the future.[8]

One may of course think of other possible constructionist threats to our unconditional predictions. Imagine for example two citizens—one with a large portion of political trust, the other an incurable political cynic—who both experience good voice opportunities in contacts with, say, public schools. To the extent that these experiences trigger political reasoning, what conclusions will be drawn? According to our hypothesis, the answer is that both these individuals will develop more positive attitudes toward the political system and its actors. However, from the constructionist perspective, the political cynic could very well deviate from the supposedly general pattern: he or she may regard the voice opportunities as new arguments for not trusting the political system. To the cynic, voice opportunities may be constructed as just another sign of political hypocrisy, as another indication that "they just pretend to care about our opinions, and then disregard them anyway." Conversely, the trusting citizen is more likely to frame experienced voice opportunities as indications of a genuine desire to incorporate citizens' views in the implementation and evaluation of public policy.

These examples demonstrate that the political meaning of comparable personal welfare state experiences is not necessarily self-evident or invariant across people. Rather, such meaning must be mentally constructed, and these constructions as well as their effects may vary.

Dynamic Theories—Static Data

In conclusion, it is likely that figure 1.1 is too parsimonious to do full justice to the complexity of experience effects. All four possibilities identified in the previous section are worth taking seriously and merit further research. Such research would teach us more about how, when, and to what extent people select, project, resist, and construct personal welfare state experiences.

While this study takes these four possibilities with utmost theoretical seriousness, it cannot pursue them to any great empirical depths. The reason, as already hinted at, is that we will use static, cross-sectional survey data collected at one point in time. Of course, from the viewpoint of selection, projection, resistance, and construction processes, this is unfortunate because all four possibilities demand some form of dynamic data. To isolate them empirically we would need to measure, not only respondents' political attitudes after experiences have occurred, but also their predispositions before the experience. Such variables would then be included as control variables and interaction variables in our statistical models. However, because we use cross-sectional data we will not be able to do this, meaning that it is not empirically possible to separate "genuine" experience effects from reciprocal selection and projection, or investigate whether the direction and strength of experience effects are conditioned by resistance and construction processes.

Having pointed out these shortcomings, there are at least two arguments for the chosen research strategy. A first point has to do with the actual purpose of this study. The main objective is not a desire to sort out once and for all the extent to which people select, project, resist, and construct personal welfare state experiences. Rather, the research task is to push the (admittedly simplistic) framework in figure 1.1 out of the economic realm and into welfare state territory. What will happen when we do this? Do personal experiences become more important than personal economic experiences have proven to be? If so, what aspects of experiences matter? And are experience effects channeled by sociotropic perceptions or not?

When these questions have been addressed in a fair amount of studies, it is reasonable to move on to testing (even) more sophisticated assumptions about how predispositions affect, and interact with, personal welfare state experiences (c.f. Krosnick 2002). But as I hope the empirical chapters will show, there is at this point a lot of illuminating cross-sectional information to be extracted. The proof of the pudding will—hopefully—be in the eating. A second point—equally important but perhaps less intellectually satisfying—has to do with the available survey data. It would of course be nice to have a panel dataset that allowed the inclusion of predispositions at t–1 for most of the analyses performed in this study. However, to the best of my knowledge, there is no Swedish panel dataset that simultaneously contains (1) nearly as much welfare state experience information as the cross-sectional datasets used here, and (2) nearly as much information about the dependent variables. Hence, we are at present not sufficiently well equipped to investigate the presence of selection, projection, resistance, and construction processes in studies of political effects of personal welfare state experiences.

The Welfare State and the Economy

Throughout the summer of 2001, Swedish newspapers reported extensively on the apparently dropping quality of public health care. For instance, the major paper in the Göteborg area arranged a phone-in where readers called journalists and shared their personal health care experiences.[1] One man told the following story: "Politicians should not use the word welfare anymore when talking about Sweden. My wife had to wait for four hours with a broken arm at the local health care central in Falkenberg. Then she was sent to Varberg for another five hours of waiting. All in all, it took twelve hours before her arm was in a cast. It's a scandal." The whole event was summarized like this: ". . . they all told similar stories. They all expressed anger, fear, and disappointment. Several said the staff should not be blamed, but rather the organization and, ultimately, the politicians."

These quotes illustrate nicely the type of effects we are looking for: Very specific personal contacts with welfare state institutions become a basis for the formation of very general political judgments and attitudes.

However, in contrast to the commonsense-feeling conveyed by these quotes, academic research concludes that politically relevant personal experiences are typically not very consequential for political attitudes. Instead, what matters to a much greater extent are "sociotropic perceptions" of the collective state of affairs. When forming political attitudes, the argument goes, citizens rarely wonder "what are my personal experiences?" They are much more inclined to ask themselves sociotropic questions like "what has the collective experienced?" and adjust their attitudes accordingly. Judging from this research, citizens in modern mass democracies are better described as "sociotropic animals," than as egocentric ones.

Furthermore, according to these studies, sociotropic perceptions are very weakly correlated with direct personal observations and experiences. People experiencing personal financial crises are not more likely than others to infer from their personal situation that the whole economy is in trouble. Collective-level perceptions do not seem to be informed by personal-level reality. In Mutz's (1998:66) words, "Despite the accessibility and obvious salience of personal experiences, they very seldom have a large or significant effect on judgments about collective-level reality." Rather, previous research concludes, sociotropic views of the collective state of affairs are the products of elite interpretations of social reality. These interpretations are typically communicated to us via the mass media.

These conclusions originate mainly in research on personal *economic* experiences. This chapter, however, studies personal experiences and sociotropic perceptions of both the economy and the welfare state. We have reasons to believe that the nature of opinion formation changes when we move out of the economic realm and into welfare state territory. More exactly, we have hypothesized that personal experiences are more consequential to political attitudes in the welfare state territory than in the economic realm.

Chapter 1 discussed two potential reasons for this difference. The first one has to do with the differing nature of political responsibility. Experiences of welfare state institutions are the immediate results of decisions taken by responsible politicians. After all, we are talking about experiences with the very institutions that are supposed to implement political decisions. In contrast, there is only an indirect and unclear political responsibility for citizens' personal economies. In Western societies, the personal economy is largely a personal, not political, responsibility. The firmer link between personal welfare state experiences and responsible political actors might be better at stimulating political thinking than the weaker link between the personal economy and political actors.

The second reason has to do with the nature of political information. The economic policy realm offers a small set of memorable and informative macroeconomic indicators ("unemployment," "budget deficits," "inflation," and so on). This set of indicators lends itself naturally to the formation of accurate economic sociotropic perceptions. We all know whether the economy is going up or down, and such views are easily separated from personal economic experiences. In contrast, the welfare state offers heterogeneous and potentially conflicting sociotropic information. Whether the welfare state is improving or deteriorating is typically a more difficult question than how the economy is doing. Welfare state personal experiences might therefore be a more important political information source than personal economic experiences.

Figure 1.1 suggested two paths by which personal experiences can be generalized into political preferences. The paths represent two potential ways in which personal experiences are more important than personal economic experiences. The first possibility is that *direct* effects of personal experiences on political orientations are strengthened as we move out of the economy and into the welfare state: People find it so difficult to form sociotropic welfare state perceptions, and personal welfare state experiences appear so easy and relevant, that sociotropic perceptions become disconnected from politics altogether. Controlling for sociotropic perceptions, differences in personal experiences then have a *direct* effect on preferences.

The second possibility is that the *indirect* effects of personal experiences increase. If so, it is still sociotropic perceptions of collective experience that are of immediate importance to political orientations, and citizens may still be accurately described as "sociotropic animals." However, sociotropic perceptions are in turn partly products of personal experience. Because of the more difficult sociotropic information, and because of the greater political relevance of personal experience, sociotropic welfare state perceptions will be more tightly linked to personal experience.

By and large, research on economic perceptions has analyzed two kinds of dependent variables: (1) support for the governing party, and (2) political trust orientations such as satisfaction with democracy and trust in politicians. The conclusion that sociotropic perceptions matter more than personal experiences has proven to hold for both. This chapter analyzes exactly these two groups of dependent variables. Of course, for reasons discussed in chapter 4, later chapters will focus entirely on overarching affect-laden political orientations, rather than more short-term and concrete opinions such as support for the governing party. However, at the moment our main concern is what happens when welfare state perceptions are added as independent variables to previously tested models. Given this concern, it would not make sense to change the models on both the independent and the dependent side, a situation in which it is unclear which change actually caused any differences compared to previous research.

Here is how the chapter is organized. First, we familiarize ourselves with the independent variables. Second, we examine the link between personal experiences and sociotropic perceptions, both in the economic realm and in the welfare state. Third, we estimate full causal models of the relations between personal experiences, sociotropic perceptions, and political attitudes in the two policy domains. Fourth, inspired by the observation that economic perceptions are more positive than views on personally experienced public services, we make a counterfactual thought experiment: How much would the percentage of government sympathizers increase if personally experienced public services were viewed as favorably as the economy? Fifth, we draw conclusions and look forward to later chapters.

Measuring Personal Experiences and Sociotropic Perceptions

Just as it would make no sense to analyze different dependent variables than previous research, it would be unwise, given our purposes, to change the format for measuring independent variables. Hence, to measure economic judgments, a question that has been included in many surveys in different countries was included in the 1999 West Sweden SOM Survey. This question asked retrospectively about trends in economic conditions: "According to your view, how have the following economic conditions changed in the last twelve months?" Respondents answered with respect to "your personal economic situation" as well as with respect to "the Swedish economy." For each item, three response alternatives were offered: "improved," "remained about the same," and "got worse."

A similar question was asked about public services: "According to your view, how has the quality of public services changed during the last two or three years?" Respondents answered with respect to both "public services I have been in contact with," and "public services in Sweden." The response alternatives were the same as for economic perceptions.[2]

As mentioned in chapter 5, I also had the opportunity to include virtually the same questions in the 1999 Swedish European Parliament Election Study. Univariate frequencies for all these independent variables may be inspected in table 6.1.

In 1999, Swedes were more satisfied with economic development than with public services.[3] For instance, between 43 and 56 percent thought the Swedish economy had gotten better, whereas only 3 percent chose the same alternative with respect to public services. The items tapping personal experiences of the economy and public services respectively registered similar differences.

People were certainly not wrong in thinking the economy was improving as Sweden had been recovering for several years after the crisis of the early 1990s. Interestingly, this crisis also resulted in sizeable cutbacks in many parts of the public sector (see Svallfors 1996). And although the governing Social Democrats, along with several other parties, built their 1998 election campaign on promises to improve public services, citizens apparently did not perceive that these expectations were being fulfilled.

There are only small percentage differences in the results from the West Sweden Survey (a mail survey conducted between October and January) and the European Parliament Election Study (face-to-face interviews conducted between June and September). The only deviation worth mentioning is that the respondents in the European Parliament Election Study

Table 6.1   Retrospective perceptions of the economy and public services in the 1999 West Sweden SOM Survey (WSOM99), and the 1999 European Parliament Election Study (EUP99)

	WSOM 99	EUP99	WSOM 99	EUP99
	Personal economy		*Personally experienced public services*	
Got better	29	30	4	5
Remained the same	51	54	67	69
Got worse	20	15	28	26
Sum percent	100	100	100	100
Number or respondents	3,615	1,268	3,448	1,168
	The Swedish economy		*Public services in Sweden*	
Got better	43	56	3	3
Remained the same	39	34	50	51
Got worse	19	10	47	46
Sum percent	100	100	100	100
Number of respondents	3,458	1,210	3,431	1,226

Note: See related main text for question wording.

viewed the economy more favorably (56 percent, versus 43 in the West Sweden Study, thought the economy had gotten better).

The Relation Between Personal Experiences and Sociotropic Judgments

Previous research on economic perceptions contends that the link between personal experiences and sociotropic judgments is weak or nonexistent. In the economic realm, people do not seem very good at drawing general conclusions from their own experiences of politically relevant phenomena. However, we have opened for the possibility that this link is strengthened when we move into welfare state territory. The relative lack of parsimonious macro indicators, coupled with the clearer connection between welfare state experiences and responsible politicians, means such experiences could be a more important source of political information than personal economic experiences. As indicated earlier, this information might affect political orientations directly, without being generalized into a sociotropic perception. However, it is also possible that personal experiences affect political orientations because experiences are an information source for sociotropic perceptions, perceptions that in turn impact on political orientations. This implies that welfare state experiences are more important than economic ones because they are more tightly linked to sociotropic perceptions.

The idea is supported by the findings presented in table 6.2. It displays correlation coefficients for pairs of items having "parallel" wording for both personal experiences and sociotropic judgments. In addition to the items introduced in table 6.1, I also included some more specific measures of experiences and sociotropic judgments. These will show up later in the book in analyses of the impact of experienced distributive and procedural justice. But for now we are only interested in the correlation between experiences and sociotropic judgments.

The classic finding in previous research is replicated by these data. There is only a rather moderate correlation between perceptions of the personal economy and sociotropic perceptions of the country's economy (between .14 and .20). However, the link is strengthened when we enter welfare state territory. Here, the correlations between personal experiences and sociotropic judgments are about twice as large or more, compared to the economic realm. The correlations between change in personal experience and change at the collective level are even three times as large in the welfare state. This latter difference was found in the West Sweden Survey (.63 versus .20), as well as in the European Parliament Election Study (.47 versus .15).

So far, the results fit the prediction. Whereas personal-level and collective-level judgments of politically relevant phenomena are fairly separate in the economic realm, they are intimately intertwined in the welfare state.

Table 6.2 The relation between personal experiences and sociotropic judgments (Pearson's *r*)

1999 West Sweden SOM survey	
The economy	
Change in personal economy—Change in Swedish economy	.20
The welfare state	
Change in personally experienced public services—Change in Swedish public services	.63
I was treated correctly—In general, people are correctly treated	.42
In my experience, public employees worked efficiently—In general, public employees work efficiently	.48
I could affect how services were run—In general people can affect how services are run	.36
I have received the service and help I have a right to—In general, people receive the service and help they have a right to	.43
1999 European Parliament Election study	
The economy	
Change in personal economy—Change in Swedish economy	.15
Change in personal economy—The situation in Swedish economy	.14
The welfare state	
Change in personally experienced public services—Change in Swedish public services	.47
Change in personally experienced public services—The situation in Swedish public services	.30

Notes: The last four welfare-state related pairs of items in the West Sweden SOM survey emanate from a question battery that is described in conjunction with tables 8.1 and 9.1. Furthermore, the sociotropic variables tapping the *situation* in the economy and in public services respectively were only included in the European Parliament Election Study. These variables have five categories: very good (coded 1), rather good (2), neither good nor bad (3), rather bad (4), and very bad (5). For information about the remaining items, see table 6.1.

Modeling Direct and Indirect Effects of Personal Experiences

We now turn to a multivariate investigation of the hypothesis that personal welfare state experiences are more important in the opinion formation process than personal economic experiences. Again, our causal scheme opens for the possibility that personal experiences may affect political attitudes both directly as well as indirectly. The indirect effects would operate through sociotropic perceptions, reflecting a process in which people generalize their experiences into collective-level judgments, judgments that play a role in the formation of political attitudes. The findings in the last section certainly underscore this last indirect possibility. Figure 6.1 reiterates our causal model graphically. Essentially, it is the same model as the one presented in chapter 1. The only difference is that perceptions of public services are now included side by side with economic perceptions.

Using OLS regression analysis, I estimated the various effects in the model for each of three dependent variables: government approval, satisfaction with the way democracy works, and trust in politicians (table 6.3). The independent variables were retrospective perceptions of changes in the economy and in public services. In addition, each equation in these causal models includes a number of control variables that are known to affect the dependent variables (as discussed in chapter 4), and that could also be suspected to influence retrospective accounts of the economy and/or the welfare state.

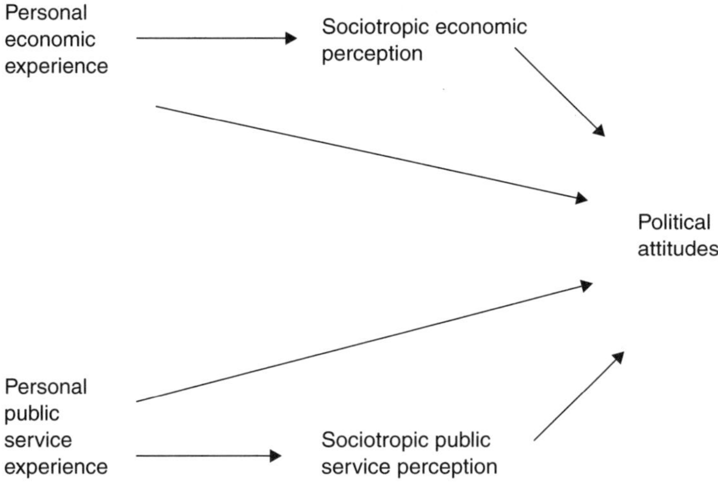

Figure 6.1   Personal experiences, sociotropic judgments, and political attitudes

Before proceeding to commenting on the results, a note on the construction of dependent variables might be in order. The government approval variable was generated by a question in the 1999 European Parliament Election Study asking how "the Social Democrats have done as a government party since the 1994 election." Respondents answered using an eleven-point scale ranging from -5 (the government has done a bad job) to $+5$ (the government has done a good job). The negative coefficients in table 6.3 mean that average government approval drops as views on the economy and the welfare state grow negative.

Furthermore, this study analyzes two indicators of political trust. Both are standard indicators employed in the literature, and both are measures of relatively concrete objects of "political support," rather than of more diffuse support toward the political community. The first indicator taps "satisfaction with the way democracy works." A second indicator of political trust taps the degree of "trust in politicians." In the parlance of the political support typology discussed in chapter 4, the former measure is most directly related to "regime performance." It is thus seen as tapping attitudes toward the democratic system as it actually functions. The second measure is concerned, not so much with the political regime itself, but rather with general support for political authorities and actors.

The 1999 West Sweden Survey offers ample opportunities to measure political trust. In order to generate a measure of overall satisfaction with democracy, I factor analyzed three items tapping the degree to which people are satisfied with how democracy works in practice in Sweden, in the Västra Götaland region, and in the municipality respectively. Similarly, to obtain a measure of trust in politicians, I factor analyzed items tapping trust in politicians in the three geographical units respectively.[4] The means of the

Table 6.3   Causal model of how retrospective perceptions affect government approval, satisfaction with democracy, and trust in politicians (unstandardized OLS estimates)

	Total effect	*Direct effect*
Dependent variable: Government approval (0–10, higher value = higher approval of the way the government is doing its job)		
Personally experienced public services	−.69***	−.26
Personal economy	−.48***	−.27**
Swedish public services	−.70***	−.70***
Swedish economy	−1.00***	−1.00***
Number of respondents	983	
Dependent variable: Satisfaction with democracy (higher value = greater satisfaction)		
Personally experienced public services	−.27***	−.17***
Personal economy	−.12***	−.09***
Swedish public services	−.12**	−.12**
Swedish economy	−.19**	−.19***
Number of respondents	2,565	
Dependent variable: Trust in politicians (higher value = greater trust)		
Personally experienced public services	−.35***	−.25***
Personal economy	−.12***	−.09***
Swedish public services	−.13***	−.13***
Swedish economy	−.19***	−.19***
Number of respondents	2,642	

$*p < .10$ $**p < .05$ $***p < .01$

Notes: The basic structure of the three causal models can be inspected in figure 6.1. For information about dependent variables, see main text. The government approval analysis was done using the 1999 European Parliament Election Study, whereas the analyses of satisfaction with democracy and trust in politicians were done using the 1999 West Sweden SOM Survey. All displayed independent variables are coded between 1 (improved) and 3 (got worse); for more details, see table 6.1. The models also contain a number of exogenous control variables, the estimates of which are not displayed (for government approval: ideological left–right self-placement, income, subjective class affiliation, education, age in years, gender, trade union membership (LO), and public sector employment. For satisfaction with democracy and trust in politicians: incumbent party preference, no party preference, education, subjective class identification, age in years, subjective life satisfaction). All these control variables were coded in the same way as in other analyses throughout the book (see e.g., table 7.6). Finally, the models also contain intercepts that are not displayed.

resulting factors equal zero, and standard deviations equal 1. They were scored so that higher values mean greater political trust.

Consistent with much previous research, voters' perceptions of economic trends matter for their attitudes toward their elected government. Holding the control variables constant, those perceiving negative trends in the economy are likely to express more dissatisfaction with the government. And just like in past studies, collective-level "sociotropic" perceptions of the country's economic affairs (−1.00) are more tightly linked to government approval than perceptions of ups and downs in the personal pocketbook (−.48). If we add to this the previously noted weak link between personal economic experiences and sociotropic views of the economy, the personal and the political appear relatively disconnected in the economic realm.

Moreover, the total effect of personally experienced public services is larger than that of personal economy (−.69 versus −.48). While this difference is not significant ($p = .31$) it is in the direction of the hypothesis. People are more likely to disapprove of the way the government is handling its job, the more people think that public services they have experienced personally have deteriorated. This effect is somewhat stronger than that of personal economic experiences.

Note that much of the impact of personal public service experiences is channeled through overall sociotropic perceptions. About two-thirds of the total personal experience impact disappears when sociotropic perceptions are added to the equation. Given this finding, and given the mainstream assumption that experiences and sociotropic perceptions correlate because the former affect the latter, it is clear that stronger personal experience effects in the welfare state are not necessarily at odds with sociotropic concerns for the collective well-being. On the contrary, judging from the relatively sizable impact of sociotropic perceptions, people still appear to consider the collective-level state of affairs when thinking about public services and incumbent performance. However, because of differences in the nature of political information and political responsibility compared to the economic policy area, personal experiences become more important as an information source in the formation of sociotropic perceptions. And because these sociotropic perceptions in turn affect government approval, personal welfare state experiences will become more influential than economic ones.

While the analysis of government approval only reveals traces of such differences, our hypotheses receive more clear-cut support in the analysis of political trust. For both satisfaction with democracy and trust in politicians, the total effects of personal public service experiences are about two to three times as strong as those of personal economic experiences ($-.27$ versus $-.12$; $p = .002$; and $-.35$ versus $-.12$, $p = .000$). Actually, for both dependent variables, the impact of welfare state experiences is also somewhat stronger than that of sociotropic economic perceptions ($-.27$ versus $-.19$ and $-.35$ versus $-.19$). This is a difference compared to the analysis of government approval, where sociotropic economic perception was still the most influential factor.

Still however, a fair share of welfare state experience effects on political orientations is channeled through sociotropic welfare state perceptions. About one-third of the impact vanishes when the sociotropic measure is entered into the models of satisfaction with democracy and trust in politicians. This observation, together with the fact that sociotropic service perceptions impact also on these dependent variables ($-.13$), means we should not throw the notion of "sociotropic animals" overboard. Citizens care about collective experiences also when it comes to drawing political conclusions of welfare state views. However, those views are more tightly linked to personal experiences than are economic collective-level views. The personal and the political spheres are less separated in the welfare state compared to the economy.

Finally, let me mention a curiosity in these causal models. I discovered that personal public service experiences affect sociotropic perceptions, not just of Swedish public services, but also of the Swedish economy. Conversely, in one of the datasets there is a certain impact of personal economic experiences on sociotropic public service perceptions. While our theoretical framework does not directly anticipate such effects, it is perhaps possible to think of reasonable explanations. For instance, some people in contact with poor public services may infer that public finances are declining and that this might have something to do with the general economic climate. Similarly, some of those experiencing personal financial decline could take this as a symptom of a more general recession, and that this is affecting public services.[5]

What if Public Services had been as Thriving as the Economy?

It is always difficult to assess effects of one survey item on the other. Whether effects should be regarded as weak, moderate, or strong is a largely arbitrary question. One part of the problem is that survey items typically lack an intuitive metric. Of course, in a statistical sense, we grasp statements such as "one unit of change along the public service experience variable produces .69 units of change along the 11-point government approval scale." However, while we understand the variable's statistical importance, we may still feel unsure of how influential it is in a more substantive sense.

A common solution is to compare effects of different variables with one another. By comparing the impact of a novel independent variable to that of a well-known one, we learn more than just looking at one single coefficient. Here, it may be argued that the most relevant yardstick for welfare state experiences variables is sociotropic economic perceptions. The latter variable is well known, it has a relatively respectable impact on government approval and political support, and it is measured using parallel question-wording and identical alternatives. This comparison has already been done, and personal public service experiences had a slightly weaker effect in the case of government approval, and a slightly stronger effect in the case of satisfaction with democracy and trust in politicians. Based on this comparison with a respected explanatory factor, personal public service experiences appear to add an element to our understanding of how these political orientations develop.

Yet, some readers might not be entirely satisfied with this relativist view on assessing effects. Indeed, it may be argued that comparing changes along one unintuitive scale with changes along another unintuitive scale does not take us where we want to go. Therefore, we now adopt an additional approach to grasping the impact of welfare state experiences. The question is how *politically important* the reported effects are.

Technically speaking, we use individual-level effect estimates to make "counterfactual comparisons" between different aggregate-level distributions along the independent variables. Based on the individual-level effect coefficients, and given our causal interpretation of those coefficients, we calculate how the percentage supporting the incumbent party ought to shift as distributions change.

The reader may recall that in 1999, Swedes were clearly more satisfied with overall economic development than with public services: whereas between 43 and 56 percent thought the Swedish economy had gotten better, only about 5 percent chose the same alternative with respect to personally experienced public services. The 1999 situation will be compared with a hypothetical—but not unrealistic—scenario: *What if people would have perceived personal public services as favorably as the economy?*

This counterfactual scenario is informative for two reasons. First, it highlights an alternative societal situation that at least many Swedes have a feeling for. In 1999, the economy had improved for several consecutive years. At least the direction of easily available macro indicators rarely gets much better. The feeling that "the tough years are over, it's time to harvest" was clearly reflected both in people's perceptions of the economy as well as in government rhetoric (Holmberg and Weibull 2000; Kumlin and Oskarson 2000). At the same time many public services had suffered badly from almost a decade of cutbacks (see Starrin and Svensson 1998). This was evident both in public opinion as well as in elite discourse. Consequently, for virtually all parties, the major emphasis in the 1998 election campaign was on public sector improvements and reforms (Swedes may remember the somewhat tedious mantra "vård-skola-omsorg").

The second reason why our counterfactual scenario is informative has to do with the simplicity of the dependent variable (the proportion of the electorate that supports the government). This is intuitive because differences between scenarios can be understood in terms of gains and losses in support for the rulers. Effects on such gains and losses are easier to grasp than effects on awkward survey scales.

The first step is the logistic regression reported in table 6.4. The dependent variable is a dichotomy taking on the value 1 if the respondent thought that the incumbent Social Democrats was the best party, and the value zero if another party was favored. Respondents who did not favor any party or had otherwise "invalid" responses were left out of the analysis.

The model includes the previously used independent variables. The one exception is sociotropic public service perceptions, which is left out. The reason is that we are now interested in grasping the *total* effects of personal service experiences. Because sociotropic perceptions are believed to partly function as a causal mechanism for personal experiences effects, and because this variable is excluded, the total effect of personal experiences is now completely contained in the personal experience coefficient. Of course, the previous analyses have already confirmed that a substantial part of these effects are channeled through collective-level sociotropic perceptions. The logit model in table 6.4 is no exception as about 50 percent of the personal experience impact vanishes when sociotropic public service perceptions are added to the equation. Finally, the model

Table 6.4 Logistic regression model of effects on preference for the incumbent Social Democratic party (logit coefficients)

	Logit coefficient
Personally experienced public services (1–3)	−.44★★★
Personal economy (1–3)	−.02
Swedish economy (1–3)	−.30★★★
Left–right self-placement (1–5)	−.82★★★
Age in years (15–80)	.01★★★
Education (1–3)	−.20★★★
Subjective class affiliation (1 = middle class)	−.46★★★
Public sector employment	−.04
Household income (1–9)	.05
Gender (1 = woman)	−.17
Trade union member (LO)	.24★
Life satisfaction (1–4)	.34★★★
Constant	3.38★★★
Model chi-square (degrees of freedom)	457.9 (12)
Pseudo *R*-squared	0.18
Number of respondents	2,166

★$p < .10$ ★★$p < .05$ ★★★$p < .01$

Notes: The data come from the 1999 West Sweden SOM Survey. The dependent variable is a dichotomy taking on the value 1 if the respondent thought that the incumbent Social Democrats was the best party, and zero if another party was favored. The public service variables, and the economy variables, are coded as in table 6.3. The left–right self-placement variable has five categories: 1 = clearly to the left, 2 = somewhat to the left, 3 = neither left nor right, 4 = somewhat to the right, 5 = clearly to the right. The education variable was coded 1 = basic primary education, 2 = second-level education, and 3 = studied at the university level. The information about subjective class comes from a question where respondents were asked to describe their present family. The variable was coded 0 = working-class family, 1 = middle-class family (white collar, farmer, academic, or private enterprise). Public sector employment is a dummy taking on the variable 1 if the respondent is employed in the public sector. The family income variable measures respondents' estimation of the annual household. It has eight categories representing intervals of 100,000 kronor, and varies from 1 = 100,000 or less, to 8 = more than 700,000. Finally, respondents were asked about how satisfied they, on the whole, are with their lives. The alternatives were coded 1 = not at all satisfied, 2 = not very satisfied, 3 = rather satisfied, 4 = very satisfied.

contains a number of control variables that have been suggested to have an impact on Social Democratic party preference.

Previous findings are underscored. Those with negative personal experiences of public services are less likely than others to favor the incumbent party $(-.44)$, whereas there is no significant corresponding effect of personal economic experiences. The impact of personal service experiences is even somewhat stronger than that of sociotropic economic perception, though this difference is not significant (Chi-square = 1.18, df = 1; $p = 0.28$).

Logistic regression coefficients are not entirely easy to understand. The reason is that they show effects on the logarithm of the odds that a respondent falls in category 1, relative to category 0. Therefore, figure 6.2 translates the results into effects on the probability of falling in category 1. More specifically, it shows how the predicted probability of supporting the incumbent Social Democrats changes as a function of evaluations of personally experienced public services and the Swedish economy.[6]

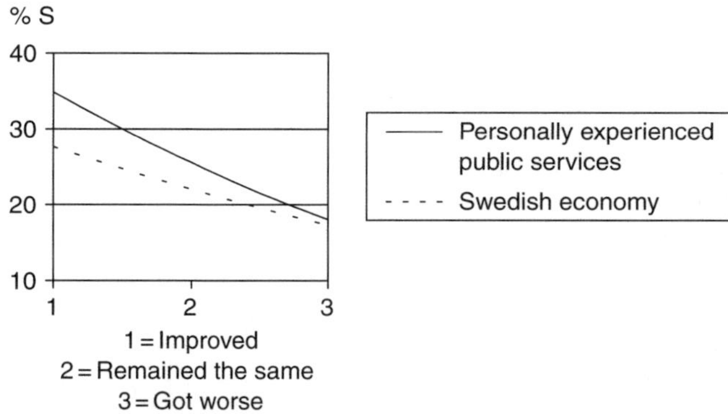

Figure 6.2   Predicted probability of supporting the incumbent Social Democrats (logit estimates)

Notes: The probabilities are based on the logit model in table 6.4. The effect of one variable is calculated holding all other variables in the model at their means. The data come from the 1999 West Sweden SOM Survey.

First, it is illuminating to look at the impact of moving between extreme categories. Looking at the graph, we see that moving from saying personally experienced services "improved," to saying they "got worse," lowers the probability of favoring the government party by 17 percentage points (from 18 to 35). The corresponding impact of sociotropic economic perceptions is 11 percentage points.

We can also use these predicted probabilities to make counterfactual comparisons. How would the percentage of Social Democratic sympathizers be affected by a certain average change along an independent variable, given that the distributions of other independent variables remain the same? Here, the model predicts that improving public service experiences from the present poor level, up to the rather positive level of sociotropic economic perceptions, would increase the percentage of Social Democrats by 4.3 percentage points. We may also make the opposite mental experiment and consider what would happen if citizens perceived the Swedish economy as unfavorably as they perceive experienced public services: The model predicts that such a change would reduce the percentage of Social Democratic supporters by 2.6 percentage points.

Let us now try the same analysis using the 1999 European Parliament Election Study. Since this is an election study we can use probability of voting for the government party as the dependent variable, rather than just probability of expressing support in a survey. A problem is that the 1999 turnout was only 38.8 percent, which means a large proportion of the sample did not actually participate in the election.[7] Luckily however, respondents who did not vote were asked what party they would have voted for had they participated. We may thus construct a dependent variable taking on the value 1 if a person voted for, or would have voted for, the incumbent Social Democrats, and the value 0 if another party was favored.

Table 6.5 Logistic regression model of effects on preference for the incumbent Social Democratic party (logit coefficients)

	Logit coefficient
Personally experienced public services (1–3)	−.47**
Personal economy (1–3)	−.09
Swedish economy (1–3)	−.20
Left–right self-placement (0–10)	−.60***
Age in years (15–80)	.02***
Education (1–3)	−.66***
Subjective class affiliation (1 = middle class)	−.55***
Public sector employment	.01
Family income (10,000 SEK)	.00
Gender (1 = woman)	−.17
Trade union member (LO)	.10
Constant	5.21***
Model chi-square (degrees of freedom)	263.0 (12)
Pseudo *R*-squared	0.27
Number of respondents	840

*$p < .10$ **$p < .05$ ***$p < .01$

Notes: The data come from the 1999 European Parliament Election Study. The dependent variable takes on the value 1 if a person voted for, or would have voted for, the incumbent Social Democrats, and the value zero if another party was favored in these respects. For information about independent variables see tables 6.1 and 6.4; the only difference to the previous analyses was that left–right self-placement was measured using an 11-point scale running from 0 (far to the left) to 10 (far to the right).

Table 6.5 reports a logistic regression analysis that is virtually identical to the previous one.[8] Again, we observe that negative personal experiences of public services lower the probability of supporting the government (log odds effect −.47). Equally consistent with the hypotheses, there is no significant impact of personal economic experiences. Furthermore, the impact of personal service experiences is somewhat stronger than that of sociotropic economic perception, though again this difference is not significant (Chi-square = 1.25, df = 1; $p = 0.26$). Also, once again, a substantial part of the effects on political attitudes appear to be channeled by collective-level sociotropic perceptions. A regression model including sociotropic service perceptions (not shown here) indicated that slightly more than 50 percent of the personal experience impact vanishes when sociotropic public service perceptions are added as an independent variable.

Figure 6.3 shows how the predicted probability of supporting the incumbent Social Democrats changes as a function of evaluations of personally experienced public services and the Swedish economy respectively.[9] The basic observation is that the graph is very similar to the previous one based on the West Sweden Survey. This time, the impact of moving from believing personally experienced services "improved," to believing they "got worse," lowers the probability of favoring the governing party by 16 percentage points (from 15 to 31). The corresponding impact of sociotropic economic perceptions is 5 percentage points.

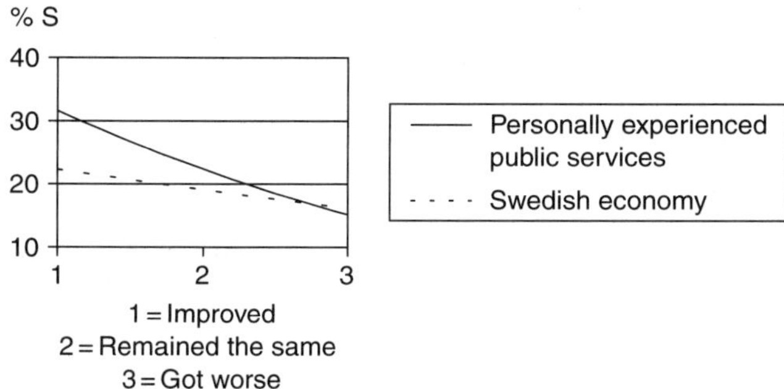

Figure 6.3 Predicted probability of supporting the incumbent Social Democrats (logit estimates)

Notes: The probabilities are based on the logit model in table 6.5. The effect of one variable is calculated holding all other variables in the model at their means. The data come from the 1999 European Parliament Election Study.

Making the same counterfactual comparisons as mentioned earlier, the model predicts that improving service experiences from the present poor level, up to the positive level of sociotropic economic perceptions, would increase the percentage of social democrats by 5.9 percentage points. Again, the opposite mental experiment is to consider what would happen if perceptions of the Swedish economy were as negative as those of experienced services: The model predicts that such deterioration would reduce the percentage of government supporters by 2.1 percentage points.

In summary, we may conclude that the effects of personal welfare state experiences seem worth taking seriously. These effects are at least as strong, and occasionally somewhat stronger than the impact of sociotropic economic perceptions (an explanatory factor that is generally respected by most political behavior researchers). Moreover, we can now conclude that while public service experiences are not the most important single explanatory factor behind government support, they are influential in a very substantial and political sense. Our estimates indicate that the governing party would have gained 4–6 percent of the electorate if public service experiences had been judged as favorably as the Swedish economy. And in 1999, such an improvement would certainly have been extremely welcome for the Social Democrats as they struggled with some of their worst poll results in history (between 30 and 35 percent throughout most of the year).

Conclusion

Previous political behavior research suffers from an economistic bias. While this research has yielded invaluable insights that will continue to be useful, the (often implicit) assumption that citizens mainly take into account economic outcomes when thinking about government perform-ance has also biased our understanding of the subject. It is telling that while economic voting is a mature research field, there is no developed parallel research program looking for "welfare state voting."

Such a program would not lack a theoretical nor empirical foundation. Our results indicate that in a service democracy like Sweden, trends and outcomes linked to the welfare state are just as important to government support and political trust as economic judgments. People appear to connect the quality of welfare state services to the way the present government is doing its job as well as to the overall functioning of the democratic system.

The results belong to a line of research indicating that our understanding of opinion formation is enriched if one simultaneously considers, not just the economy, but also other salient policy areas (Huseby 2000). Of course, we are not suggesting that economic perceptions are any less consequential than they have seemed in previous research. Indeed, in the first model of government approval, sociotropic economic perception was the most powerful of the four independent variables at focus. Rather, our argument is that previous research has examined retrospective judgments of government performance and policy output through a too narrow lens. Future researchers may want to consider how citizens perceive performance in yet other policy domains such as the environment, law and order, and so on. As Newton and Norris (2000:73) emphasize, we need to answer "the important question of which measures of government performance matter most to citizens. . . ."

The economistic bias has not only limited our view on *what* matters in public opinion formation. It has also formed our view on *how* the process works. Economic voting research portrays modern citizens as "sociotropic animals." When thinking about politics, such animals care more about collective-level experiences than about personal experience. They are not willing and/or able to translate personal events into political judgments. This makes them dependent on the mass media and elite actors for politically relevant information. The personal and the political are believed to constitute separate life spheres.

In contrast, we predicted and supported empirically that the opinion formation process changes when we move out of the economic realm and into welfare state territory. Because welfare state experiences are more immediate results of decisions taken by responsible politicians, and because welfare arrangements offer heterogeneous and potentially conflicting sociotropic information, personal welfare state experiences are a more important source of political information than personal economic experiences. Empirically, we have seen stronger correlations between personal experiences and sociotropic judgment, as well as stronger total effects of experiences on political attitudes, in the area of public services. Again, this does not mean that sociotropic perceptions are unimportant in the welfare state. Rather, it means that sociotropic public service perceptions are informed by personal experiences to a much greater extent than economic perceptions. Whereas personal-level and collective-level judgments are fairly separate in the economic realm, they blend together in the welfare state.

★ ★ ★

So far, we have only scratched the surface of personal welfare state experience effects on political attitudes. We want to know more about the causal processes that the uncovered effects represent. What have those discontent with "public services I have been in contact with" really gone through? The following three chapters tackle this problem from three different theoretical angles: Chapter 7 investigates the role of self-interest. Chapter 8 then adds the distributive justice perspective: Does it matter whether people think they have personally received the service and help that they have a right to? In chapter 9, we broaden the conceptual horizon further and look at political consequences of procedural voice aspects of welfare state experiences.

CHAPTER SEVEN

Self-Interest

It's always the same. Come election year, political commentators begin to criticize governments for trying to buy votes with increased welfare state spending. The nastiest critics portray the ministers as a bunch of populists focused on staying in power, even if it takes irresponsible short-term increases in public spending on services and transfers. Such spending, it is argued, is irresponsible because it threatens economic stability and the long-run health of public finances.

In Anglo-Saxon countries, alleged attempts to buy votes with welfare are referred to as "pork barrel," whereas Swedish commentators tend to use the equally derogatory expressions "valfläsk" (election pork) or in recent years "väljargodis" (voter candy). These metaphors conjure up the image of irresponsible power-maximizing politicians, as well as that of irresponsible citizens who do not care to consider the common good or the long-run impact of political choices. Rather, according to the cynics, citizens are naïve and self-centered kids who cling to any political alternative that for the moment offers more voter candy.

Both nasty commentators and populist politicians assume that citizens react politically to differences and changes in how much they get from the welfare state. This assumption is also shared by many social scientists. In fact, "pork barrel" and "voter candy" are just cynical symptoms of the perhaps most basic mental tool for thinking about political effects of welfare state experiences: *the self-interest perspective*. From this theoretical vantage point, welfare state experiences have a political impact on citizens by affecting their personal, material, short-term interests.

As we shall soon see, almost all Swedish citizens have occasional contacts with at least one welfare state institution or the other. Still, some people gain more than others in terms of personal services and transfers from these institutions. This variation in welfare-state related self-interest is believed to structure political attitudes. According to the self-interest perspective, then, opinion formation in modern welfare states is not mainly about labor versus capitalism, economic ups and downs, religious cleavages, or center versus periphery. Rather, the crucial feature is "who gets how much from the welfare state."

In this spirit, Swedish sociologist Hans Zetterberg (1985) argued that the most important voter group for the Swedish Social Democrats is no longer the industrial working class. Rather, public sector employees and recipients of public services and transfers make up the crucial voters. In Zetterberg's parlance, the Swedish electorate has become "an electorate in the grips of the welfare state." The generosity of welfare state institutions coupled with the short-sighted egoism of individual citizens mean that seriously antiwelfare parties and ideological viewpoints can no longer receive extensive support.

We have seen that the self-interest perspective is adopted by influential students of welfare state development at the macro level (Esping-Andersen 1990; Baldwin 1990; Pierson 1994; Rothstein 1998). While these researchers differ from each other in terms of focus, theory, and methods, they share the assumption that citizens to a significant extent adjust their political leanings to their welfare state interests. It is believed that people consuming a large quantity of welfare state services will differ politically from those consuming a small amount. Typically, high-level consumers are considered more likely to stand to the left ideologically, more likely to support state intervention in the market economy, and more likely to vote for leftist parties. This assumption underlies for instance, Esping-Andersen's (1990:27–28) account of how the political left and its universal social policies draw support in Scandinavian welfare states: "All benefit; all are dependent; and all will presumably feel obliged to pay."

Empirical research at the individual level sends radically different signals. Sears and Funk (1991:76) summarized the literature like this: "The conclusion is quite clear: self-interest ordinarily does not have much effect upon the ordinary citizen's sociopolitical attitudes." Evidence suggests that people do not calculate the personal benefits and costs implied by every new concrete political choice. Instead, in order to arrive at specific opinions, people tend to fall back on "symbolic orientations" such as party identification, general ideology, or group identification. Symbolic orientations, the argument goes, have typically been shaped by socialization processes occurring long before any future interests could be calculated.

However, some scholars have discussed the possibility that symbolic orientations themselves are in turn affected by short-term self-interest. This is the question dealt with in this chapter. To what extent can general political orientations such as left–right self-placement, state-intervention orientations, satisfaction with democracy, and trust in politicians be explained by variables measuring short-term welfare-state related self-interest?

In the next section, I notice that previous research on self-interest and symbolic orientations has used rather rough indicators of welfare state interests. I will then go on to a conceptual distinction not yet considered: that between objective and subjective self-interest. After that, we are ready to look at the empirical indicators and hypotheses tests. In the concluding section I discuss the viability of the self-interest perspective on welfare state experiences.

Rough Measurement in Previous Research

If people make self-interested political choices, there will be political differences between people with different interests. But how can we measure differences in interest? Actually, given that the dependent variable is concrete, it may not be all that difficult. Consider for instance, attitudes toward increased spending on public child care. A simple dichotomy separating those with children in child care from other respondents would take us a long way. We would then have two groups that are radically different in terms of how personal short-term well-being is affected by increased spending on child care. Granted, there may still be some within-group variation in terms of self-interest. For instance, among current users some may utilize services more than others, and we would ideally wish to capture this variation too. Nevertheless, it would appear that the self-interest variation between the two groups is much larger than that within the groups, so that we have a useful measure of variation in self-interest.

But here we are interested in very general political orientations. We want to know for instance, if those who currently use a lot of welfare state services and transfers are more inclined to embrace leftist ideology. It then becomes more difficult to measure self-interest, as such large and general political choices have implications for one's personal short-term well-being in a great number of ways. In principle, when assessing the impact of self-interest on generalized attitudes toward the welfare state and the political system, the whole gamut of welfare state institutions becomes potentially relevant.

Much previous research has been forced to use data—typically from election studies—that were not collected specifically for these purposes. Because a wide range of theoretical considerations inspires such studies, they rarely contain extensive information about personal welfare state usage. Such data constraints have forced scholars to rely on rather rough measures of short-term welfare state self-interest.

For instance, Dunleavy (1979) drew far-ranging conclusions about the importance of sectoral cleavages for voting behavior based only on two types of indicators: public housing and car access. The absence of a car was taken as an indication that a respondent in fact used public transportation. The study thus ignored fundamental components of public intervention in private consumption patterns, such as education, health care, public insurance systems, child care, leisure activities, and many others.[1] Similarly, Hadenius (1986) used a small number of dummy variables as indicators of welfare state self-interest (whether people were pensioners, had received sickness benefits, had children at home, or whether they had received unemployment benefits). These indicators proved to have weak effects on attitudes toward public expenditure and taxation. Hadenius (1986:104) concluded that "there hardly exists any exclusive 'client-based' demand for public expenditure" and that "People appear to a very minor extent to assess the public sector from the viewpoint of personal utility" (1986:121).

Finally, based only on information about whether Danish respondents were unemployed, disabled, early retired, or old-age pensioners, Goul Andersen (1993:37–38) "found virtually no evidence confirming that people's personal relationship to the welfare state [...] has any impact upon their welfare state attitudes." He concluded that "interests are almost irrelevant as determinants of welfare state support in Denmark" (Goul Andersen 1993:43).

It is possible that using so few indicators facilitates less than optimal tests of the impact of self-interest. After all, citizens receive services and transfers from the welfare state in a multitude of shapes and situations, and ideally this should be reflected as clearly as possible by measures of welfare state interest.

The data analyzed here certainly have their limitations too. But they do offer more complete information about personal welfare state self-interest than those typically used in previous research. The datasets contain extensive information about current usage of a large number of public service institutions. All in all, we will be able to tap whether respondents have a short-term self-interest invested in each of about twenty-five different welfare state services and transfers. It is believed that this puts us in a more fortunate situation than many previous studies when it comes to assessing the impact of welfare state interest.

Objective and Subjective Self-Interest

A self-interest effect denotes the process by which a person becomes more likely to support a political alternative (a party, an ideological point of view etc.) because that alternative has the most positive implications for her personal, material, short-term situation. Based on this definition we may now discern two ways of conceptualizing and measuring welfare-state related self-interest. *Objective self-interest* refers to differences between individuals in the extent to which their short-term self-interest is actually satisfied by welfare state arrangements. Here, the question is to what extent and with what frequency an individual actually enjoys benefits and services emanating from the welfare state. This variable, typically measured using quite sparse information, taps objective characteristics in the sense that respondents do not have to be aware of them.[2]

Subjective self-interest, on the other hand, denotes perceptions of the extent to which one gains from welfare state arrangements and public services. To measure subjective self-interest, then, the researcher must get inside the minds of people. Does the citizen think of herself as someone who gains nothing, a little, or a lot, from the public sector? To what extent does she think she would win or lose if welfare state spending was increased or decreased?[3]

In this chapter, we will have the possibility to measure both objective and subjective self-interest. This is fortunate not the least as it allows us to get a handle on the full causal chain specified in figure 1.1. Whereas several other chapters only have access to perceptions of personal experiences, this chapter has access to information also about "actual" experiences.

The standard model of self-interest depicts objective and subjective self-interest as nothing but different phases in one causal process (see Green 1988:25):

Objective self-interest → *Subjective self-interest perceptions* → *Political choices*

According to this model, differences in objective interest give rise to different subjective interest perceptions, which in turn have attitudinal or behavioral effects. Objective interests are thus temporally distant from the final political choice, whereas subjective interests are close to it. In the welfare state context, the model implies that citizens have well-developed subjective perceptions, in the sense that they are substantially correlated with actual objective interests. Self-interest effects on political orientations occur when people consciously match such perceptions with political choices ("I support government spending on welfare state services because I'm a person who benefits greatly from such spending," "I trust and support the existing democratic system because the output of the system is of great benefit to me"). Or as Dunleavy (1980c:14) explained the process in his work on consumption cleavages and voting behavior: "voters can be seen as aligned instrumentally towards the party most clearly identified with the interests of their consumption location."

A critique against the standard model is that subjective interest perceptions are difficult to form. This becomes a problem especially when the dependent variable is general political orientations. The generality opens for a multitude of interest sources, basically the whole gamut of welfare state institutions. Forming welfare state interest perceptions based on a multitude of sources may be a too demanding or too uninteresting exercise for many citizens, and perceptions may therefore not be formed at all. Alternatively, individuals may form incorrect perceptions, in the sense that they do not correlate with objective self-interest.

In this vein, Franklin and Page (1984) and Taylor-Gooby (1986) criticized "consumption cleavage theory" as formulated by Dunleavy (1979, 1980a,b,c) for being silent on how objective differences in patterns of public consumption are translated into differences in political preferences. Whereas traditional cleavage theory emphasizes that it all depends on which social differences are politicized by the party system, as well as on socialization within primary groups, consumption cleavage theory seems to suggest that objectively existing social differences between citizens automatically translate into differing political preferences. Franklin and Page (1984:526) formulated the critique like this: "Existing research provides no evidence to support the presence of a mechanism which would ensure that people became aware of their 'objective interests' [...] Indeed one of the distinctive contributions that political science has made to the social sciences has been in its treatment of the relationship between social stratification and political cleavages, especially electoral alignments, as problematic. [...] This caution required in equating social differences with political conflicts does not appear in the consumption approach to electoral behavior."

However, Franklin and Page (1984:527) also identified two ways to escape the criticism. First, if party platforms clearly politicized different consumption interests, people might develop meaningful subjective interest perceptions accurately reflecting their objective interests. This would entail that some parties to a greater extent than others explicitly profile themselves as protectors of the interests of public service users. However, while the authors acknowledged that this precondition "may indeed have existed at times for issues related to consumption cleavages," they also argued that it is by no means consistently present.

A second possibility would be that objective interests translate into political preferences through socialization mechanisms. Of course, this is the micro-foundation of classic cleavage theory: individuals belonging to the same class, religion, or geographic area have more contact with each other than they have with people from other groups. Moreover, because political preferences within a group are socially contagious, a strong correlation between objective interests and political preferences may emerge, even if nobody but a few sophisticated "opinion leaders" have clear perceptions of their interests (see e.g., Katz and Lazarsfeld 1955).

But again there are problems. First, socialization processes are very different to the standard model shown earlier, as effects of objective interests are not channeled through subjective interest perceptions. Indeed, as pointed out by Franklin and Page (1984:528), socialization processes would not lead us to expect "that perceptions of objective interests have any part to play in the process." Second, the socialization explanation seems far-fetched, as groups with similar welfare state interests are not necessarily concentrated to a particular social environment. Indeed, the whole point of consumption cleavage theory is that public consumption patterns are weakly correlated with traditional social bases of political alignment, such as the workplace, the neighborhood, geographic areas, and religious affiliation. This means that whereas, say, industrial workers live and work in the same places, heavy welfare state users are more "spread out" in society. It is therefore not obvious where and how they would gather to socialize each other. Of course, some categories of public service users such as parents of schoolchildren have natural places to meet. But then again numerous other groups such as beneficiaries of social insurances appear rather isolated from each other. Socialization theory is therefore not entirely credible as an account of how objective welfare state interests translate into political preferences. This difficulty is also recognized by proponents of consumption cleavages. As Dunleavy (1979:413) stated, "We cannot simply assume that political alignment brushes off by rubbing shoulders in the street."

So we still need to explain how objective differences in objective welfare state interest could translate into attitudinal differences. The "on-line" model of opinion formation that was introduced in chapter 4 provides such an explanation. It suggests that, in the light of new relevant information, citizens *gradually* update a small set of general political orientations. They then forget the information that caused the update, remembering only the affective imprint on the political orientation left behind by the information (Lodge, McGraw, and Stroh 1989; Lodge, Steenbergen, and Brau 1995). The model means that even if people never perceive their welfare state–interest use as a whole, it could nevertheless have political effects. Objective interest effects are then achieved by piecemeal, gradual updating rather than by means of a sophisticated one-shot synthesis of many experiences.

Imagine a mother who receives a sum of money in the form of public child allowance. Given that this experience triggers some political reasoning at all, and given that self-interest is her political driving force, she will react politically on the basis of how much her material well-being was improved by the experience. According to the on-line model, she does this by updating her political preferences so as to integrate the new information into these preferences. After the process, she remembers the updated preferences but forgets the information that caused the update. Thus, if later an interviewer asks for the reason behind her preference she would not think of the experience. This process is reiterated whenever she encounters another welfare state service that makes some contribution to her self-interest. The result will be a correlation between objective interests and political orientations.

Note how different the on-line process is compared to the standard model of self-interest effects. According to the latter, people have memorized perceptions of the overall extent to which they gain from the welfare state, perceptions which in turn affect political variables. In contrast, according to the on-line model, effects of objective self-interest bypass subjective self-interest perceptions, provided the final choice to be explained is general "updateable" orientations.

It has been suggested that people update mainly overarching, affectively based, and repeatedly used political orientations that will probably be of use in the future (Feldman 1995; Huckfeldt et al. 1999). Chapter 4 argued that ideological left–right orientations and political trust orientations constitute "updateable" political judgments into which new information may gradually be incorporated.

Below we use measures of both objective and subjective self-interest as independent variables. We estimate full causal models that take into account, not only the direct impact of interest variables on political orientations, but also the internal relation between objective and subjective self-interest. This allows us to analyze both the extent to which objective interests affect orientations, as well as the extent to which such effects are channeled by subjective interest. If effects are largely indirect, flowing throw subjective interest, then the two variables simply denote different locations in one causal process as suggested by the standard model. However, if objective effects are largely direct, thus bypassing subjective perceptions, we would regard this as support for the on-line model of opinion formation.

Measuring Self-Interest

To create a measure of objective welfare state self-interest in the 1999 West Sweden SOM survey, I used the following question: "Please indicate below which of the following services you yourself or a family member use." Respondents were presented with a list of welfare state institutions, mainly locally distributed human services. For each service, there were three response alternatives: "I use the service myself," "I don't use the service, but a family member does," and "neither I, nor a family member, use the service." Second, I took advantage of the question "Please indicate to which of the following groups you belong at present." Among other things, respondents indicated if they were pensioners, early retired, or participated in labor market schemes. The objective welfare state interest measure was then created by counting the number of public service institutions that individual respondents use.[4] The measure may be inspected in table 7.1.

The table nicely illustrates the pervasiveness of the Swedish welfare state: less than 5 percent do not define themselves as users of any of the measured public services. The mean number of currently used institutions is 4.6. Still, there is enough variation around this mean to make the variable interesting as a potential explanatory variable in analyses of political orientations: only 15.8 percent fall in the modal category (4), and the standard deviation is 2.6.[5]

Subjective self-interest was measured by asking respondents about the extent to which a reduction of the public sector would benefit them

Table 7.1 Univariate distribution of the objective welfare state self-interest variable in the 1999 West Sweden SOM survey (percent)

Number of utilized services	Percent
0	4.7
1	6.8
2	10.4
3	14.2
4	15.8
5	14.4
6	10.9
7	8.8
8	6.5
9	3.7
10 or more	3.8
Sum percent	100
Number of respondents	3,685
Mean	4.6
Standard deviation	2.6

Notes: The variable counts the number of public service institutions that individual respondents receive service from. See text for a more detailed description. The proportion of respondents with values larger than 10 is less than 1 percent.

personally. A five-category scale running from 1 ("would be of no benefit") to 5 ("would be of great benefit") was used. The head question was: "How do you think the following suggestions would affect *your own personal situation*, and the situation of *the Swedish people in general*, if they were realized? To what extent do you think they would be of benefit to yourself and for the Swedish people respectively?" For each of seven political suggestions, respondents simultaneously indicated the extent to which they think they would gain personally, as well as the extent to which the Swedish people in general would benefit.[6]

We are interested in perceptions of overall welfare state interest. The analysis is therefore based on the item concerning the extent to which a reduction of the public sector would benefit them personally. The univariate distribution can be inspected in table 7.2. To get an intuitive scoring, the variable was reversed so that it varies from low to high subjective welfare state interest.

The results show that we are not only dealing with a pervasive welfare state in the objective sense. Many of its citizens apparently also perceive a welfare state interest: no less than 41 percent think that a reduction of the public sector would not at all be of benefit to them personally. Another 11 percent chose the category next to this extreme alternative. Only 19 percent perceive that they would benefit personally from a reduction in the public sector, in the sense that they place themselves on the low-interest side of the mid-point.

The SOM data contain mainly information about local human services. This is natural since the academic focus of the West Sweden SOM surveys is on local sociopolitical issues and processes (see Nilsson 1999, 2000a). However, from our perspective this is slightly problematic since our hypotheses cover also state transfer systems such as unemployment insurances, sick leave benefits, child allowances, student aid, and so on.

Table 7.2   Perception of how the personal situation would be affected if the public sector were reduced (subjective welfare state interest) in the 1999 West Sweden SOM survey (percent)

1 Benefit greatly	10
2	9
3	29
4	11
5 Not at all benefit	41
Sum percent	100
Number of respondents	3,457

Notes: See text for exact question wording and construction. The variable has been reversed compared to the questionnaire, so that higher values reflect greater perceived welfare state interest.

Therefore, I will also take advantage of a dataset containing information about contacts with such transfer systems. More exactly, while the 1999 SOM data focus on local human services, the 1992 Swedish Living Standard Survey (SLEV) highlights usage of central public insurance systems. I thus test the same basic predictions using information about a different kind of welfare state interest.

The SLEV data on welfare state usage were collected differently compared to the SOM data (see Halleröd et al. 1993; Halleröd 1994). Public records rather than survey questions were used to gather information about reception of social transfers in 1991.[7] (Interviews were carried out in spring 1992.) In contrast to the SOM survey, then, respondents did not provide information about welfare state usage themselves. The available information was used to create a variable counting the number of welfare state institutions that respondents had received transfers from. The distribution of this indicator of objective self-interest is displayed in table 7.3.

What we see is yet an alternative illustration of how pervasive the Swedish welfare state is. No less than 85 percent of the sample had in the previous year received benefits from at least one of the institutions for which there was information in the dataset. The single most common situation was to have received a benefit from one of the measured institutions (49 percent).

The subjective interest measure in SLEV can be inspected in table 7.4. It was generated by the following question: "Do you think you would win or lose if income equality were increased in Sweden?" The response alternatives were "win" (coded 3), "neither win nor lose" (2), "lose" (1), and "don't know" (2). A variable was thus created, which varies from low subjective welfare state interest (1) to high subjective welfare state interest (3).

Again, it seems that many Swedes perceive that they have interests invested in the welfare state. Only 12 percent think they would lose if

Table 7.3 Univariate distribution of the objective welfare state interest-level variable in the 1992 SLEV survey (percent)

Number of utilized transfers	*Percent*
0	15
1	49
2	19
3	12
4 or more	5
Sum percent	100
Number of respondents	789
Mean	1.5
Standard deviation	1.1

Notes: The variable counts the number of welfare state transfers that the respondent received service from. See text for a more detailed description. The proportion of respondents with values larger than 4 is less than 2 percent.

Table 7.4 Perceptions of how the respondent would be affected if income equality were increased in Sweden (1992 SLEV survey) (percent)

1 would lose	12
2 neither win nor lose	53
3 would win	35
Sum percent	100
Number of respondents	757

Notes: The variable measures the extent to which respondents perceive that they would win if "income equality were increased in Sweden." It is coded 1 = would lose, 2 = neither win nor lose/don't know, 3 = would win. Ten respondents answered don't know. See text for exact question wording. The variable has been reversed compared to the questionnaire.

income equality were increased. More than one-third think they would win if such a change occurred.

There are some notable differences compared to the question used in SOM. For example, the SLEV question concerns changing income equality rather than the size of the public sector as such. Hence, in order for the variable to be a valid measure of subjective welfare state self-interest, respondents must themselves make the connection to the welfare state. Although the question makes no reference to welfare state services, people must "understand" that it is the public sector and its transfer programs that are supposed to influence income equality. The usefulness of the measure thus builds on the premise that frequent beneficiaries infer that they are the ones who will benefit the most if the state decides to spend more on transfers.

Moreover, given that respondents make this connection, the phrase "income equality" probably shifts the attention from the entire public sector to certain parts of it. Particularly transfer systems redistributing actual money, rather than human services, spring to mind. This is, however, less of a problem since the measure of objective welfare state outcome in SLEV focuses on exactly such parts of the welfare state. We are thus still in a situation where, in addition to estimating direct effects, it makes sense to investigate the relationship between objective and subjective interest.

I close this section by considering a further problem related to the subjective measures. The problem is that the wordings of subjective interest items are very close to those of items used to tap ideological orientations. Closely interrelated words such as "public sector," "privatization," "left/right," and so on will be employed to measure both subjective interest as well as ideology variables. In one case, the subjective interest measure is generated by a question about how much one thinks one would be affected if the "public sector were reduced." One empirical indicator of state-intervention orientations in the SOM survey will be based on virtually the same phrase ("reduce the public sector").

While these questions are not tautological it is still possible that some respond to both of them based on ideological considerations. A strong correlation then emerges even though subjective interest does not have a causal effect. In the terminology of Sears and Funk (1991:69–70), the subjective measure is then "reactive" in relation to dependent ideology variables. The latter explain the former, not the other way around. Fortunately however, the problem is much smaller when orientations like "satisfaction with democracy" and "trust in politicians" serve as the dependent variables. The problem is smaller as the linguistic difference between words such as "democracy" and "politicians" on one hand, and "the public sector" on the other, is greater than that of "left/right" and "privatization" on one hand, and "the public sector" on the other. This observation parallels Sears and Funk's (1991:70) goal "to make the subjective measures as unreactive as possible," by ensuring "that the subjective measures of self-interest have not simply been slightly altered versions of the dependent variable."

These remarks provide a minimum criterion for when statistical effects of subjective interest measures can be taken seriously. More specifically, it becomes difficult to interpret effects as reflections of causality if they only appear when problems of "reactiveness" are great (as in the case of ideological orientations), but not when such problems are smaller (as in the case of political trust). In other words, we mistrust subjective self-interest measures if they do not affect variables such as satisfaction with democracy and trust in politicians.[8]

The Impact of Self-Interest

We now begin to analyze the impact of self-interest on political trust and ideology. The former is measured by the "satisfaction with the way democracy works" and "trust in politicians" factors that were introduced in chapter 6. Moreover, throughout the rest of this book, state-intervention orientations will be measured by an additive index summing responses to questions about suggestions to "reduce the public sector" and "introduce more private health care."[9] These two items are widely used in Swedish electoral research as reliable measures of state-intervention orientations, as indicated by a quite strong cross-sectional correlation between the two items ($r = .46$), and by the reoccurring observation that their aggregate distributions change in a very similar fashion over time (see Johansson, Nilsson, and Strömberg 2001; Kumlin 1997). The index, which ranges from 1 to 9, was scored so that higher values mean greater support for state intervention.

Left–right self-placement, furthermore, was generated by the following question: "It is sometimes said that political opinions can be placed on a left–right scale. Where would you place yourself on such a scale?" The response alternatives were "clearly to the left" (coded 1), "somewhat to the left" (2), "neither left nor right" (3), "somewhat to the right" (4), and "clearly to the right" (5).

Finally, the access to dependent variables is more limited in the 1992 SLEV survey. However, there are sufficient opportunities to measure state-intervention orientations. To achieve this, I factor analyzed three opinion items from two different question batteries. A unidimensional factor solution was obtained, and the first factor was saved for future analysis.[10]

Before proceeding to multivariate analysis, table 7.5 shows bivariate correlations between self-interest measures and political orientations. Several of the hypothesized relationships emerge. Looking first at the SOM data, individuals with a high objective welfare state interest are more likely to place themselves further to the left than others (−.11), more likely to support state intervention (.09), and to be satisfied with democracy (.07). While none of these relationships are exceedingly strong, they are stronger than the significant, but very weak, bivariate correlation between objective interest and trust in politicians (.04).

Moreover, the subjective self-interest variable has sizeable bivariate correlations with left–right placement (−.33) and state-intervention orientations (.55), but weak correlations with satisfaction with democracy (.03) and trust in politicians (.05). So far, then, it seems that the subjective variable does not pass the test with respect to political trust.

It is also interesting to note that the link between objective and subjective welfare state interest is not strong (.10). This is interesting as we have noted that at the aggregate level many Swedes benefit from welfare state arrangements both in the objective sense, as well as in the subjective sense that many perceive a welfare state interest. Now we see that this relationship does not necessarily hold at the individual level. Perceptions of self-interest are only weakly related with the objective extent to which people consume services. The SOM data, then, support the suspicion that accurate subjective perceptions of objective interests cannot be taken for granted (Franklin and Page 1984). We shall get back to this finding.

Table 7.5 Objective self-interest, subjective self-interest, and political orientations (Pearson's *r*)

1999 West Sweden SOM survey	
Objective welfare state interest/Left–right self placement	−.11
Subjective welfare state interest/Left–right self placement	−.33
Objective welfare state interest/State-intervention orientations	.09
Subjective welfare state interest/State-intervention orientations	.55
Objective welfare state interest/Satisfaction with democracy	.07
Subjective welfare state interest/Satisfaction with democracy	.03
Objective welfare state interest/Trust in politicians	.04
Subjective welfare state interest/Trust in politicians	.05
Objective welfare state interest/Subjective welfare state interest	.10
1992 SLEV survey	
Objective welfare state interest/State-intervention orientations	.19
Subjective welfare state interest/State-intervention orientations	.24
Objective welfare state interest/Subjective welfare state interest	.25

Notes: Correlation coefficients are calculated based on 3,162 (SOM) or 747 (SLEV) respondents or more. For information about variable constructions, see main text.

Shifting the attention to the SLEV data, we find the expected positive relationship between both objective (.19) and subjective (.24) interest and state-intervention orientation. Also, the link between objective and subjective interest is somewhat tighter in this dataset (.25).

The data thus suggest that at least some orientations are affected by welfare state self-interest. But there are reasons to be cautious, as bivariate correlations might be biased by omitted "third variables." Such variables might have an impact on both the independent and the dependent variable. For instance, the strong correlations between subjective variables and ideological orientations might be exaggerated by spurious influences of income and class; we know that the poor and the working class tend to stand further to the left ideologically, and they might score higher on interest variables. By a reversed logic, omitted third variables could suppress some of the correlations between interest and political trust; we know that the poor and the working class tend to distrust the political system and politicians somewhat more than others (Nye, Zelikov, and King 1997; Norris 1999; Holmberg 2000). To come to terms with the third variable problem I now proceed to multivariate tests. The task is to examine the relationships between welfare state self-interest and political orientations, under control for a number of potential third variables, the theoretical background of which were discussed in chapter 4. This means that the multivariate analyses yield interesting information about how strong interest effects really are compared to those of some previously well-researched control variables. Moreover, we pay attention not only to direct effects, but also to indirect effects of objective interest channeled by subjective interest.

The remainder of this chapter reports five estimated causal models. The first two contain effects on satisfaction with how democracy works and trust in politicians in the 1999 West Sweden SOM survey. The third and fourth models are based on the same dataset and deal with effects on left–right self-placement and state-intervention orientations respectively. The fifth model estimates effects on state-intervention orientations in the 1992 SLEV survey.

Figure 7.1 shows the conceptual structure of these models. First, they involve direct effects of objective and subjective self-interest on the dependent political orientation measures. Second, we model the indirect effects of objective self-interest flowing through subjective perceptions. Third, the model contains exogenous control variables of mainly socio-economic/demographic character, which are included as independent variables in all equations. The short triple headed arrows illustrate this feature without cluttering the picture.

We are now ready to look at results from the first model (table 7.6). We see that the objective self-interest variable has a significant total effect on both satisfaction with democracy (.02) and on trust in politicians (.02). The more public services individuals consume, the more democratic satisfaction and political trust they tend to express.

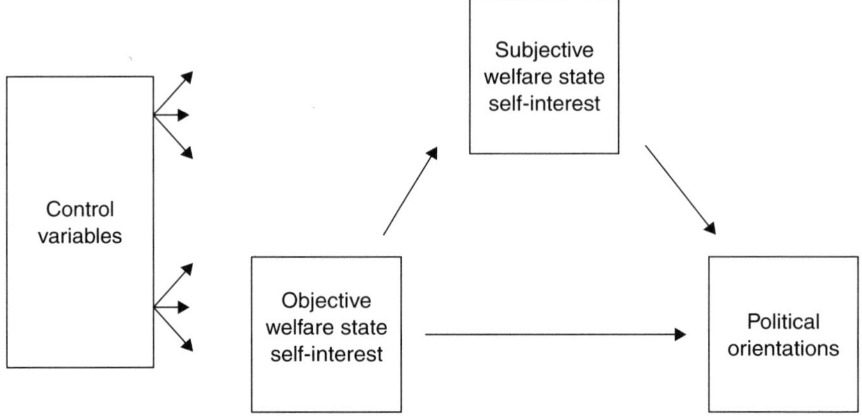

Figure 7.1   Conceptual diagram of estimated causal models reported in tables 7.6–7.8

Table 7.6   Causal models of self-interest effects on satisfaction with democracy and trust in politicians (unstandardized OLS estimates)

	Dependent variable: Satisfaction with democracy (higher value = more satisfaction)		Dependent variable: Trust in politicians (higher value = more trust)	
	Direct effect	Total effect	Direct effect	Total effect
Objective welfare state interest (0–10)	.02***	.02***	.02**	.02**
Subjective welfare state interest (1–5)	.01	.01	.02*	.02
Perception of Swedish economy	−.20***	.20***	−.22***	−.21***
Preference for incumbent party	.37***	.38***	.42***	.43***
No party preference	−.16**	−.16**	−.19***	−.19***
Age in years (15–80)	−.004***	−.005***	.00	.00
Education (1–3)	.02	.03	.06**	.05**
Subjective class affiliation (1 = middle class)	.06	.06	.05	.04
Life satisfaction (1–4)	.19***	.19***	.18***	.17***
Adjusted R-squared	.09		.10	
Number of respondents	2,630		2,710	

*$p < .10$ **$p < .05$ ***$p < .01$

Notes: The data come from the 1999 West Sweden SOM Survey. For more information about the interest variables, see tables 7.1 and 7.2, and related text. The dependent variables were described in chapter 6. Preference for incumbent party was coded 1 = Social Democrats, 0 = other party. For information about how other independent variables were coded, see tables 6.3 and 6.4.

In contrast, subjective welfare state interest has weak and mostly statistically insignificant coefficients. In turn, this means that little of the impact of objective self-interest can be channeled through subjective interest perceptions. The direct effects of objective interest are equal to its total effects. This indicates that the reason why high-level welfare state consumers tend to display greater political trust is not that they perceive a greater welfare state interest. Rather, the data support the idea that citizens gradually update their political orientations at the time of each new welfare state experience. After this process has taken place, they seem to forget the information that made them update the initial orientation.

How strong is the impact of objective welfare state self-interest? One way of answering the question is to compare with effects of other, better known, variables. For example, as described in chapter 4, three factors that are known to have respected effects on political trust are perceptions of the country's economy (Huseby 2000), preference for the incumbent party (Miller 1974; Borre 1995; Holmberg 1999), and personal life satisfaction (Kornberg and Clarke 1992). These variables provide yardsticks against which interest effects may be assessed.

When comparing coefficients for objective self-interest with those of economic perceptions, one discovers that the self-interest impact is smaller than economic effects. For instance, the predicted difference in democratic satisfaction between someone who does not use any of the measured public institutions, and someone using 10 of them, is .20 (.02 × 10).[11] In comparison, the predicted effect of shifting from perceiving that the economy has "gotten worse," to perceiving that it "improved," is .40 (.20 × 2). Alternatively, we may compare with the effects of preferring the incumbent party (.37). This reveals that the influence of a maximum change in objective interest is about half that of shifting between the incumbent party and the opposition. Finally, a comparison with personal life satisfaction (.57 = .19 × 3) is even less flattering for the objective self-interest effect on political trust; the impact of the former is about three times as large as the latter.

We now move on to the third and fourth models in table 7.7. They involve effects on state-intervention orientations and left–right self-placement.[12] A main finding is that the more public services individuals consume, the more likely they are to support state intervention (.07) and to be located to the left (−.04).

These effects of objective interest are partly indirect, flowing throw subjective interest perceptions. However, while not all of the impact is direct, more than half of it is. Again, we interpret this as support for the notion of gradual updating and on-line opinion formation: Much of the objective interest effect does not seem to arise because people integrate many welfare state contacts into a meaningful overall interest perception that is stored in memory and subsequently used in opinion formation.

How strong are the objective interest effects? Here, the toughest yardstick in the model is the total effect of subjective class affiliation. It is a suitable yardstick as many readers have a feeling for political differences between workers and the middle class (see Petersson 1982; Franklin 1985; Oskarson 1994).[13] When comparing someone not using any of the measured public institutions, and someone using ten, the predicted total effect on state-intervention orientations is .70, which approaches the impact

Table 7.7 Causal models of self-interest effects on state-intervention orientation and left–right ideology (unstandardized OLS estimates)

	Dependent variable: State-intervention orientation (higher value = greater support for intervention)		Dependent variable: Left–right self-placement (higher value = further to the right)	
	Direct effect	*Total effect*	*Direct effect*	*Total effect*
Objective welfare state interest (0–10)	.04**	.07***	−.03***	−.04***
Subjective welfare state interest (1–5)	.82***	.82***	−.24***	−.24***
Employed in public sector	.54***	.92***	−.14***	−.26***
Subjective class affiliation (1 = middle class)	−.58***	−.83***	.57***	.65***
Family income (1–8)	−.08***	−.10***	.05***	.06***
Gender (1 = woman)	−.07	.12	.02	−.06
Education (1–3)	−.07	−.10*	−.02	−.02
Adjusted *R*-squared	.34		.20	
Number of respondents	2,559		2,625	

*p < .10   **p < .05   ***p < .01

Notes: The data come from the 1999 West Sweden SOM Survey. For more information about the interest variables, see tables 7.1 and 7.2, and related text. For information about how other independent variables were coded, see tables 6.3 and 6.4. The dependent variables were described previously in this chapter.

of subjective class. The corresponding predicted change in left–right ideology is −.40, which amounts to about two-thirds of the class effect (.65).

Looking at effects of subjective interest perceptions, one discovers that these are very strong (.82 and −.24). However, there is the risk that subjective interest is affected by political orientations rather than the other way around. The problem, as we have noted, is that the wordings used to measure ideology are very similar to those used for subjective perceptions: Expressions such as "public sector" are employed to tap both dependent and independent variables and it is therefore possible that many respond to the subjective interest questions based on ideological considerations. Borrowing the language of Sears and Funk (1991:69–70), the subjective measure is potentially "reactive" in relation to the dependent ideology variables. A strong correlation might thus result although subjective interest has no causal effect on ideology.

We have cautioned against interpreting subjective effects as genuine reflections of causality if such effects only appear when the problem of "reactiveness" is great (as in the case of ideological orientations), but not when the problem is smaller (as in the case of political trust). Unfortunately, this is exactly the situation at hand. While subjective interest strongly correlates with state intervention and left–right self-placement, it does not correlate much with satisfaction with democracy and trust in politicians. Since subjective interest effects were nonexistent when "reactiveness" was

Table 7.8 Causal model of self-interest effects on state-intervention orientation (unstandardized OLS estimates)

	Dependent variable: State-intervention orientation (higher value = greater support for intervention)	
	Direct effect	Total effect
Objective welfare state interest (0–4)	.13***	.15***
Subjective welfare state interest (1–3)	.24***	.24***
Employed in public sector	.33***	.36***
Occupational class	−.31***	−.38***
Monthly household income (1000 SEK)	−.009**	−.011**
Gender (1 = woman)	.08	.25***
Education (1–3)	−.10*	−.09*
Age in years	.012***	.009***
Adjusted R-squared	.16	
Number of respondents	720	

*$p < .10$ **$p < .05$ ***$p < .01$

Notes: The data come from the 1992 SLEV Survey. For more information about the interest variables, see tables 7.3 and 7.4 and related text. The dependent variable was described previously in this chapter. Occupational class is coded 0 for workers and 1 for middle class (tjänstemän, företagare jordbrukare, ledande befattningar, fria yrkesutövare med akademiyrken). The household income variable measures monthly income after tax in thousands of SEK (mean = 16208, SD = 8409). The education variable was coded 1 = basic primary education, 2 = second-level education, 3 = studied at the university level.

slightly less problematic, I suspect that much of its covariation with dependent ideology variables may be generated by a reversed causal impact.

Let us look at the fifth model (table 7.8). It is based on data from the 1992 SLEV survey and uses state-intervention orientations as the dependent variable. The pattern is similar to that revealed by the SOM data. Objective welfare state interest has a significant positive effect on support for state intervention. Most of its total effect (.15) is direct and does not flow through subjective interest. Moreover, subjective self-interest once again has a rather strong independent impact on support for intervention (.24). Still, however, the problem of reactiveness is large as the term used to tap subjective interest ("equality") is indeed similar to the state intervention indicators ("social reforms," "income differences," and so on.)

These findings, too, are consistent with the notion that people do not walk around with meaningful overall perceptions of their welfare state interest. Rather, since objective self-interest is nevertheless influential, it seems that orientations have been gradually updated as suggested by the on-line model.

On-Line Opinion Formation or Poor
Measures of Subjective Self-Interest?

It should be admitted that the measures of subjective self-interest used in this chapter are not perfect. Perhaps people do think in terms of welfare state interests, though in less abstract and "academic" concepts than the ones I have used to capture this thinking. For instance, it would be interesting to analyze questions about interest perceptions that somewhat clarify the connection between proposed policies on the one hand, and everyday life and personal self-interest on the other. This could entail asking about "public services" instead of the public sector, or something like "public safety net" instead of "income equality." One could also imagine trying somewhat longer questions containing explicit references to various concrete institutions. Perhaps they would indicate that subjective interest indeed affects dependent variables where the problem of reactivity is reasonable? And perhaps such variables would show that there is indeed a strong relationship between objective interests and subjective interest perceptions?

We cannot rule out these possibilities. What we can say is that this study, just like much past research, has rather negative experiences with subjective self-interest measures: Effects are typically weak when question wordings for interest perceptions are clearly different from those used to measure dependent variables, thus diminishing the problem of "reactiveness" (Sears and Funk 1991:69–70). Our results point in a similar direction.

So far, then, there is little evidence that people do have consequential overarching welfare state self-interest perceptions that are not just reflections of already developed political orientations. Rather the uncovered effects of objective welfare state interest appear to operate in a more piecemeal fashion, where self-interest effects are the results of gradual updating, rather than the results of synthesizing perceptions of the totality of one's welfare state self-interest.[14]

Services, Transfers, and the Visibility of Stakes

The effects of objective interest appear stronger in the analysis of the SLEV data compared to that of the SOM data. The predicted difference in intervention support between someone who does not use any of the measured institutions, and someone using four of them, is .60 (.15 × 4).[15] This effect is greater than both that of occupational class (−.38), as well as that of public sector employment (.36).

Why are effects of objective welfare state interest stronger in the SLEV data than in the SOM data? First, there is a difference in the measurement of welfare state usage. The fact that the SLEV data come from records about benefit reception should reduce measurement error substantially. In contrast, SOM respondents provide information about public service usage themselves. It is likely that (some) people forget, lie, or otherwise underestimate the extent to which they use welfare state services.

Second, there is a difference between the experience of receiving money (such as unemployment benefits) and the experience of receiving a human service (such as using libraries). As noted, the SLEV measure taps mainly reception of monetary benefits, whereas the SOM survey is focused on human services. And as discussed in chapter 4, previous research on self-interest contends that the impact of personal economic concerns rises with the *visibility of stakes* (Sears and Citrin 1982; Green 1988; Sears and Funk

1990, 1991). Further, transfer systems make personal stakes less difficult to discover compared to human services. After all, it is quite easy to tell whether and how much one gains from an institution like the unemployment insurance. In contrast, it is more difficult to tell when it comes to an institution like libraries, as "benefits" are not clearly spelled out in monetary terms. Because of the difference in the visibility of stakes, interests emanating from transfer systems might be more politically salient to citizens than those emanating from human services. If so, it makes sense that the effects of the latter are weaker.

Conclusion: A Half-Full, Half-Empty Glass

We conclude that objective welfare state self-interest has statistically and substantially significant effects on political ideology and political trust. These effects are present both for transfers as well as for services. The more such arrangements satisfy citizens' short-term self-interest, the more likely people are to embrace leftist ideology and to display higher levels of political trust.

The effects are quite decent compared to those of some respected variables representing other theoretical perspectives. For example, objective interest effects on support for state intervention and left–right ideology are sometimes at par with those of the working-class/middle-class dichotomy. Having said this, welfare state interest was still not the most influential variable in the multivariate analyses. There was usually some other variable that was more important, such as class or sociotropic economic perceptions.

So do we have a half-full or half-empty glass at hand? As usual, the answer to such questions depends entirely on one's initial expectations. Given previous public opinion research, the self-interest glass looks at least half-full. This research contends that short-term self-interest effects on general, "symbolic" political orientations are negligible or nonexistent. In the welfare state context, results have indicated that "interests are almost irrelevant as determinants of welfare state support," (Goul Andersen 1993:43) which in turn has suggested that people seem "to a very minor extent to assess the public sector from the viewpoint of personal utility" (Hadenius 1986:121). Similarly, Sears and Funk (1991:56) noted, "Materialist theorists often propose that ideology, party preferences [...] are themselves mere creatures of real economic interests." But summarizing empirical research they found that "In fact, self-interest proves to be almost uncorrelated with these symbolic predispositions." To be very exact, they noted that the median correlation in these studies "was a nonsignificant +.05."

This chapter has painted a somewhat different picture. In plain empirical language, we have noted correlations between objective welfare state interest and political orientations up to +.19. This suggests that interest effects on general political orientations have been somewhat underestimated in previous research: interests are certainly not "irrelevant," and "symbolic" orientations appear somewhat less symbolic, and more rational also in the short-term-sense, than they have often seemed.

Actually, this point is twofold. First, effects on previously analyzed ideological orientations appear somewhat stronger than those typically reported. Second, objective welfare state interest also influences variables that have rarely been placed under the magnifying glass: In addition to effects on ideology, we have seen a certain impact on satisfaction with how democracy works and trust in politicians.

What is the reason for the partial discrepancy between our conclusions and those of many past studies? In my view, the most plausible reason is that much previously analyzed data—typically national election studies—contain too little information about welfare state interests. By necessity, objective self-interest has been tapped with information about usage of a small number of institutions. The data used here have allowed for more detailed and valid measurement.

This measurement-related argument has received support elsewhere. Drawing on more recent Danish data, Goul Andersen (1999) has somewhat modified his previous clear-cut conclusion that welfare state self-interests are "irrelevant." He analyzed a more elaborate independent self-interest variable referred to as "labor market position." This index contained four categories: privately employed with no unemployment experience, privately employed with some unemployment experience, public employees, and publicly supported (essentially consisting of the unemployed, the disabled, people on parental or maternity leave etc., and early retirement pensioners). He finds that both public employees as well as the publicly supported display higher general welfare state support and are more likely to vote for socialist parties than other categories and that these effects approach those of social class. Goul Andersen (1999:27–28) concluded, "we face a polarity between a minority of 'core insiders' in the private sector at the one pole, and a minority of publicly supported at the other [. . .] Clearly, this polarity is politically important, in some respects equally important as social class [. . .] Clearly, then, labor market position is a quite important interest factor."

Results such as these fit well with those presented here: More detailed measurement reveals stronger self-interest effects. Yet, we did not have access to one dataset offering information about the entire welfare state: In a perfect scientific world there would have been a survey that simultaneously focused on both human services (like the SOM survey) and on transfer systems (like the SLEV survey). Based on my findings, I would expect indices covering the full welfare state range to further tighten the relation between interests and orientations.

But let us close this chapter in a more self-critical fashion: If the self-interest glass seems half-full from the perspective of previous opinion research, it appears half-empty from the viewpoint of much macro welfare state theory. While we have seen statistically and substantially significant interest effects, this impact is still not enormous or dominant. Even when self-interest is given a really fair chance, then, it fails to provide the single best explanation for variation in political orientations. Rather, welfare state interest is but one of several independent variables telling us something about how political orientations are formed. It would therefore appear that many scholars exaggerate the potency of welfare state interests in structuring political alignments. Given our results, it seems too simple to assume that just because "All benefit," then all will "feel obliged to pay" (Esping-Andersen 1990:27–28). By the same token, general support for welfare state arrangements depends on much more than just "the outcome of narrowly based battles between antagonistic interests" (Baldwin 1990:293–94).

In conclusion, to say that the Swedish electorate is "an electorate in the grips of the welfare state" (Zetterberg 1985) is to overstate the case for self-interest. Rather, Swedes seem to have a healthy—but not perverse—taste for voter candy.

CHAPTER EIGHT

Distributive Justice

The self-interest perspective is a parsimonious theory. Because of its parsimony it is not surprising that it fails to explain certain portions of political attitudes and behavior (Mansbridge 1990; Lewin 1988; Green and Shapiro 1994; Udéhn 1996). One parsimonious assumption is that public service delivery always has positive effects on support for leftist ideology and political trust. This assumption underlies the hypotheses tested in chapter 7, which claimed that heavy public service usage generates support for the system and the institutions providing services. The self-interest perspective thus ignores the possibility that welfare state usage sometimes reduces support through negative experiences: Given that citizens are driven by short-term, economic self-interest when evaluating the welfare state and the political system, and given that welfare state services make at least some minimal contribution to that self-interest, it follows that yet another welfare state experience will always be conducive to greater system support. Adapting Zetterberg's (1985) language, citizens are "in the grips of the welfare state" in the sense that they must always react positively to service experiences—that is, by increasing their support for the system providing the service.

A More Subtle Perspective

We now begin to acknowledge that welfare state experiences might involve more action than just assessments of personal, material, short-term outcomes. In all the remaining empirical chapters this idea is present in one way or the other. For example, the *social justice perspective* assumes that people do not necessarily react positively to the level of welfare state outcome they receive, as assumed by the self-interest perspective. Rather, what they want out of their contacts with public institutions is different forms of social justice. People do not just want as much welfare state out-come as possible for themselves. They also want to experience fairness and justice. Since the perceived fairness of personal welfare state outcomes and procedures can vary, so can the political effects of experiences. Sometimes experience effects on support for the system are positive and sometimes they are negative. In this sense, the social justice perspective is a subtler and less deterministic theoretical perspective.

In this chapter we investigate effects of distributive justice judgments ("have I received what I have a right to"). In chapter 9, we deal with one particular aspect of procedural justice: experienced voice opportunities.

Based on past social psychological research on social justice, we have hypothesized that higher degrees of experienced distributive justice produces more ideological leftism, more state-intervention support, more satisfaction with democracy, and more trust in politicians. Conversely, experiences of poor distributive justice ("I did not get the service I have the right to") tend to produce ideological support for the right, less positive views on state intervention, less satisfaction with democracy, and less trust in politicians.

These predictions deserve some qualification. More specifically, we expect experienced distributive justice to be more influential for political trust orientations than for ideological orientations. In chapter 4, we reviewed literature suggesting that self-interest matters more when the political choices have greater and more visible implications for one's personal, economic, short-term situation (Sears and Citrin 1982; Green 1988; Sears and Funk 1991). As economic "stakes" get larger and more visible, self-interest considerations become more influential. And given that citizens have limited cognitive capacity and motivation for careful political deliberation, arguments pertaining to distributive and procedural justice should be crowded out in the process. Since the choice between, for example, trusting politicians or not has small implications for short-term material self-interest, experienced distributive justice should have its greatest effects on such variables. In contrast, because the choice between leftist and rightist policies has substantial implications for citizens' personal economies, self-interest considerations will matter more, and social justice considerations will matter less, for such choices.

Before the empirical analysis begins, I will briefly remind the reader about a couple of theoretical considerations, which have implications for how the impact of experienced distributive justice should be analyzed and thought about.

Self-Interest in Disguise?

The social justice perspective assumes that people in contact with public services have a normative expectation as to what constitutes a fair service outcome or procedure. It is when the expectation is compared with the actual experience that a judgment of experienced social justice is formed (see Tyler et al. 1997:45–50).

The self-interest perspective challenges this idea. People are not believed to compare normative expectation with actual experience in an intellectually honest way. Rather, judgments of experienced justice are but reflections of the extent to which experiences have served one's short-term material self-interest (Tyler 1990:173). It is more socially acceptable to assess public institutions using arguments of social justice than arguments relating to self-interest. Because people are essentially driven by self-interest, and because they usually seek a politically and socially correct disguise for that interest, citizens who gain a lot from the welfare state will typically say that they have experienced distributive and procedural justice. Conversely, those who gain less will tend to judge justice aspects of experiences unfavorably. The self-interest perspective thus predicts that higher levels of individual gain from public services will be strongly correlated with positive perceptions of experienced justice. Moreover, once self-interest has been controlled for, there is no independent political effect of perceptions of experienced justice.

In this chapter, and in chapter 9, I try to assess empirically the extent of the damage these objections do to the social justice perspective. For instance, I look at the correlation between the level of welfare state interest and judgments of experienced justice: The social justice perspective predicts that this correlation is not exceedingly strong. Also, I control effects of justice judgments on political orientations for self-interest: The social justice perspective predicts that there are significant effects also when controlling for self-interest.

Personal Experience and Sociotropic Judgment

Chapter 1 introduced the basic model that has inspired most previous research on the relation between personal experiences and political attitudes and behavior (see figure 1.1). This model links personal experiences to dependent variables in two ways: First, there is a potential direct effect of experiences. In this case, citizens react politically to experiences in a direct manner. They form political attitudes based on personal experiences that are particular to the person in question. Second, there is a possibility of an indirect effect component flowing through sociotropic judgments of how the nation as a whole is doing and what the collective as a whole has experienced. Here, people are more inclined to look at sociotropic judgments of common experiences. While personal experiences are not the decisive causal trigger, sociotropic judgments are in turn partly affected by specific personal experiences. According to this second account, then, personal experience effects are perfectly compatible with the prevailing image of the modern voter as a "sociotropic animal," with the addition that sociotropic judgments are in turn partly informed by personal experiences.

In chapter 1, I suspected that the link between experiences and sociotropic judgments might be tighter in the welfare state territory than in the economic realm. One argument was that macro information about the welfare state is less accessible than macro information about the nation's economy. A second argument was that there is a clearer political responsibility for personal welfare state experiences, as opposed to private economic experiences. Taken together, worse accessibility of sociotropic information and greater political relevance make welfare state experiences more influential in attitude formation than economic experiences. This hypothesis received empirical support in chapter 6.

In some of the analyses presented in this chapter we will have access to measures of personally experienced distributive justice, as well as measures of sociotropic perceptions of what people in general experience. Hence, to the extent that personally experienced distributive justice affects attitudes, we can continue to track which of the two described paths effects take.

Overall Judgments of Experienced Distributive Justice

Experienced distributive justice was measured in two ways. The first strategy involved asking about people's overall experience with public services. The second strategy was to ask about "institution-specific" experienced distributive justice in contacts with six different public services. The overall measure will be analyzed in this section, while the institution-specific items are used in the two sections to come.

The overall measure of experienced distributive justice was included in a question battery with the following head question: "If you look back on your own personal contacts with public authorities and services during the last twelve months, to what extent do the following statements fit with your own experience." The response alternatives were "fits very well," "fits rather well," "fits rather poorly," "fits very poorly," and "have not been in contact." As can be seen in table 8.1, 43 percent of respondents reported positive experiences ("fits very or rather well"), while 20 percent reported experiences on the negative side.

Interestingly, 37 percent placed themselves in the "have not been in contact" category. This should not be taken as a sign that many Swedes do not have any actual personal public service contacts during a year. We know from chapter 7 that only 5 percent of respondents had managed to avoid all the public services for which actual personal usage was measured. Rather, it seems likely that "have not been in contact" functions as a residual category for people who do not know or do not remember either positive or negative experiences. It seems reasonable to assume that most of these people have actually had relatively neutral experiences that did not stick out from the ordinary. Consequently, the no contact category will be treated as a middle category in the analyses to come (coded 0). The other categories will be coded: fits very well ($+2$), fits rather well ($+1$), fits rather poorly (-1), and fits very poorly (-2).

The measure of sociotropic distributive justice in table 8.1 was included in a question battery with the following head question: "If you instead think about how public authorities and services function in general, how well do the following statements fit with your general view." The response

Table 8.1 Experienced and sociotropic distributive justice perceptions (percent)

Experienced distributive justice	
"I have received the service and help I have the right to"	
Fits very well	8
Fits rather well	35
Fits rather poorly	13
Fits very poorly	7
Have not been in contact	37
Sum percent	100
Number of respondents	3,460
Sociotropic distributive justice	
"In general, people receive the service and help they have the right to"	
Fits very well	4
Fits rather well	43
Fits rather poorly	25
Fits very poorly	8
Don't know	20
Sum percent	100
Number of respondents	3,531

Notes: The data come from the 1999 West Sweden SOM Survey. The measure of experienced distributive justice was included in a question battery with the following head question: "If you look back on your own personal contacts with various public authorities and services during the last twelve months, to what extent do the following statements fit with your own experience?" The measure of sociotropic distributive justice was included in a question battery with this head question: "If you instead think about how public authorities and services function in general, how well do the following statements fit with your general view?"

alternatives were "fits very well," "fits rather well," "fits rather poorly," "fits very poorly," and "don't know." In the analyses to come, the variable will be coded in the following manner: fits very well (+2), fits rather well (+1), don't know (0), fits rather poorly (−1), and fits very poorly (−2).[1]

Interestingly, experienced distributive justice does not correlate much with the various measures of welfare state self-interest used in chapter 7. It has a nonsignificant correlation with "objective" welfare state interest (less than .01), and a significant but weak correlation with "subjective" welfare state interest (.05).[2] Apparently, there are many people consuming small quantities of public service who nevertheless believe that they receive the service they have a right to. Conversely, there are many people who use lots of public services and nevertheless feel that they do not get distributive justice in their contact with public institutions. These low correlations are a problem for the assumption that perceptions of experienced justice are mainly a politically correct way of expressing content or discontent with the extent to which one's economic self-interest is satisfied. Rather, the low correlations strengthen the social justice perspective, which considers perceptions of experienced justice to be results of intellectually honest comparisons between actual experience and normative distributive justice expectations.

Moreover, there is a strong correlation between experienced distributive justice and sociotropic judgments as to whether people in general get the service and help they have the right to (.43).[3] This observation fits the suspicion that the link between personal experience and sociotropic judgment is tighter in the area of the welfare state than it has proven to be in the economic realm (Mutz 1998). To the extent that sociotropic judgments affect attitudes, sociotropic judgments may channel parts of the effect of personal experience.

What are the effects of experienced distributive justice on political orientations? Table 8.2 answers this question with respect to state-intervention orientations and left–right ideology. For each of these dependent variables I estimated three OLS regression equations. The first model contains the bivariate effect only. The second model controls that effect for the same control variables that were used previously. Model 3 adds the measure of sociotropic distributive justice, thus allowing us to see how much of the effect of experiences is direct and how much is indirect, flowing through sociotropic judgments.

There are significant direct effects of experienced distributive justice on support for state intervention (.08) and on left–right self-placement (−.05). As we have hypothesized, the tendency is that the greater distributive justice people feel they have experienced, the more they tend to support state intervention and leftist ideology. These effects, however, are weak. And taken on its own experienced distributive justice explains less than 1 percent of the variation in the dependent variables. Moreover, there are no effects of sociotropic distributive justice judgments on state-intervention orientations and left–right self-placement. In sum, neither personal experiences of distributive justice, nor sociotropic judgments of collective experience are overly related to political ideology.

What is the impact on political trust? Table 8.3 answers this question with respect to satisfaction with the way democracy works and trust in politicians. Here the impact of experienced distributive justice is greater. This shift is in line with the hypothesis that social justice concerns are more important for political trust than for ideological left–right orientations. When the control variables are included the experience variable still has a relatively sizable impact on satisfaction with democracy (.15) and on trust in politicians (.19). Taken on its own, experienced distributive justice explains 4 and 6 percent respectively of the variation in the dependent variables.

It is interesting to compare the total effects of experienced distributive justice with those of perceptions of the economy. Of course, the effects of the latter variable are the single most important reason why previous research has come to the conclusion that modern voters are "sociotropic animals." When forming political judgments, such animals are prone to consider collective information about the population as a whole, rather than information generated by personal experience. In the economic area, this has proven to be a valid conclusion both for vote choice and

Table 8.2 The impact of experienced distributive justice in contacts with public agencies on state-intervention orientation and left–right ideology (unstandardized OLS estimates)

	Dependent variable: State-intervention orientation (higher value = greater support for intervention)			Dependent variable: Left–right self-placement (higher value = further to the right)		
	Model 1: Experienced distributive justice	Model 2: Model 1 + control variables	Model 3: Model 2 + Sociotropic distributive justice	Model 4: Experienced distributive justice	Model 5: Model 4 + control variables	Model 6: Model 5 + Sociotropic distributive justice
Experienced distributive justice (−2–2)	.07*	.08*	.08**	−.03**	−.05**	−.05**
Objective welfare state interest (0–10)	—	.06***	.06**	—	−.03***	−.03***
Employed in public sector	—	.91***	.91***	—	−.25***	−.25***
Subjective class affiliation (1 = middle class)	—	−.86***	−.85***	—	.64***	.64***
Family income (1–8)	—	−.10***	−.11***	—	.06***	.06***
Gender (1 = woman)	—	.08**	.07**	—	−.02	−.02
Education (1–3)	—	−.11**	−.11**	—	−.01	−.01
Sociotropic distributive justice (−2–2)	—	—	.003	—	—	.001
Constant	6.82***	7.17***	7.17***	2.94***	2.66***	2.67***
Adjusted R-squared	.001	.11	.11	.001	.12	.12
Number of respondents	2,487	2,487	2,487	2,591	2,591	2,591

* $p < .10$ ** $p < .05$ *** $p < .01$

Notes: The data come from the 1999 West Sweden SOM Survey. For more information about the two distributive justice measures, see table 8.1, and related text. For information about the objective welfare state interest variable, see table 7.1 and related text. For information about how other independent variables were coded, see tables 6.3 and 6.4. The dependent variables were described in chapter 7.

Table 8.3 The impact of experienced distributive justice in contacts with public agencies on satisfaction with democracy and trust in politicians (unstandardized OLS estimates)

	Dependent variable: Satisfaction with democracy (higher value = more satisfaction)			Dependent variable: Trust in politicians (higher value = more trust)		
	Model 1: Experienced distributive justice	*Model 2: Model 1 + control variables*	*Model 3: Model 2 + Sociotropic distributive justice*	*Model 4: Experienced distributive justice*	*Model 5: Model 4 + control variables*	*Model 6: Model 5 + Sociotropic distributive justice*
Experienced distributive justice (−2–2)	.19***	.15***	.07***	.24***	.19***	.12***
Objective welfare state interest (0–10)	—	.02***	.02**	—	.01*	.01
Perception of Swedish economy (1–3)	—	−.19***	−.18***	—	−.18***	−.17***
Preference for incumbent party	—	.34***	.32***	—	.39***	.37***
No party preference	—	−.14**	−.13**	—	−.18***	−.17***
Age in years (15–80)	—	−.005***	−.005***	—	.00	−.00
Education (1–3)	—	.01	.01	—	.04	.04
Life satisfaction (1–4)	—	.17***	.15***	—	.14***	.13***
Subjective class affiliation (1 = middle class)	—	.06	.04	—	.07	.06
Sociotropic distributive justice (−2–2)	—	—	.19***	—	—	.18***
Constant	−.03	.65***	.62***	−.06***	.29**	.26**
Adjusted *R*-squared	.04	.11	.15	.06	.13	.16
Number of respondents	2,580	2,580	2,580	2,653	2,653	2,653

★ *p* < .10   ★★*p* < .05   ★★★ *p* < .01

Notes: The data come from the 1999 West Sweden SOM Survey. For more information about the two distributive justice measures, see table 8.1, and related text. For information about the objective welfare state interest variable, see table 7.1 and text. For more information about other independent variables, see tables 6.3, 6.4, and 7.6. The dependent variables were described in chapter 6.

government approval (see Lewis-Beck 1988), as well as for political trust (see McAllister 1999; Huseby 2000).

It turns out that personally experienced distributive justice has stronger effects on both satisfaction with democracy and trust in politicians than do sociotropic perceptions of the Swedish economy. For satisfaction with democracy, the total effect of moving between the extreme categories along the experience variable is .60 (= .15 × 4). The corresponding effect of economic perceptions is .38 (= .19 × 2). Likewise, for trust in politicians, the effect of moving between the extreme categories along the experience variable is .76 (= .19 × 4). Here, the corresponding effect of economic perceptions is .36 (= .18 × 2).

These findings do not imply that Swedes do not consider collective information in the welfare state area. On the contrary, sociotropic distributive justice has a strong impact on both dependent variables; as a matter of fact, it has a stronger maximum effect than that of economic sociotropic judgments. We also see that the coefficients of the experience variable decrease when the sociotropic measures are entered. This observation, together with the strong correlation between personal experience and sociotropic judgment (.43), means a sizable chunk of the total personal experience effect is in fact channeled through collective sociotropic judgments. Such indirect effects demonstrate that personal experience effects and sociotropic considerations do not necessarily constitute rival pictures of opinion formation.

Having said this, it is also clear that experienced distributive justice has direct effects. Among people who make the same sociotropic judgments, personal experiences still significantly affect orientations. More precisely, between half and two-thirds of the experience effect remains even when sociotropic judgments are controlled for (see models 3 and 6). We interpret this as evidence that a more direct generalization of personal experiences has also taken place, a process that is independent of sociotropic judgments.

In conclusion, the total effects of experienced distributive justice on political trust seem to travel along both the suggested generalization paths. The data are consistent both with the idea of an indirect generalization process, in which experiences inform sociotropic judgments, as well as with a direct generalization process, in which experience effects bypass sociotropic judgment. These findings fit well with those of chapter 6.

Experienced Distributive Justice in Six Institutions

Thus far, we have measured experienced distributive justice using a single question about overall experiences with public service institutions. There is something to be said for this method as it is an economic way of getting at meaningful information. On the other hand, it is not necessarily an easy question for respondents. For instance, those who have been in contact with two or more public services must construct a rather strange average of experiences or otherwise strike a balance between different experiences with different institutions. This introduces difficulties on top of the pure memory problems that arise when survey respondents are asked to recall their own past.

Respondents who do not care to go through that difficulty have at least two options, both of which introduce additional measurement error. First, people can choose the "have not been in contact" category. We noted that 37 percent ticked this option when confronted with the general distributive justice item, although virtually all Swedes are in contact with one welfare state institution or the other on a regular basis. Second, there is an increasing risk for the "projection" processes that chapter 5 warned of. Because the question is relatively imprecise and general, it may bring to mind preexisting stereotypes about how the public sector treats people, rather than recollections of actual experiences.

To partly come to terms with these difficulties I tried an alternative method. I included in the questionnaire a question battery with this head question: "If you look back on your contacts with the following services in the last twelve months, to what extent do you feel you have received the service and help you have the right to?" For each of six institutions, respondents were asked to answer along a five-point scale between 1 (have not received the service and help I have the right to) and 5 (have received the service and help I have the right to). Also, people could indicate that they had not been in contact with the service in question.

The advantage of this measurement strategy is that people will not be forced to construct error-prone averages of different experiences of different institutions. This should reduce the risk that they flee to the "have not been in contact" category. Also, because the question refers to concrete institutions, it should stand a greater chance of calling actual experiences to mind, rather than stereotypes and prejudice.

But there are also drawbacks. Due to space limitations in the questionnaire, it was impossible to include all conceivable public service institutions in the battery. A selection had to be made. The following six public institutions were included: health care, kindergartens, social welfare, public transportation, job agencies, and housing allowance. Table 8.4 shows the univariate distributions.

Experienced distributive justice varies substantially; between 55 and 27 percent of those who have been in contact think they have received what they have a right to. I urge readers who find these differences interesting to hold their horses. Such institutional differences will play a key role in chapter 10. At the moment, we are interested in the effects on political orientations of these institution-specific measures of experienced distributive justice. As a first step toward this end, table 8.5 shows effects of single items among users of the institution in question. Specifically, the first column displays bivariate correlation coefficients. The second column contains unstandardized OLS coefficients for the same bivariate relation. The third column controls for the variables included in previous analyses in this chapter. The fourth column shows how many respondents have had contact with a particular institution *and* have a valid value on the dependent variable.

Table 8.4 Experienced distributive justice in personal contacts with six welfare state institutions (percent)

	Experienced distributive justice						
1 ←					→ 5		
I have not received the service and help I have a right to					*I have received the service and help I have a right to*		
	1				*5*	*Sum percent*	*N*
Health care	6	6	15	21	52	100	2,836
Child care	5	5	10	25	55	100	613
Social assistance	2	12	23	16	27	100	198
Public transportation	3	5	16	28	48	100	1,977
Job agency	1	13	21	24	27	100	676
Housing allowance	1	10	17	13	45	100	375

Notes: The data come from the 1999 West Sweden SOM Survey. The question was formulated as follows: "If you look back on your contacts with the following services in the last twelve months, to what extent do you feel you have received the service and help you have the right to?" For each of the six institutions, respondents answered using a five-point scale between 1 (have not received the service and help I have the right to) and 5 (have received the service and help I have the right to). Also, people could indicate that they had not been in contact with the service in question. This group has been left out of the table.

This time we do not have parallel sociotropic judgment measures for the six institution-specific experience items. So here we do not have the possibility to investigate whether experience effects are direct or whether they are indirect, flowing through sociotropic perceptions of what people in general experience.

The impact of experienced distributive justice on state-intervention orientation and left–right ideology is largely absent. While there are small but significant effects on the state-intervention index in one case (public transportation), there is no significant impact whatsoever on left–right self-placement.

As in the previous analysis, experienced distributive justice has stronger effects on political trust variables, compared to the ideology variables (the only exception being that experienced distributive justice in housing allowance contacts does not significantly affect satisfaction with democracy). Hence, once again the findings fit the assumption that social justice concerns will be crowded out by self-interest as the economic implications of political choices increase. Self-interest becomes more influential, and social justice less so as "the stakes" go up (Sears and Citrin 1982; Green 1988; Sears and Funk 1991).

The multivariate OLS estimates of the impact of experienced distributive justice on satisfaction with democracy range from .07 (kindergartens

Table 8.5 The impact of experienced distributive justice in contacts with six institutions on political orientations

	Pearson's r	Bivariate b	Multivariate b	Number of respondents (bivariate)
Dependent variable: State-intervention orientation				
Health care	.04	.07**	NS	2,622
Kindergarten	.03	NS	NS	568
Social welfare	.02	NS	NS	180
Public transportation	.03	.07***	.05*	1,868
Job agency	.01	NS	NS	623
Housing allowance	.03	NS	NS	335
Dependent variable: Left–right self-placement				
Health care	−.01	NS	NS	2,777
Kindergarten	.02	NS	NS	601
Social welfare	.02	NS	NS	190
Public transportation	−.03	NS	NS	1,943
Job agency	.04	NS	NS	654
Housing allowance	−.02	NS	NS	360
Dependent variable: Satisfaction with democracy				
Health care	.16	.13***	.10***	2,592
Kindergarten	.12	.10***	.07*	567
Social welfare	.21	.17***	.16**	175
Public transportation	.17	.16***	.15***	1,819
Job agency	.12	.09***	.07**	621
Housing allowance	.12	.09**	NS	323
Dependent variable: Trust in politicians				
Health care	.15	.13***	.08***	2,671
Kindergarten	.06	.05	.07*	582
Social welfare	.21	.16***	.14**	182
Public transportation	.19	.18***	.17***	1,883
Job agency	.15	.12***	.11***	635
Housing allowance	.16	.11***	.08*	336

* $p < .10$ **$p < .05$ *** $p < .01$ NS = not significant, p-value $> .10$

Notes: The data come from the 1999 West Sweden SOM Survey. The analyses were done among people having been in contact with the institution in question. For more information about the experienced distributive justice measure, see table 8.4, and related text. The multivariate effects are controlled for the same variables that were included in tables 8.2 and 8.3 respectively. The dependent variables were described in chapters 6 and 7.

and job agency) to .16 (social welfare). The exact same pattern is found for trust in politicians. As these independent variables have five categories one must only multiply the coefficients with four to arrive at the impact of moving between extreme categories. For instance, among users of public transportation, the maximum effect of experienced distributive justice on satisfaction with democracy is .60 (.15 × 4). In other words, the predicted satisfaction with democracy decreases by about half a standard deviation as we move from public transportation users who have experienced distributive justice, to public transportation users who have not. (Recall that the standard deviations of the political trust factors equal 1.)

Are reports of experienced distributive justice nothing but self-interest in disguise? Or in other words, does experienced distributive justice correlate with welfare state interest so that people who consume more welfare state services than others are also more inclined to claim they have only received what is fair? Again, the answer seems to be no.

I arrived at this conclusion by performing two separate tests. First, I looked at correlations between the six experience items and the general welfare state–interest variables used in the chapter on self-interest. For objective welfare state interest there were (weak) positive correlations with only two of the six distributive justice items (kindergarten, $r = .08$ and housing allowance, $r = .07$). Similarly, for subjective welfare state interest, there were (very modest) tendencies for greater interest to covary with greater experienced distributive justice for three of the six items (health care, $r = .05$, kindergartens, $r = .05$, and public transportation, $r = .08$).[4]

In a second test of the self-interest-in-disguise hypothesis I used a set of more focused measures of subjective self-interest. For each institution, respondents were asked to indicate the extent to which they would benefit personally if more resources were given to the specific institution in question.[5] A five-point scale was used ranging from 1 (would not at all be of benefit) to 5 (would be of great benefit). Table 8.6 reports five regression analyses in which these subjective interest measures are used as independent variables. The dependent variable in each regression is the extent to which respondents in contact with the respective institution have experienced distributive justice.

Table 8.6 Effects of institution-specific subjective self-interest on institution-specific experienced distributive justice (unstandardized OLS estimates)

	Pearson's r	*b*	*Number of respondents*
Health care	.05	.05**	2,738
Public transportation	.02	.01	1,927
Kindergartens	−.03	−.02	602
Social welfare	−.04	−.02	189
Housing allowance	.12	.12**	351

$\star\, p < .10$ $\star\star\, p < .05$ $\star\star\star\, p < .01$

Notes: The data come from the 1999 West Sweden SOM Survey. The dependent variables in the six OLS regression analyses are the institution-specific measures of experienced distributive justice that were reported in table 8.4. Each of these institution-specific items was regressed on an independent variable measuring subjective perceptions of the extent to which increased public spending on the institution in question would be of personal benefit. These perceptions were measured on a five-point scale from 1 (would not at all be of benefit) to 5 (would be of great benefit). See Nilsson (2000a) for the exact wording of individual items. Respondents who had not been in contact with the institution in question are not included in the analyses.

Again, we discover weak or nonexistent links between the extent to which one gains from welfare state institutions and experienced distributive justice. For only two out of five institutions is experienced distributive justice significantly affected by the extent to which one perceives an invested self-interest in that institution (this time as measured by perceptions of how much one would gain from increased public spending on the particular service). These effects, however, are a matter of weak tendency at best.[6]

Combining Institution-Specific Experiences into One Index

The results in table 8.5 offered a detailed insight into effects of institution-specific distributive justice measures on political orientations. However, a limitation was that analyses were performed only among citizens who had been in contact with the institution in question. After all, the hypotheses are concerned with the overall impact of experienced distributive justice among the whole population. Therefore, we now bring together all the information contained in the items into a summary measure of experienced distributive justice in these six institutions. This measure will then be related to the dependent variables.

The summary index of experienced distributive justice was constructed by adding the six five-point scales into a single additive index. When doing this one needs to decide how to treat the "have not been in contact" category for each of the items. In the analysis that follows I treated noncontacts as "neutral experiences." That is, I gave such responses the value 3. Each of the six institution-specific items thus varies between 1 (have not received the service and help I have the right to) and 5 (have received the service and help I have the right to). The mid-point category contains people who either reported neutral experiences, or had not been in contact at all.[7] The resulting index varies between 6 and 30 (mean = 19.8, standard deviation = 2.2). A value of six means the respondent has been in contact with all six institutions and reports having experienced maximum distributive injustice in all six cases. A value of 30 means the respondent has been in contact with all six institutions and reports having experienced maximum distributive justice for all of them.

The described index of experienced distributive justice was included as a dependent variable in four regression analyses reported in table 8.7. The dependent variables were satisfaction with democracy and trust in politicians. State-intervention orientation and left–right self-placement are left out as the six institution-specific items on which the index is based had virtually no effects on ideology.

The results fit the previous findings. Experienced distributive justice has both statistically and substantially significant effects on political support variables. Recalling that both dependent variables have standard deviations of 1, it is interesting that the maximum effect of the experienced distributive justice index is 1.38 for both dependent variables (.06 × 23 category leaps). This is the effect of moving from someone experiencing maximum

Table 8.7 The impact of experienced distributive justice in contacts with six public agencies on satisfaction with democracy and trust in politicians (unstandardized OLS estimates)

	Dependent variable: Satisfaction with democracy (higher value = more satisfaction)		Dependent variable: Trust in politicians (higher value = more trust)	
	Model 1: Experienced distributive justice	Model 2: Model 1 + control variables	Model 3: Experienced distributive justice	Model 4: Model 3 + control variables
Experienced distributive justice index (6–30)	.08***	.06***	.08***	.06***
Objective welfare state interest (0–10)	—	.01	—	.01
Perception of Swedish economy (1–3)	—	−.19***	—	−.19***
Preference for incumbent party	—	.35***	—	.41***
No party preference	—	−.13**	—	−.18***
Age in years (15–80)	—	−.005***	—	.00
Education (1–3)	—	.02	—	.04*
Life satisfaction (1–4)	—	.18***	—	.16***
Subjective class affiliation (1 = middle class)	—	.07	—	.07
Constant	−1.56***	−.58***	−1.60***	−.91***
Adjusted *R*-squared	.03	.10	.03	.11
Number of respondents	2,604	2,604	2,686	2,686

* $p < .10$ ** $p < .05$ *** $p < .01$

Notes: The data come from the 1999 West Sweden SOM Survey. See main text for information about the experienced distributive justice index. For information about the objective welfare state interest variable, see table 7.1 and related text. For more information about other independent variables, see tables 6.3, 6.4, and 7.6. The dependent variables were described in chapter 6.

injustice in contacts with all six institutions to a person experiencing maximum justice with all six institutions. Of course, it is unusual to find people that extreme. In fact, there are only seven of them in the dataset. A more interesting comparison might be that between the 5th and 95th percentiles respectively; that is between the values 16 and 24. Such an eight-step move along the independent variable changes both dependent variables by .48 (.06 × 8). Looking at the table, one sees that this total effect is on par with those of some other variables emphasized by the political support literature, such as perception of the economy, incumbent preference, or life satisfaction.

As in other analyses in this chapter, the explanatory variables only manage to account for 10–11 percent of the variation in satisfaction with democracy and trust in politicians. Experienced distributive justice explains 3 percent in the bivariate analysis. While this may sound low it should be kept in mind that the institution-specific experience index used here is based on only six welfare state institutions. It is likely that the strength of the effect would have gone up if we had institution-specific experienced distributive justice measures for more welfare state services.

Still, some readers might not be satisfied with the explanatory power of experienced distributive justice. However, previous research clearly indicates that variation in political trust is a multifaceted phenomenon that cannot be entirely explained by one single theoretical perspective. Very different types of variables are usually needed to reach reasonable explanatory power in these types of analyses (Norris 1999; Holmberg 1999). Therefore, when assessing the explanatory success of experienced distributive justice, the most relevant yardstick appears to be the impact of variables representing other theoretical perspectives, rather than the absolute level in the proportion of explained variance. Experienced distributive justice does rather well, though not necessarily much better, in comparison with variables representing other theoretical perspectives that are taken seriously in research on political trust.

Why Weak Effects on Ideology?

A central finding in this chapter is that experienced distributive justice has sizeable effects on political trust, but very weak and rare effects on political ideology. We have provided the explanation that since issues related to redistribution and equality lie at the heart of the left–right conflict, such ideological positions are more related to potentially large self-interest stakes. Previous research contends that larger and more visible stakes mean that self-interest considerations tend to occupy more space in citizens' political thinking (Green 1988; Sears and Funk 1991). From this point of view, the explanation for the weaker impact of experienced distributive justice on ideology is that social justice concerns are "crowded out" by self-interest because stakes are high and visible.

But there is an alternative interpretation. It starts with the observation that it is not self-evident what ideological conclusions are drawn from experienced distributive justice. While social psychological findings indicate that injustice generally produces *weaker* support for collective institutions (Tyler et al. 1997), exactly the opposite is logically possible. It has been suggested that, in the welfare state context, deficiencies such as distributive injustice may actually *strengthen* willingness to accept public spending and state intervention in order to come to terms with the problems (see Kaase and Newton 1995; Huseby 1995; Pettersen 1995; Svallfors 2001; Johansson, Nilsson, and Strömberg 2001). Moreover, this reverse effect could be especially common among people who already display a good amount of support. Among such people, the natural reaction to distributive injustice may be an even greater willingness to protect and support welfare state arrangements. Victims of injustice may draw the conclusion that such arrangements have in fact too few resources and should receive more—not less—support in the future. This alternative hypothesis is a nice example of the possibility that different people actively "construct" very different political meanings from very similar experiences.[8]

The alternative hypothesis poses a threat to the conclusion that experienced distributive injustice has weak negative effects on support for leftist ideology. The crux is not just that the effect could theoretically have turned out to run in the opposite direction. Rather, the problem is that the impact could have a different direction depending on what ideological leanings a person had before experiences occurred. People who already subscribed to an antiwelfare state ideology could react to personal distributive injustice by becoming even more negative, whereas those who already supported it draw the conclusion that welfare state arrangements are in trouble and need even more support. If this is what is going on, a weak overall effect could hide a great impact that has different signs in different subgroups.

As discussed in chapter 5, we are not that well equipped to empirically assess "constructionist" predictions. The reason is that we use static, cross-sectional survey data, which are collected at a single point in time. In order to assess the alternative hypothesis, we would need panel data. One would want to measure, not only respondents' ideological orientations after experiences have occurred, but also orientations before the experience. Such "t-1" variables would be included as control variables and interaction variables, so as to check whether the weak overall coefficients mask an impact that has different signs depending on political orientations at t-1.

We will have to wait for definitive longitudinal studies of this particular question. As it stands, however, the current evidence arguably provides more support for the hypothesis that poor distributive justice *reduces* ideological support, as well as the hypothesis that these effects are weaker than those on political trust. On the occasions when we have found an effect on ideology, the results have indeed indicated negative effects of negative experiences on general ideological support. For instance, using the overall measure of experienced distributive justice, table 8.2 showed a weak tendency for negative experiences to produce effects in a rightist direction. The same goes for effects of the institution-specific measures related to health care and public transportation on state-intervention orientations (table 8.5). On no occasion did we find negative experiences to produce overall coefficients indicating increased support for leftist ideology. These findings are a problem for the hypothesis that negative experiences are constructed as arguments for increased ideological support.

Of course, one could object that the coefficients for the entire sample do not tell us what we want to know. Rather, according to the "constructionist" hypothesis, it is mainly people who already displayed considerable doses of leftist support before experiences occurred that should react to distributive injustice by developing even more support. Again, it is difficult to respond in a definitive way to this, as we do not have the right sort of longitudinal data.

But a couple of preliminary points can be made. First, if it were true that people who already support state intervention react to negative experiences by further increasing their support, one would have expected this process to at least occasionally produce overall coefficients with the right sign, especially as welfare state policies are typically popular among a majority of Swedes (Svallfors 1996, 1999). Therefore, even if it were true that different subgroups react differently, one would have expected the effect of this type of "construction" to at least occasionally be the dominant one, producing overall coefficients indicating that distributive injustice strengthens support. Moreover, in a "poor man's" attempt to simulate the desired t-1 interactions, I performed split-sample versions of the regression analyses in tables 8.2 and 8.5. These analyses compared results for the whole sample with those among the extreme quartiles along the state-intervention variable, assuming that these two groups were different in terms of ideology also before experiences occurred. Admittedly, this is a crude test. Nevertheless, for what it is worth, the results did not reveal any great differences in the direction of the effects on political ideology among pro- and antistate-intervention respondents respectively. Effects were typically insignificant in both groups for most institutions. Having said this, two interesting exceptions may be noted: for public transportation and job agencies, experienced injustice did indeed push people slightly toward the left on the self-placement scale. However, this effect was not present for state-intervention orientations, or for any other of the measured institutions. Also, the impact was still very weak, for instance considerably weaker than that of objective self-interest. These results, then, are still consistent with the interpretation that self-interest dominates over social justice when stakes are high.

Finally, it is crucial to remember that the aforementioned discussion is concerned with general ideological orientations ("a large public sector is a good thing"), not concrete opinions about specific services and institutions (such as "more resources to kindergartens"). It would appear that those suggesting that poor distributive justice increases welfare state support are usually talking about rather short-term and specific opinions, rather than general ideological orientations. In fact, it is perfectly possible that poor distributive justice simultaneously produces both increased and decreased welfare state support, albeit at different levels of abstraction. For example, think of someone having a highly negative health care experience (involving long waiting times and, after a quick examination, being sent home with painkillers). This negative experience may very well simultaneously result in both demands for increased short-term spending on public health care, as well an increased general skepticism toward the public sector, state intervention, "big government," and the like.

This is indeed the empirical picture that emerges if we add the findings presented here with those of previous studies. Whereas we have found that experienced distributive injustice has (very weak) negative effects on support for leftist ideology, we know from previous research that public service dissatisfaction indeed tends to breed demands for *more* spending on those *concrete* services that are targets for dissatisfaction (Johansson, Nilsson, and Strömberg 2001:148). This pattern was further corroborated when I investigated the effects of the institution-specific measures of distributive justice on whether one prefers increased spending on the same institutions. Poor experienced distributive justice with a welfare state institution seems to make people more willing to give public resources to that particular institution. However, to the extent that more general ideological orientations are at all affected, the impact on support seems to be negative.

Conclusion

Experienced distributive justice affects political orientations. However, while on occasion we have seen significant effects on support for state intervention and left–right self-placement, the effects appear to operate mainly on political trust. Social justice concerns, it seems, are more important when self-interest stakes involved in political choices decrease.

Moreover, the extent to which citizens experience distributive justice is not the same empirical thing as the extent to which welfare state institutions satisfy citizens' economic self-interest. Rather, in addition to being conceptually distinct, self-interest and experienced distributive justice constitute two quite independent empirical dimensions of personal welfare state experiences. We have seen that the empirical link between the two is generally weak and that distributive justice effects on attitudes are clearly present also when controlling for welfare state interests. That is, among citizens having roughly the same self-interest invested in the welfare state, experienced distributive justice still varies greatly, a variation that has respectable effects on political trust. These findings do not fit with the idea found in public choice theory that personal justice judgments are merely socially and politically correct rationalizations of self-interest. Instead, the findings are more in line with the distributive justice perspective, from which people are believed to make intellectually honest comparisons between a normative welfare state expectation and actual experiences. In short, experienced distributive justice is not self-interest in disguise.

Much previous opinion research contends that citizens in modern developed democracies can be described as "sociotropic animals." When forming political attitudes, such animals consider overall sociotropic information about collective rather than personal experiences. At first glance one might think that effects of experienced distributive justice are incompatible with the notion of "sociotropic animals." But this is not true. Sociotropic judgments of collective distributive justice also have a respectable impact on political trust. In addition, corroborating findings from chapter 6, quite a lot of the total impact of experienced distributive justice is in fact *channeled* via sociotropic judgments, though there is also evidence of a more direct generalization mechanism. In summary, welfare state experiences and sociotropic welfare state judgments "blend together" much more than has proven to be the case in studies of economic perceptions and political preferences (see Mutz 1998). Because simple quantifiable information about collective welfare state experiences is hard to come by, and because there is direct political responsibility for what people experience in welfare state contacts, sociotropic welfare state judgments are more experience-driven than sociotropic economic judgments.

The self-interest perspective implicitly assumes that welfare state experiences always have positive effects on system support. Given that citizens are driven by short-term, economic self-interest, and given that services make at least some minimal contribution to that self-interest, it follows that yet another welfare state experience will always be conducive to greater system support.

Of course, things look different from the social justice perspective. Whether experiences have positive attitude effects hinges on whether experiences match normative expectations concerning various forms of social justice. If experiences fall short of expectations, extensive welfare state usage will be detrimental to system support. Hence, citizens are not "in the grips of the welfare state" in the sense that they can only respond to welfare state experiences by developing more positive attitudes toward the system they are experiencing.

This chapter provides a certain dose of empirical support for these theoretical ideas in the context of political trust orientations. Whether heavy consumers of welfare state services are satisfied with democracy and trust politicians depends, not only on self-interest but also on whether they see their personal outcome as just. The same goes for citizens who get little or nothing from the welfare state.

Voice

Every winter morning during the past few years I have taken the tram to the university in downtown Göteborg. It is usually a dull trip, offering no excitement and no surprises. But one day, while on my way to continuing this chapter, I caught sight of a fascinating commercial sign in the tram:

> THE GÖTEBORG JOB AGENCY
> NOW COMING CLOSER TO YOU!
> EASIER TO GET SERVICE!
> EVERYTHING IN ONE PLACE!

Below the large headlines there was information in small print as to how accessible and user-friendly public job agencies would now be. Interestingly, there was no information about the actual services that job agencies might offer, such as job opportunities.

Now recall the Chicago woman from chapter 2. As the reader might remember, she was charged with a minor traffic offence and the court decided losing a day's work was a cruel enough penalty for the insignificant offence. The woman thus escaped getting fined altogether, which must be seen as a personal victory. Yet, she was very angry and made unflattering remarks about the judge. The reason was that, although she escaped the fine, court procedures did not allow her the possibility to show some photographs that relieved her from suspicion (Lind and Tyler 1988).

Neither the theories of self-interest tested in chapter 7, nor those of distributive justice investigated in chapter 8, make these episodes understandable. Both the Chicago woman and Gothenburgers in contact with job agencies appear to care about more than just the results, outcomes, and decisions they eventually receive from public institutions. More exactly, both stories highlight *procedural* aspects of the processes generating outcomes and results. Procedural aspects of experiences are not directly related to the outcomes or end results of that interaction. For instance, the Göteborg job agency believes that citizens care about the agency being "close," and that everything is "in one place," and not just about what the agency delivers once citizens get there. Similarly, the Chicago woman was primarily interested in having the opportunity to communicate her personal view to the jury, rather than in not being punished.

In the beginning of chapter 8, I remarked that the social justice perspectives are more subtle than theories of self-interest. The reason is that the former links personal outcomes and gains from the welfare state with a normatively charged expectation of what the individual has a right to in a given situation. The procedural justice perspective takes us yet another step away from pure self-interest effects. Unlike the chapters on self-interest and distributive justice, we are no longer concerned with the material outcomes and end results people get from institutions. Rather, we now bring into focus various procedural aspects of the interaction process between citizen and institutions.

Chapter 2 discussed several procedural aspects that have been highlighted in previous research (see Tyler 1997:chapter 4). One particular procedural aspect will be analyzed here: the extent to which citizens have the opportunity to make their voices heard and exercise influence in the process. Such procedural values have increasingly been at the forefront of debates on the future of the welfare state (see Petersson, Westholm, and Blomberg 1989; Schneider and Ingram 1997; Petersson et al. 1998; Lindbom 1998; Goul Andersen, Torpe, and Andersen 2000; Jarl 2001). It is assumed that citizens do not just want satisfactory service outcomes from their welfare state experiences. People also want to have their opinions and views recorded in the process leading up to outcomes, and they want to affect how these public institutions operate. Citizens have an independent desire to "have a say," and "to make a difference."

This chapter proceeds in several steps. First, I elaborate the independent variable—experienced voice opportunities. I then present the first of two different indicators of the independent variable, and bring up some measurement-related difficulties. Third, we analyze whether experienced voice opportunities are in fact nothing but "self-interest in disguise," and, fourth, the extent to which they correlate with experienced distributive justice. Fifth, we ask ourselves whether there is an interaction effect between experienced voice opportunities and service satisfaction. The next two sections then investigate the relationship between the various indicators of experienced voice and political orientations. The concluding section summarizes the findings and establishes a link to chapter 10.

Conceptual Remarks and Hypotheses

Let me put experienced voice opportunities in their conceptual context. Hirschman (1970) made a generally useful distinction between two different methods of signaling discontent, which are at the disposal to those dissatisfied with what an organization does for them: exit and voice.[1] First, people may turn their backs on the organization to either the benefit of a comparable service or, at times, to no service at all (exit). Alternatively, individuals may stay with the organization and communicate their complaints with the aim that things change for the better (voice). Generally speaking, it is voice opportunities—as perceived by citizens—that constitute the independent variable in this chapter.

Our independent variable can be specified further using the concept of *political efficacy*. This concept has been developed in research on voting behavior and political participation (see Campbell, Gurin, and Miller 1954; Almond and Verba 1963), and may be defined as "the feeling that individual political action does have, or can have, an impact on the political process [...] It is the feeling that political and social change is possible, and that the individual citizen can play a part in bringing about this change" (Campbell, Gurin, and Miller 1954:187).

Moreover, it is customary to distinguish between *internal* and *external* efficacy.[2] Internal efficacy has to do with the citizen's personal political confidence and competence. The question is: to what extent do individuals think that they themselves have the knowledge, the resources, and the strength to be able to make a difference. External efficacy refers to whether people feel that a political institution is interested in, and responsive to, one's opinions. ("If I tried to influence this institution, would it consider my views and weigh them into its decisions?") Here, we are interested in external efficacy.

Finally, it is useful to distinguish between political efficacy at different political levels. For example, people may have great political efficacy at, say, the local government level, whereas the regional or national political systems might be perceived as harder to influence (Goul Andersen 2000). Also, the situation can be different depending on whether we are talking about elected politicians and parliaments, high ranking civil servants, or street-level bureaucrats with which citizens have face-to-face contact.

In sum, we are interested in external efficacy in personal contacts with public services. To what extent do people perceive that the welfare state institutions and services they have been in contact with have offered possibilities to affect institutions and services? I will refer to this independent variable as "experienced voice opportunities."

The hypotheses to be tested is that greater experienced voice opportunities create more support for the welfare state, for leftist ideology, more satisfaction with democracy, and greater trust in politicians. As was discussed in chapter 2, the underlying assumption is that people put great value on the voice aspect of procedural justice in their personal welfare state experiences. If this is true, people who experience poor voice opportunities may use such experiences as general arguments against the leftist idea of a large welfare state ("bureaucracies are unresponsive and have little interest in the views and needs of ordinary people"). And since the responsibility for such matters ultimately resides with elected politicians, dissatisfaction with experienced voice opportunities may also foster negative views on how democracy and its policies function in practice.

As in the chapter on distributive justice, the expectation is that procedural justice has greater effects on political trust variables than on ideological left–right variables. More specifically, self-interest should matter more when political choices have greater and more visible implications for one's personal, economic, short-term situation (Sears and Citrin 1982; Green 1988; Sears and Funk 1991). As such "stakes" increase, economic self-interest becomes more influential and experienced distributive and procedural justice less so. Of course, we believe that the choice between, for example, trusting politicians or not has small implications for short-term economic self-interest. Therefore, experienced justice should have its greatest effects on such variables. In contrast, because ideological choices between left and right, or between little state intervention or a lot of state intervention, have potentially substantial implications for one's material situation, self-interest will matter more, and social justice less, for such variables.

Just like theories of distributive justice, the procedural justice perspective acknowledges the possibility that welfare state experiences can have both positive and negative effects on support for the welfare state and for democratic institutions and actors. This is a crucial difference compared to the self-interest perspective, which builds on the parsimonious assumption that public service delivery always has positive effects on these variables: Given that citizens are driven by short-term, economic self-interest when evaluating the welfare state and the political system, and given that welfare state services make at least some minimal contribution to that self-interest, welfare state experiences will always be conducive to support. The electorate is "in the grips of the welfare state" (Zetterberg 1985) as they must always react to welfare state contacts by increasing their support for the system and the institutions providing the service. The procedural justice perspective continues to challenge this notion by claiming that whether experiences will have positive effects on support depends on whether experiences meet procedural expectations.

Overall Judgments of Experienced Voice Opportunities

Experienced voice opportunities will be tapped in two ways. A first strategy involves asking about people's overall experience with public services. Second, we will analyze five institution-specific indicators of experienced voice.

Two aspects of overall experienced voice opportunities will be analyzed. First, recent debates on collective user influence highlight what we can call *formal* voice opportunities. Here, it is seen as important that people have real power to affect institutions. A radical and increasingly popular solution is that users of an institution (a school, a day care center, or a home for elderly) are given the opportunity to elect representatives to a user board. This board is given real decision-making power, or sometimes an advisory function, in local matters (see Sørensen 1997; Goul Andersen, Torpe, and Andersen 2000; Jarl 2001). Such institutional arrangements have been widely implemented in Denmark and are under way in for instance, the Swedish school system. These changes are interesting to us as they highlight a direct and "real" aspect of voice opportunities: that citizens feel that they—collectively or individually—can have a real impact on a public service institution in question. Empirically, we will measure such formal voice opportunities by tapping citizens' perceptions of their possibilities to actually affect how experienced welfare state institutions are run.

Second, we analyze a more *informal* voice aspect. The idea is that experiences involving possibilities to express opinions and feelings to a public employee stand a greater chance of producing system legitimacy, even if these voice opportunities are not obviously, visibly, or directly linked to actual decisions and changes. Consistent with this idea, both researchers and political actors emphasize the importance of institutions being interested in recording citizens' views in the interaction process, regardless of citizens' actual power to influence real decisions. Writing in the Danish context, Goul Andersen (2000:47)[3] notes, "One of the most important formal changes in the 1990s has been the introduction of user boards [...] But parallel to formal user influence, politicians have encouraged citizens and public employees to also informally put users and their preferences at focus."[4]

The distinction between formal and informal voice has interesting parallels in American research on procedural justice and voice in the legal system. A basic finding is that informal voice opportunities are as important as formal opportunities to have a real impact on decisions. For instance, Lind, Kanfer, and Early (1990) found that giving people the opportunity to present evidence after relevant decisions had been made—thus rendering voice opportunities meaningless from an instrumental point of view—nevertheless enhanced their judgments of procedural justice. Tyler and his colleagues (1997:90) summarize the significance of informal voice opportunities: "people value the opportunity to speak even when they think they are having little or no influence on the decision-maker. People's desire to have a voice [...] is not simply instrumental. They also value the opportunities to speak for other reasons."

Both aspects of voice opportunities were measured in the question battery with overall experience items in the 1999 Western Sweden SOM survey.[5] The item "I have had the possibility to affect how services are run" tapped the more formal and instrumental aspect of voice, whereas "employees have been helpful and listened to what I had to say" measured the informal aspect. For both items, the response alternatives were "fits very well," "fits rather well," "fits rather poorly," "fits very poorly," and "have not been in contact."

Table 9.1 tells us that informal voice opportunities are judged more favorably than the formal ones. While 46 percent reacted positively to the "employees listened" item, only 8 percent did so with respect to "affect services."[6] This is perhaps understandable as the more direct means to influence schools, kindergartens, and elder care institutions, are only in the beginning of their development. Also, it is probably easier for employees to convey the feeling that someone records opinions, rather than the feeling that those opinions have real effects on actual decisions or bring about change in how institutions operate.

Table 9.1 Experienced voice opportunities in contacts with public institutions (percent)

	Employees were helpful and listened to me	I had opportunities to affect how services are run
Fits very well	10	6
Fits rather well	36	2
Fits rather poorly	12	15
Fits very poorly	4	26
Have not been in contact	38	51
Sum percent	100	100
Number of respondents	3,469	3,435

Notes: The data come from a question battery with the following head question: "If you look back on your own personal contacts with various public authorities and services during the last twelve months, to what extent do the following statements fit with your own experience?" The data come from the 1999 West Sweden SOM survey.

As noted in chapter 8, many respondents placed themselves in the "have not been in contact" category. Again, this does not mean that many Swedes do not have personal public service contacts during a year. Rather, "have not been in contact" appears to function as a residual category for people who do not know, or remember neither positive nor negative experiences. It seems reasonable to assume that most of these people have actually had relatively neutral experiences that did not stick out from the ordinary. Consequently, just like in chapter 8, the no contact category will be treated as a middle category (coded 0). The other categories will be coded like this: fits very well $(+2)$, fits rather well $(+1)$, fits rather poorly (-1), and fits very poorly (-2).[7]

Let us pause for a minute and consider what we want these variables to measure. We are interested in *experienced* voice opportunities. That is, we hope to register how people actually felt while at the social welfare office, while in the hospital, when calling the children's schoolteacher, and so forth. However, there is a risk that the questions do not make people remember and report actual experiences, but instead evaluate aspects of political efficacy that are less relevant for us. These aspects include personal administrative and bureaucratic capabilities and general political self-confidence. People might thus take the questions to mean, not "did you experience voice opportunities?" but rather "generally, can you make your voice heard?" If so, there will be a strong correlation between our voice measures and other measures of political efficacy, and it becomes difficult to argue that we are measuring actual *experiences* of voice opportunities.

Beyond these wording-related difficulties, there are causal reasons for why experienced voice and internal efficacy could correlate. Even if everybody understands the meaning of the questions, it is still likely that those high in competence and confidence *truly experience* greater voice opportunities. Such persons should exercise greater influence, as they are better at making complaints and otherwise communicating their views to employees.

How serious are these problems? The data offer some opportunities to investigate the relation between indicators of experienced voice and political efficacy–related variables. First, education is known to strongly affect people's subjective competence and confidence in contacts with public services (see Petersson, Westholm, and Blomberg 1989:190–94). People with higher education are much more likely to feel they can make their voice heard and be influential than those with low education.[8] However, the correlation between education and the *experienced* voice measures was low (education/affect services = .11; education/employees listened = .05). Furthermore, the survey included a question battery asking people about their possibilities to affect political decisions at different government levels.[9] Responses regarding two of these levels—Sweden and the municipality— were combined into an additive index. The correlation between this general political efficacy index and experienced voice was not exceedingly high (political efficacy/"affect services" = .12; political efficacy/employees listened = .15). The same goes for a measure of general "political sophistication" (sophistication/affect services = −.12; sophistication/employees listened = .09).[10]

None of these correlations between experienced voice opportunities and efficacy-related measures are particularly high, and one even has the wrong sign. Hence, the experienced voice measures appear to capture a variation that is reasonably independent from other efficacy-related variables. Of course, whether this variation is meaningful in the sense that it impacts on political orientations remains to be seen. And naturally, given the arguments and results presented earlier, it will be important to investigate such effects controlling for the other efficacy-related factors. We are interested in whether experienced voice opportunities affect orientations among citizens at the same levels of other efficacy variables.

Such controls, however, introduce one further curiosity. Internal political efficacy can probably not be regarded as entirely exogenous in relation to experienced voice. In fact, variables such as administrative competence and bureaucratic self-confidence could be one of the mechanisms through which experienced voice affects political orientations. It is then experiences of poor voice that have a negative impact on internal political efficacy, rather than the other way around. In turn, reduced internal efficacy might have a negative effect on variables such as satisfaction with democracy and trust in politicians. Consequently, controlling experienced voice effects for internal efficacy could make estimates of the former too conservative. The reason is that we then hold constant one of the mechanisms that could channel the effect of experienced voice. Portions of the bivariate effects removed by efficacy controls may thus nevertheless still be consistent with the idea that experienced voice has a causal impact on orientations. Therefore, to the extent that we still find voice effects under control for variables such as education, engagement, and political efficacy, one would conclude that the hypotheses have passed rather tough tests.

Self-Interest in Disguise?

A basic assumption in the social justice perspective is that social justice judgments can be distinguished from personal outcomes and self-interests (see Lind and Tyler 1988:chapter 1). Judgments of distributive and procedural aspects of experiences are not merely rationalizations of the extent to which one has benefited personally. Rather, they constitute independent dimensions of judgment, which are distinct from outcomes and self-interest in the process of attitude formation.

These arguments have empirical implications. More exactly, even among people who do not differ in terms of self-interest, experienced voice opportunities should (1) vary substantially, and (2) affect sociopolitical attitudes and behavior. Expressed differently, if experienced voice is not merely self-interest in disguise, there should not be an exceedingly strong correlation between measures of self-interest and measures of experienced voice. Also, to the extent that there is a correlation, we still expect experienced voice to impact on orientations when self-interest variables are controlled.

At least the first implication is supported by the data. The correlations between the overall measures of experienced voice opportunities and the previously used welfare state–interest variable were all very weak.[11] Overall perceptions of voice opportunities do not seem to be self-interest in disguise. To find out if the second implication holds, I will later control experienced voice effects for the self-interest measures.

Different Dimensions of Experienced Justice?

Experienced distributive justice and experienced procedural justice are also potentially related to each other. Such a correlation could be the result of a reciprocal causal process in which people blur the academic distinction between distributive and procedural justice. In fact, when it comes to services like child care, elder care, and public education, service outcomes are delivered during an extended period of time. At the same time, there is an interaction process going on between the citizen and the public institution. When procedures and outcomes are not temporally distinct, judgments of the two aspects might be partly intertwined. For instance, people might infer judgments of outcomes from judgments of procedures. In particular, fair procedures might have a legitimizing effect on judgments of outcomes. It is easier to look favorably at what one gets if one is also treated fairly in the process. Likewise, those who are unsure of whether it was possible to "affect services," or whether "employees listened," might still have an idea of whether the outcome seemed fair, and they might reason, "if the result is fair, then the procedures probably were too."

Such processes are conducive to a pattern where those reporting positive experienced distributive justice will also report positive experienced voice opportunities. And this pattern is exactly what we find. However, judgments about the more instrumental/formal aspect of voice opportunities are more independent from experienced distributive justice than judgments of informal voice: While there is a strong correlation between "received the service and help I have a right to" and "employees listened" (.60), there is a much weaker one between distributive justice and "affect services" (.20).[12]

These correlations mean that we will want to control the effects of experienced voice opportunities for distributive justice judgments. The crucial issue is whether there is an independent effect of experienced voice, once experienced distributive justice is taken into account. If the answer is yes, the procedural justice perspective adds to our understanding of the political impact of welfare state experiences.

Procedural Justice: General Value or an Instrumental Tool for Self-Interest?

In addition to examining the relation between procedural judgments and outcome variables such as self-interest and distributive justice, we also investigate whether attitudinal *reactions* to procedures are related to outcome variables. The question is whether voice effects differ in magnitude depending on how personally beneficial outcomes are.

This analysis informs the question of how generally applicable the procedural justice perspective is. One view is that procedural fairness is a general human yardstick for evaluating common sociopolitical institutions. Therefore, its impact on attitudes and behavior toward such institutions does not vary much across individuals and contexts. As Tyler et al. (1997:209) explain, "One model of the psychology of the person suggests that a concern for justice is an inherent human characteristic. [...] If justice concerns arise from basic human motivations, we would expect to find common justice concerns across people, social groups, and societies."

One implication of these assumptions is that experienced voice opportunities should have *the same* impact on political orientations regardless of how personal outcomes from experiences are perceived. In statistical parlance, outcome-related variables such as quality judgments will *not* interact into the link between experienced voice opportunities and political orientations, so that this link will be stronger at certain levels of outcome satisfaction than at others. The absence of such an interaction effect would indicate that voice is a procedural value that matters to people even when personal outcomes from the process are more or less perfect. Procedural justice, in this case voice, would then not appear as a mere tool for improving personal outcomes.

The literature on voice opportunities in the welfare state often challenges this universal view.[13] Researchers do not think of the voice aspect of procedural justice as a reflection of a basic human inclination toward voice values. Rather, voice opportunities become important to people *only if they are dissatisfied with service quality*. Only then does the need arise for citizens to be able to affect how institutions are run and to have their opinions about them recorded by responsive public employees. Satisfactory service quality, on the other hand, means all is well and in that case people do not care much about "having a say." Voice is a tool for improving outcomes, and the quality of this tool is irrelevant as long as outcomes are perfectly satisfactory.

This was the view taken by Albert Hirschman (1970) in his influential book *Exit, Voice, and Loyalty*. Indeed, the subtitle was *Responses to Decline in Firms, Organizations, and States*, which reflects Hirschman's economic consumer perspective on relations between individuals and service providers. People are instrumentally oriented toward the organization and the goods it provides. Voice and exit are nothing but "responses to decline." That is, voice is an instrumental strategy for improving service quality. Hence, these mechanisms kick in only when service delivery is perceived as unsatisfactory. Voice is not regarded as a basic human procedural fairness value, but rather as an instrumental tool for improving personal outcomes from the procedure.

This instrumental view on voice opportunities has received some empirical support. For instance, Möller (1996:375)[14] conducted in-depth interviews with Swedes using elder care and child care and concluded: "Service delivery is the central factor. And as long as it meets expectations, the risk for system distrust is nonexistent. [...] Voice opportunities are also important but dissatisfaction in this respect is not enough to trigger distrust. [...] The political system 'should,' according to citizens, deliver services and as long as this is done there are no problems."

Moreover, Scandinavian survey research on voice opportunities has reported a positive correlation between dissatisfaction and actual attempts to affect public service institutions (see Petersson, Westholm, and Blomberg 1989; Hoff 1993; Goul Andersen 2000). Such attempts involve for example, active complaints such as contacting a public employee. This correlation, too, may be regarded as consistent with the idea that voice opportunities are more important for dissatisfied people.

We will explicitly test for an interaction effect between experienced voice opportunities and service satisfaction. Is voice only important for attitudes toward the welfare state and the political system among the dissatisfied? Or do such opportunities constitute more general yardsticks that are used in the opinion formation process regardless of what one thinks of public service quality? The answers inform us about how generally applicable the procedural justice perspective is: To what extent are we talking about a truly outcome-independent procedural dimension of personal welfare state experiences?

Overall Voice Opportunities and Political Orientations

Do the overall measures of experienced voice opportunities affect political orientations? Table 9.2 answers this question with respect to state-intervention

Table 9.2 The impact of experienced voice opportunities in contacts with public agencies on state-intervention orientation and left–right ideology (unstandardized OLS estimates)

	Dependent variable: State-intervention orientation (higher value = greater support for intervention)		Dependent variable: Left–right self-placement (higher value = further to the right)	
	Model 1: Experienced voice opportunities	Model 2: Model 1 + control variables	Model 3: Experienced voice opportunities	Model 4: Model 3 + control variables
Employees listened (−2–2)	.17***	.16**	−.07***	−.07**
I could affect how services are run (−2–2)	.01	.01	.00	.00
Experienced distributive justice (−2–2)	—	−.01	—	.00
Objective welfare state interest (0–10)	—	.06**	—	−.03***
Employed in public sector	—	.87***	—	−.22***
Subjective class affiliation (1 = middle class)	—	−.94***	—	.68***
Family income (1–8)	—	−.06***	—	.06***
Gender (1 = woman)	—	.11*	—	−.05
Political efficacy index (1–9)	—	.00	—	−.01
Education (1–3)	—	−.13**	—	.01
Political sophistication	—	.17	—	−.10***
Constant	6.77***	7.22***	2.96***	2.66***
Adjusted *R*-squared	.004	.12	.002	.13
Number of respondents	2,364	2,364	2,450	2,450

*p < .10   **p < .05   ***p < .01

Notes: The data come from the 1999 West Sweden SOM Survey. The dependent variables were described in chapter 7. For more information about the voice variables, see previous section on measurement. For more information about the distributive justice measure, see table 8.1, and related text. The objective welfare state interest variable was described in table 7.1 and related text. The political efficacy scale is an additive index summing responses to two questions about the possibilities of affecting political decisions in Sweden and in the municipality, respectively. The political sophistication measure (higher values = higher sophistication) was obtained through a factor analysis. Both the efficacy measure and the sophistication measure are described in more detail in a footnote in this chapter. For more information about other independent variables, see tables 6.3, 6.4, and 7.6.

orientations and left–right self-placement. For each dependent variable, two OLS models were estimated: one with only the two overall experienced voice measures, and one that adds a number of control variables to the equation. For reasons discussed earlier, we include the measures of political efficacy and political sophistication in addition to the controls used in previous chapters.

The "affect services" variable is wholly unrelated to the dependent ideology variables, whereas the "employees listened" item has weak significant effects. Looking at the controlled equations, it has an effect on both the state intervention index and on left–right self-placement (.16 and −.07). It thus seems as it is the more informal and less instrumental version of experienced voice that influences the ideology variables: People who have been in contact with responsive and helpful public employees are more likely to endorse leftist ideology and state-intervention policies.

However, even the impact of informal voice is quite limited in this analysis. Taken on its own, the "employees listened" item explains less than

1 percent of the variation in the dependent variables. And when comparing
its maximum effect with the impact of the subjective class dummy, one
notices that the effect of "employees listened" amounts to between two-
thirds and half of the class effect (.16 × 4 = .64 versus −.94 for state intervention, and .07 × 4 = .28 versus .68 for left–right self-placement).
According to this comparison, then, experienced voice opportunities, are
clearly less important for ideological orientations than the class dummy. Of
course, these comparisons are still quite kind to the voice variable as we are
moving between empirically unusual extreme categories.

Let us now look at the impact of experienced voice opportunities on
satisfaction with democracy and trust in politicians (table 9.3). The main
observation matches the hypothesis: People that experience responsive and
helpful public employees, and who perceive possibilities to affect services,
exhibit more political trust. An exception is that "affect services" is not significantly related to satisfaction with democracy.

It is informative to compare the maximum effect of the voice variables
with that of other theoretical perspectives, such as incumbent party preference and economic perception. For instance, the maximum effect of voice
variables on trust in politicians is .40 (.04 × 4 + .06 × 4). This might be
compared with the effect of moving from a citizen opposing the ruling
party *and* disapproving of the economy, to someone who favors the incumbent *and* approves of the economy. This effect amounts to .66. When it
comes to trust in politicians, then, it takes two competing variables representing two theoretical perspectives in order for the effect of experienced
voice to be clearly exceeded.

Remember that these effects are under control for variables such as welfare state interest and perceptions of experienced distributive justice. The
impact of experienced voice does not disappear when one investigates it
among people at the same welfare state interest level who make the same
distributive justice judgments about their outcomes. Hence, the voice
aspect of procedural justice seems to add an element to our understanding
of welfare state experience effects that was missing in chapters 7 and 8. This
element is independent in the sense that it matters to political orientations
also when objective outcomes and peoples' justice-based judgments of such
outcomes are taken into account.

Furthermore, it is notable that, taken on their own, the experienced
voice variables manage to explain more of the variation in political trust
variables than was the case for the ideology variables. This provides some
support for the hypothesis that social justice aspects of experiences become
more influential as the economic stakes involved in political choices
decrease. I will get back to this point in later sections.

We also want to know if the impact of experienced voice opportunities
varies with the level of service satisfaction. Here, one theoretical position is
that procedural justice is a general human yardstick for judging social experiences and common institutions. Voice should therefore matter regardless
of whether citizens are dissatisfied or not. A different position is that, in the
welfare state, people look at voice opportunities as something that produces

better outcomes. If this latter instrumental attitude toward voice prevails, one would expect a stronger impact of poor voice opportunities among those dissatisfied with services. Conversely, if the former general-value model of voice is the more accurate one, there should be no interaction effect of service satisfaction.

To test these hypotheses I used two measures of service satisfaction. The first one was the retrospective personal service satisfaction measure used in chapter 6. A dummy variable was created, which separates people who thought personally experienced public services had "become worse" during the last 12 months from those choosing other alternatives. I then ran the OLS models reported in tables 9.2 and 9.3 separately within the two

Table 9.3 The impact of experienced voice opportunities in contacts with public agencies on satisfaction with democracy and trust in politicians (unstandardized OLS estimates)

	Dependent variable: Satisfaction with democracy (higher value = more satisfaction)		Dependent variable: Trust in politicians (higher value = more trust)	
	Model 1: Experienced voice opportunities	Model 2: Model 1 + control variables	Model 3: Experienced voice opportunities	Model 4: Model 3 + control variables
Employees listened (−2–2)	.17★★★	.04★	.20★★★	.04★
I could affect how services are run (−2–2)	.03★★	.00	.10★★★	.06★★★
Experienced distributive justice (−2–2)	—	.10★★★	—	.13★★
Objective welfare state interest (0–10)	—	.01	—	.01
Perception of Swedish economy (1–3)	—	−.19★★★	—	−.16★★★
Preference for incumbent party	—	.31★★★	—	.34★★★
No party preference	—	−.16★★	—	−.17★★★
Age in years (15–80)	—	−.004★★★	—	.00
Education (1–3)	—	.00	—	.03
Life satisfaction (1–4)	—	.14★★★	—	.09★★★
Subjective class affiliation (1 = middle class)	—	.08★	—	.07
Political efficacy index (1–9)	—	.12★★★	—	.16★★★
Political sophistication	—	−.04	—	.00
Constant	−.03	.14	−.03	−.39★★★
Adjusted R-squared	.03	.16	.05	.22
Number of respondents	2,464	2,464	2,536	2,536

★*p* < .10   ★★*p* < .05   ★★★*p* < .01

Notes: The data come from the 1999 West Sweden SOM Survey. The dependent variables were described in chapter 6. For more information about the voice variables, see previous section on measurement. For more information about the distributive justice measure, see table 8.1, and related text. The objective welfare state interest variable was described in table 7.1 and related text. The political efficacy scale is an additive index summing responses to two questions about the possibilities of affecting political decisions in Sweden and in the municipality, respectively. The political sophistication measure (higher values = higher sophistication) was obtained through a factor analysis. Both the efficacy measure and the sophistication measure are described in more detail in a footnote in this chapter. For more information about other independent variables, see tables 6.3, 6.4, and 7.6.

groups along the satisfaction dummy. Also, I added to the original regressions multiplicative interaction terms together with the main effect of the satisfaction dummy.

The results did not support the hypothesis that voice effects grow with dissatisfaction. The only prominent exception was that the effects of "employees listened" among the dissatisfied on left–right self-placement and state-intervention orientation were significant, but virtually zero among the satisfied. However, these findings were contradicted by the fact that there was an impact of "affect services" on state-intervention orientations among the satisfied, but no effect among the dissatisfied. When it comes to political trust, there was no interaction effect whatsoever on satisfaction with democracy. For trust in politicians, the pattern was again reversed with somewhat stronger effects of experienced voice opportunities among the satisfied.

I also tried the same procedure using an alternative measure of service satisfaction. This second item tapped people's retrospective evaluations of how public services have worked in the municipality during the last 12 months. People who answered "rather badly" or "very badly" were separated from other responses and the same analysis as the one reported earlier was performed. Again, the data did not support the hypothesis that voice effects grow with dissatisfaction. For left–right self-placement, satisfaction with democracy, and trust in politicians, no significant differences in the impact of the voice variables could be observed across different levels of service satisfaction. The exception was the state intervention factor on which there were significant positive effects of both "employees listened" and "affect services" among the dissatisfied, but no such effects among the satisfied.

In summary, the effects of experienced voice opportunities on political orientations do not seem to depend much on whether citizens are satisfied with services and outcomes. Voice seems to be something from which people draw political conclusions regardless of whether they are satisfied with the actual quality of services. The model of procedural justice, and the idea that voice opportunities in particular are independently valued by citizens regardless of outcome quality, thus receives support.

Institution-Specific Voice Opportunities

The overall experience measures used so far are very general. They cover practically the whole welfare state as respondents are asked to look back at their "experiences with public authorities and services." As noted in chapter 8, people who have been in contact with several institutions might find it difficult to compute an average across experiences. And to the extent that the task is too difficult, they may opt for the no contact category, or report preexisting stereotypes and prejudice rather than actual experiences. Both options produce measurement error.

In order to partly escape these problems, we now begin to analyze institution-specific voice items. Unfortunately, because of limited space and

Table 9.4 Institution-specific voice opportunities among people having been in contact with public service institutions (percent)

	Very good	Rather good	Neither good nor bad	Rather bad	Very bad	Don't know	Sum percent	N
Child care	5	28	26	17	17	7 (50)	100	423
Leisure time activities/ culture	2	12	23	18	18	27 (48)	100	1,763
Health care	1	4	18	20	30	27 (32)	100	2,496
Public transportation	2	7	18	20	28	25 (35)	100	1,505
Schools	4	26	26	16	16	12 (38)	100	706

Notes: The data come from the 1998 West Sweden SOM Survey. The question was formulated as follows: "What opportunities do you think you have to affect how these services are run, if needed." The alternatives were "very good opportunities," "rather good," "neither good nor bad," "rather bad," "very bad opportunities," and "don't know." The table shows results only for people who have been in personal contact with a given institution, with the exception of don't know percentages within parentheses, which are calculated for the whole sample.

resources, it was not possible to include such variables in the 1999 West Sweden SOM survey. Instead, we use a set of measures available in the 1998 dataset. The head question was: "What opportunities do you think you have to affect how these services are run, if needed." For a number of public services, respondents then indicated whether they perceived "very good," "rather good," "neither good nor bad," "rather bad," or "very bad" opportunities, or whether they did not know. Table 9.4 contains univariate distributions for the institutions that will be analyzed here.[15] For reasons that will soon become clear, the table shows results only for people who have been in personal contact with the institutions.[16]

These institution-specific voice items are attractive as they avoid artificial averages across experiences with different institutions. In addition, the references to concrete institutions might stand a better chance in stimulating people to think about personally experienced situations. But these questions are certainly not flawless, given our purposes. One readily apparent problem is that, unlike the overall battery, they make no reference to actual personal experiences. They simply ask people to rate their voice opportunities without specifying that we are interested in a particular voice channel, namely the direct encounter between the citizen and the institution. Of course, one may think of several other voice channels, including voting and traditional forms of political participation. However, while the question makes no explicit reference to direct personal contacts, it was asked toward the end of a section in the questionnaire that focused heavily on such contacts. The section included questions about personal usage of a great number of services, as well as satisfaction with these services. Because the institution-specific items were preceded by such questions, it becomes less likely, though still possible, that answers do not reflect direct personal experience.

Also, the fact that experiences are not mentioned might increase the risk that effects on political orientations are due to, not just experiences, but also to internal political efficacy. As discussed earlier, responses to questions about experienced voice opportunities may reflect both actual experiences, as well as assessments of one's own resources, abilities, and political self-confidence. Therefore, in order to avoid spurious effect interpretations, one should control experience effects for political efficacy variables. Certainly, this recommendation is not less important when using questions that do not explicitly ask people about their direct, personal experiences.

Of course, these measurement-related problems should be worst among people with no personal experiences of a given institution. Indeed, their answers cannot even logically be regarded as reports of experienced voice opportunities. Rather, their responses should entirely be the products of internal efficacy, prejudice, or stem from alternative information sources, such as the media or interpersonal communication.

Consequently, I estimate the effects of experienced voice opportunities *only among people who have actually recently been in contact with the institutions in question.* The risk that responses reflect preexisting internal efficacy feelings rather than recollection of experiences, or are mainly assessments of voice channels other than direct contacts, should reasonably be smaller in these groups. Some support for this idea is provided by the observation that the proportion of "don't know" answers to the questions is (sometimes greatly) reduced among people having experienced institutions.

Looking at table 9.4, child care and schools were perceived the most favorably. About one-third are satisfied in the sense that they have "very" or "rather" good opportunities to affect services. These two institutions clearly receive better voice evaluations than leisure time activities/culture (14 percent), public transportation (9 percent), and health care (5 percent).

The "don't know" alternative was popular. Among institution users, up to approximately one-fourth ticked this category.[17] The high percentages of don't know answers come as no surprise. Our previous findings indicate that relatively large groups choose categories such as "no contact" or "don't know" when asked about experienced distributive or procedural justice. Many seem to have had neutral experiences that do not deviate from the ordinary, or that have not produced any perception at all.

We are now ready to analyze the effects of institution-specific voice on political orientations. Table 9.5 shows bivariate correlations, as well as bivariate and multivariate effects of voice items on the dependent variables. As left–right self-placement was not included in the 1998 questionnaire we now only have three dependent variables. Apart from this deviation, the dependent variables were identical to the ones in the 1999 survey.

Again, the results apply only to people who had actually been in contact with the various institutions. In this analysis I collapsed the "don't know" and the "neither/nor" categories, thus creating a five-point independent variable ranging from "very good" (1), "rather good" (2), "neither good nor bad/don't

Table 9.5 The impact of poor voice opportunities (unstandardized OLS estimates)

	Pearson's r	Bivariate b	Multivariate b	Number of respondents (bivariate)
Dependent variable: State-intervention orientation				
Child care	NS	NS	NS	401
Leisure time activities/culture	NS	NS	NS	1,657
Health care	.06	.13***	.09*	2,306
Public transportation	NS	NS	NS	1,394
Schools	NS	NS	NS	654
Dependent variable: Satisfaction with democracy				
Child care	−.27	−.23***	−.19***	391
Leisure time activities/culture	−.15	−.15***	−.14***	1,578
Health care	−.14	−.14***	−.15***	2,216
Public transportation	−.11	−.11***	−.10***	1,336
Schools	−.16	−.15***	−.10**	639
Dependent variable: Trust in politicians				
Child care	−.30	−.25***	−.20***	408
Leisure time activities/culture	−.18	−.18***	−.17***	1,680
Health care	−.20	−.20***	−.19***	2,348
Public transportation	−.13	−.12***	−.10***	1,423
Schools	−.21	−.19***	−.13***	684

$*p < .10$ $**p < .05$ $***p < .01$ NS = not significant, p-value $> .10$

Notes: The data come from the 1998 West Sweden SOM Survey. The OLS regression analyses were estimated only among people having been in contact with the institution in question. For more information about the experienced voice measures, see table 9.4, and related text. The multivariate effects are under control for the same variables that were included in tables 9.2 and 9.3. To the extent that it was possible, these variables were constructed on the basis of questions that were identical to the ones used in the 1999 questionnaire. The only significant alteration has to do with political sophistication, which is now measured by an additive political interest index (Cronbach's alpha = .83) summing responses to three questions as to how interested respondents are in politics "generally," "in your municipality," and "in the Västra Götaland region." Compared to tables 9.2 and 9.3, political efficacy and experienced distributive justice were missing in the 1998 data set.

know" (3), "rather bad" (4), to "very bad" (5). Just like in previous analyses, the collapsed middle category is permissible as there are no significant differences between the two categories with respect to dependent variables.[18]

One main observation is that the institution-specific voice items do not have many significant effects on attitudes toward state intervention.[19] Again, we see this as support for the hypothesis that social justice aspects of experiences become more influential as the economic stakes involved in political choices decrease.

The pattern changes when we shift our attention to political trust. The institution-specific voice items impact significantly on satisfaction with democracy and trust in politicians. Citizens who have been in personal contact with institutions, and who have perceived poor voice opportunities, are more dissatisfied with democracy and less trustful in politicians, than those perceiving good voice opportunities.

The multivariate effects range from −.19 to −.10 (satisfaction with democracy) and −.20 to −.10 (trust in politicians). And as we are dealing with five-point independent variables, one gets maximum effects by multiplying these estimates by four. How strong are these effects? Again, one gets a feeling for these coefficients when comparing with previously estimated effects of moving from a citizen opposing the ruling party *and* disapproving of the economy, to someone who favors the incumbent *and* approves of the economy. This effect amounts to .66. If we accept this comparison as interesting, then, experienced voice opportunities appear to have a rather respectable impact on political trust.

Finally, we turn to the question of whether there is an interaction effect between the institution-specific voice measures and service satisfaction. To find out, I used institution-specific measures of the extent to which respondents were satisfied with services. These measures formed the basis of five dummies separating those dissatisfied with the service ("very" or "rather" dissatisfied") from other valid responses. Furthermore, for each institution, an interaction term was generated by multiplying experienced voice opportunities with the service dissatisfaction dummy. Finally, for each of the three dependent variables, the regression coefficient of the interaction term was estimated together with the main effects of voice and satisfaction respectively. This analysis, which was performed only among respondents in personal contact with an institution in question, resulted in 15 regression equations (5 institutions $\times$ 3 dependent variables).

Again, there was very little support for the hypothesis that the impact of voice grows with service dissatisfaction. In fact, only one of the 15 equations contained a voice $\times$ dissatisfaction interaction that was significantly larger than zero. More specifically, in the leisure time/culture area, the interaction term revealed a negative effect of poor voice on state-intervention support among the dissatisfied. This effect was invisible when the dissatisfaction interaction was not taken into account (see table 9.5). Also, there were three equations where the interaction coefficient had the correct sign and was rather substantial, but not statistically significant.[20]

Conclusion

Experienced voice opportunities affect political orientations. This conclusion holds for both of our rather different indicators of the independent variable—overall experienced voice opportunities, as well as for institution-specific voice opportunities. The effects are sometimes at par with, but rarely stronger than, those of variables representing different theoretical perspectives such as incumbent party preference and economic evaluations. This reinforces findings from previous chapters. Welfare state experiences are but one of quite a number of explanatory factors behind the political orientations dealt with here.

The conclusion, however, does not hold for all the investigated political orientations. Consistent with Assarson's (1995) and Möller's (1996) conclusions we found an impact of experienced voice opportunities on political trust variables such as satisfaction with democracy and trust in politicians. However, experienced voice was not related to ideological variables such as left–right self-placement and state-intervention orientations. This pattern fits with that found in chapter 8, which showed that experienced distributive justice affects political trust but not ideological orientations. Both chapters are consistent with the notion that social justice concerns become more important as the self-interest stakes in political choices decrease. Conversely, the relative importance of self-interest increases when stakes are higher, such as in the case of ideological left–right orientations.

Both formal and informal voice opportunities matter. Citizens appear to care both about having real instrumental power to affect experienced institutions, as well as about being paid attention to and having one's opinions recorded. In fact, in the one case where we could compare the two voice versions, differences in informal opportunities (employees listened) turned out to be more important for political trust than formal ones (I could affect how services are run). This indicates that public employees who wish to use direct encounters with citizens to generate system legitimacy are well advised to signal that the institution is interested in their opinions, even if there is no simple or direct mechanism through which those opinions eventually affect the institutions.

Taken together, chapters 9–11 corroborate one of our theoretical cornerstones: Personal welfare state experiences are not one-dimensional events. Rather, we find support for the notion that at least three theoretical perspectives—self-interest, distributive justice, and procedural justice—simultaneously enrich our understanding of how and why citizens react politically to welfare state contacts.

In this spirit, chapters 8 and 9 have been unkind to the public choice–inspired idea that social justice–related evaluations of experiences are nothing but self-interest in disguise. We have reported weak or nonexistent correlations between variables tapping self-interest aspects of welfare state contacts and, on the other hand, variables tapping experienced distributive and procedural justice. This indicates that people's perceptions of experienced social justice are relatively honest in the sense that they do not reflect the extent to which welfare state institutions satisfy their personal, short-term economic interests. Contrary to what public choice theory would predict, social justice judgments of experiences are not just a politically correct disguise for self-interest.

However, the two different dimensions of experienced social justice overlap internally. Specifically, there is a correlation between citizens' views on whether they received the service they are entitled to and views on the quality of voice opportunities. Reasonably, this correlation is created by a reciprocal causal process, in which some people make inferences about judgments of one experience aspect to another. Having said this, it is still the case that the two experience dimensions affect political trust, controlling one for the other. In other words, despite the correlation between the two types of experienced justice, each makes an independent contribution to our understanding of how experiences affect orientations.

Interestingly, this contribution is unrelated to people's service satisfaction. That is, the impact of experienced voice opportunities is about the same among those satisfied with the overall quality of services, compared to those dissatisfied. This finding is not compatible with Hirschman's (1970) and Möller's (1996) view that voice opportunities are mainly an instrument to achieve satisfactory service delivery; their view implies that voice only matters to people when service delivery fails. Instead, the data sustain the notion that voice is a general value. This value is used as an outcome-independent yardstick for evaluation of public institutions even when the output of those institutions is perfect. Accordingly, poor voice opportunities hamper system legitimacy even if the quality of the services are deemed to be good. In short, voice opportunities seem to be more than mere instruments for improving personal outcomes.

This finding tells us, not just that people care about voice opportunities, but also something about *why* they care. Judging from the results, voice opportunities are not just an instrument for achieving accurate service delivery. Rather, they seem to be important in themselves. Much like the Chicago woman who was not allowed to show photos in court, Swedes appear to be interested in voice opportunities, not just in the passive reception of satisfactory goods and services. And if the opportunities to exercise influence are poor, welfare state experiences will have negative effects on political trust, no matter how satisfactory services are.

CHAPTER TEN

The Customer, the User, and the Client

Welfare state experiences have both positive and negative effects on system legitimacy. This theoretical possibility is a major point of disagreement between the self-interest perspective and those of social justice. Whereas the former parsimoniously assumes that any service delivery is always better than no service delivery, the latter imply that things can "go either way," depending on whether experiences of distribution and procedures match expectations. The results presented in previous chapters support this idea. At least when it comes to political trust, the Swedish electorate is not "an electorate in the grips of the welfare state," in the sense that they must always react to welfare state experiences by increasing their level of support. Rather, to a great extent the impact on political trust depends on whether people feel they have experienced distributive and procedural justice.

This chapter will elaborate a similar point. The empirical concern is whether the nature and effects of personal welfare state experiences vary systematically across different kinds of welfare state institutions. Specifically, we are interested in the extent to which institutional interfaces empower citizens in relation to employees. The theory and concepts behind our expectations were laid out in chapter 3. Based on the extent to which institutions involve discretion and exit-options, three basic categories of institutions were identified. These categories were labeled *customer institutions* (higher degree of empowerment), *user institutions* (medium degree of empowerment), and *client institutions* (lower degree of empowerment). It was hypothesized that the more empowerment that is built into institutional designs, the more positive effects do personal contacts tend to have on perceptions of personal experiences. In other words, customer experiences are thought to have more positive effects than user experiences, which are in turn predicted to have more positive effects than client experiences. This is the prediction to which we turn first. At the end of the chapter, we investigate whether empowering institutional interfaces, by virtue of their more positive effects on experiences, are also better at building general ideological support for state intervention and political trust.

Does Welfare State Design Shape Personal Welfare State Experiences?

In order to tap justice judgments, the questionnaire included two detailed question batteries concerning experiences with specific institutions. The first battery had the following head question: "If you look back on your own personal contacts with the following public services during the last twelve months, to what extent do you think you were treated correctly?" The head question of the second battery was "If you look back on your own personal contacts with the following public services during the last twelve months, to what extent did you receive the service and help you think you have the right to?" This latter question battery is familiar as it was used in chapter 8.

As the reader may remember, respondents answered along a five-point scale for each of six institutions. The scale ranged from 1 = "not at all correctly treated/did not receive the service and help I have a right to," to 5 = "completely correctly treated/have received the service and help I have a right to." Also, respondents could answer that they had not been in contact with the institution in question. The public services covered by the two batteries were health care, child care, social assistance, public transportation, job agencies, and housing benefits. Univariate results can be inspected in table 10.1.

Three institutions—health care, child care, and public transportation—receive clearly positive personal experience judgments. Their averages along the five-point scale are all over 4, and the opinion balance measures are around +70. However, three institutions—social welfare, job agency, and

Table 10.1 Personal experiences of particular public service institutions

	Opinion balance	Mean	Standard deviation	Number of respondents
"I was treated correctly"				
Health care	+65	4.10	1.12	2,892
Child care	+71	4.17	1.05	651
Social assistance	+7	3.10	1.48	220
Public transportation	+68	4.12	1.03	2,025
Job agency	+27	3.42	1.35	692
Housing allowance	+29	3.54	1.51	383
"I have received the service and help I have a right to"				
Health care	+62	4.08	1.19	2,836
Child care	+71	4.21	1.10	613
Social assistance	+10	3.15	1.50	198
Public transportation	+69	4.14	1.03	1,977
Job agency	+23	3.34	1.39	676
Housing allowance	+34	3.65	1.49	375

Notes: The data come from the 1999 West Sweden SOM Survey. For information about questions and response alternatives, see main text. The opinion balance was calculated by subtracting the proportion of respondents on the negative side of the middle alternative (1 and 2) from the proportion on the positive side (4 and 5). Hence, more positive opinion balance values indicate more positive personal experiences.

housing assistance—produce more lukewarm judgments, with averages between 3 and 4. Interestingly, all the institutions receiving comparatively poor experience judgments are client institutions with a low degree of institutionalized citizen empowerment: These institutions all perform a significant amount of discretionary means-testing at the same time as exit-options are scarce. The institutions receiving positive judgments are either user institutions (health care and child care) or customer institutions (public transportation).

What do the questions measure? While the second formulation ("received service I have a right to") lies close to the definition of distributive justice, it is less obvious what is tapped by the first formulation ("treated correctly"). Here, respondents can interpret it as "received service I have a right to." Alternatively, in addition to distributive judgments, people can choose to let also procedural concerns color the responses. To test whether "correct treatment" is in fact interpreted as something partly different from "received service I have a right to," I correlated corresponding items among people who had responded to both. Since all the six resulting correlation coefficients were exceedingly high (over .76), it seems unlikely that respondents differentiate between the two questions in table 10.1. A more plausible interpretation is that they both measure distributive justice concerns.[1]

The questionnaire also included a series of items with the following head question: "If you look back on your own personal contacts with various public authorities and services during the last twelve months, to what extent do the following statements fit with your own experience?" The question battery contained several items tapping distributive and procedural aspects of experiences. For each of the items, the following response options were offered: "fits very well," "fits rather well," "fits rather poorly," "fits very poorly," and "have not been in contact." To familiarize ourselves with these variables—three of which have already appeared in chapters 8 and 9—let us look at their univariate distributions in table 10.2. For the sake of simplicity, the percentages indicate the proportion of respondents reporting negative experiences, positive experiences, and have not been in contact respectively.

For each of the items, between one-third and half of the respondents reported positive experiences with public services and agencies. The exception is "I had opportunities to affect how services are run," where only 8 percent indicated positive experiences. Moreover, we see that between 37 and 51 percent place themselves in the "have not been in contact" category. As discussed in chapters 8 and 9, this does not mean that many Swedes do not have any actual personal contacts with public services during a year. Rather, "have not been in contact" appears to function as a residual category for people who do not know, or remember neither positive nor negative experiences.

What we want now is an analysis in which answers to these questions can be compared among people exposed to different kinds of institutions. It has

Table 10.2 "If you look back on your own personal contacts with various public authorities and services during the last twelve months, to what extent do the following statements fit with your own experience?" (percent)

	Positive experiences	Have not been in contact	Negative experiences	Sum percent	Number of respondents
Difficult finding the right person	31	42	27	100	3,437
Employees were helpful and listened to me	46	38	16	100	3,469
Written messages were difficult to understand	32	44	24	100	3,444
I had opportunities to affect how services are run	8	51	41	100	3,435
Employees worked fast and efficiently	29	41	30	100	3,426
I was treated correctly	49	37	14	100	3,541
I have received the service and help I have a right to	43	37	20	100	3,460

Notes: The data come from the 1999 West Sweden SOM Survey. For each item, respondents were offered the following response options to the statements in the table: "fits very well," "fits rather well," "fits rather poorly," "fits very poorly," and "have not been in contact." Positive experience means that the respondent answered "fits very/rather well" when items had a positive formulation, and proportion of "fits rather/very poorly" when items had a negative formulation. Conversely, negative experience means that the respondent answered "fits very/rather well" when items had a negative formulation, and proportion of "fits rather/very poorly" when items had a positive formulation.

been hypothesized that institutions with higher degrees of institutionalized citizen empowerment yield more positive experiences. While we have seen some bivariate evidence of such an effect, there are "third variables" that must be controlled. Specifically, resource variables such as education, class, income, and political engagement might affect the power balance between institutions and citizens. Highly educated, politically knowledgeable, well-off middle-class citizens usually have more bureaucratic confidence and competence than others. The same could be true for citizens who are public employees themselves. Because these groups of citizens are more likely to know their rights, to protest, and to otherwise put pressure on institutions, they are more likely to be "winners" in contacts with public agencies (Sjoberg, Brymer, and Farris 1966; Petersson, Westholm, and Blomberg 1989; Bleiklie 1990; Möller 1996). Their behavior increases institutions' and employees' incentives to adjust distributive and procedural aspects of experiences to these citizens' preferences. Since usage of various kinds of institutions can be expected to correlate with social status and engagement variables, it is important to include the latter ones as controls in analyses of institutional effects on welfare state experiences.

The first step in the analysis is to create three independent variables measuring personal exposure to customer, user, and client institutions respectively. More precisely, based on the classification in table 3.1, the three

Table 10.3 Number of contacts with customer, user, and client institutions (in percent)

Number of customer experiences	
0	13
1	18
2	19
3	19
4	15
5	11
6	5
Sum percent	100
Number of respondents	3,685
Number of user experiences	
0	25
1	25
2	37
3	7
4	6
Sum percent	100
Number of respondents	3,685
Number of client experiences	
0	68
1	24
2	5
3 or more	3
Sum percent	100
Number of respondents	3,615

Notes: The data come from the 1999 West Sweden SOM Survey. The proportion of respondents with more than three client experiences is less than 1 percent.

indicators count the number of customer, user, and client institutions respectively that respondents were in contact with at the time of answering the questionnaire.[2] Univariate distributions may be inspected in table 10.3.

Most respondents (87 percent) were in contact with at least one of the customer institutions for which usage was measured. Similarly, 75 percent were using at least one of the measured user institutions. In contrast, only about one-third had been in contact with a client institution. This last observation underscores the universal character of the Swedish welfare state. At a given point in time most people are not exposed to bureaucratic discretion and means-testing. Interestingly, some scholars have suspected that this might be changing slowly (see Svallfors 1996; Lindkvist 1998; SOU 2001:79). We shall get back to this in the concluding chapter.

The next step in the analysis is reported in table 10.4. It contains results from seven multinomial logit analyses in which the seven measures of personally experienced distributive and procedural justice serve as the dependent variables. These dependent variables were coded as follows: 1 = positive experiences, 2 = have not been in contact, and 3 = negative experiences.

Table 10.4 Multinomial logistic regression analysis of perceived procedural and distributive justice in contacts with the public sector

	Difficult finding the right person	Employees were helpful and listened to me	Written messages were difficult to understand	I had opportunities to affect how services are run	Employees worked fast and efficiently	I was treated correctly	I have received the service and help I have a right to
Number of client experiences	.20***	.32***	.07	.00	.18***	.39***	.32***
Number of user experiences	−.12**	.01	.06	.02	−.06	.06	.01
Number of customer experiences	.01	−.08**	−.02	.00	−.01	−.04	−.02
Gender (1 = woman)	.19	.10	.12	.11	−.05	−.13	.06
Age in years	−.01	−.02***	.01	−.01*	−.02***	−.03***	−.02***
Education	−.15**	−.04	−.15**	−.02	.07	−.13	−.15*
Public sector employment	−.18	−.24*	−.21*	−.13	−.35***	−.01	−.17*
Subjective class affiliation	−.22*	−.04	−.26**	−.07	−.05	−.13	−.06
Household income	−.02	.02	−.06*	.04	.03	.01	.00
Political efficacy index	−.13***	−.17***	−.13***	−.25***	−.16***	−.17***	−.20***
Political sophistication	.10*	.04	−.18***	.01	.01	.08	.06
Constant	.87**	.48	.39	2.88***	1.56***	.84**	1.08***
Chi-square improvement	454.2	479.5	392.6	425.2	474.9	494.9	491.4
(df)	(22)	(22)	(22)	(22)	(22)	(22)	(22)
Number of respondents	2,497	2,512	2,507	2,500	2,488	2,537	2,506

Table 10.4 *Continued*

The entries below are likelihood ratio tests comparing the unconstrained models reported above with models where pairs of coefficients were forced to be equal (Chi-square decrease, *p*-values)

In the top row, bold text indicates (some) evidence that client institutions yield more negative experiences than do user institutions

In the bottom row, bold text indicates (some) evidence that user institutions yield more negative experiences than do customer institutions

Equality constraint	*Chi-square decrease resulting from equality constraint (p-values)*						
Client effect = User effect	**14.89** **(.000)**	**12.60** **(.000)**	.00 (.953)	.04 (.841)	**8.62** **(.003)**	**13.93** **(.000)**	**13.46** **(.000)**
User effect = customer effect	Wrong direction of difference	**1.48** (.224)	**1.52** (.218)	.05 (.826)	0.61 (.433)	**2.01** **(.157)**	.25 (.616)

*p < .10 **p < .05 ***p < .01

Notes: The data come from the 1999 West Sweden SOM Survey. Entries are multinomial logit coefficients. The dependent variables were coded 1 = reported negative experience, 2 = have not been in contact, 3 = negative experience (for further information, see table 10.2 and related text). The coefficients show effects on the log-odds of reporting a negative experience relative to the odds of reporting a positive experience. The client-, user-, and customer variables were described in table 10.3 and related text. The political efficacy scale is an additive index summing responses to two questions about the possibilities of affecting political decisions in Sweden and in the municipality, respectively. The political sophistication measure (higher values = higher sophistication) was obtained through a factor analysis. Both the efficacy measure and the sophistication measure are described in more detail in a footnote in chapter 9. For more information about other independent variables, see tables 6.3, 6.4, and 7.6.

The crucial independent variables are the three indices from table 10.3, counting how many client, user, and customer institutions respectively a person has experienced.

Since these independent variables are included at the same time, we adjust for the fact that individuals might simultaneously use client, user, and customer institutions respectively. What we are interested in—and what the models in table 10.4 give us—is effects of contacts with one type of institution controlling for the level of individual contact with other types of institutions. Hence, we utilize more detailed information about the "institutional mix" that an individual has actually experienced, compared to studies using nationality as a proxy for institutional exposure. In addition, unlike the previous univariate data, these models take into account that our independent variables are conceptually continuous: Since the assumption is that institutions communicate political information to citizens during experiences, *the degree* of individual exposure to institutions should matter for the extent to which people notice, remember, and politicize various aspects of these experiences.

A multinomial logit model estimates effects on a dependent variable measured at the nominal level. Estimated parameters show effects on the log-odds of respondents being in a category on the dependent variable, relative to the odds of being in a reference category (Long 1997:chapter 6). Here, our direct substantive interest is effects on the odds of reporting negative experiences, relative to the odds of reporting positive experiences. The coefficients in table 10.4 thus show how the relative mix of positive and negative experiences changes as we move from few to many contacts with a certain type of institution. A positive sign means the odds of reporting negative experiences increase as the number of contacts with a given type of institution increases.[3]

In order to understand table 10.4 it is helpful to look at the model in which "I was treated correctly" constitutes the dependent variable. Here, the results support our predictions in a relatively clear-cut manner. Client institution contacts tend to increase the odds of not feeling treated correctly (.39). The same goes for exposure to user institutions, though this effect is smaller than that of client institutions and not quite significant (.06). In contrast, the customer coefficient is negative ($-.04$). In other words, more personal exposure to customer institutions tends to decrease the odds of not feeling treated correctly.

These differences are exactly what have been hypothesized. The larger the dose of empowerment built into institutional designs, the lower the risk of negative welfare state experiences: Client institution contacts increase the risk of negative welfare state experiences more than contacts with user institutions, which in turn increase the risk more than customer institution contacts.

At the bottom of the table one finds formal statistical tests of these differences between coefficients. The entries are likelihood ratio tests comparing the unconstrained models reported in the table with models where one pair of coefficients at a time was forced to be equal. For instance, looking at the "treated correctly" column, we observe that the client effect is indeed significantly larger than the user effect (Chi-square $= 13.93$; $p = .000$). Similarly, the difference between the user effect and the customer effect approaches significance (Chi-square $= 2.01$; $p = .157$).

In general, the hypotheses receive rather firm support with respect to differences between client institutions and user institutions. For five of the seven dependent variables, client institutions increase the risk of negative experiences more than user institutions. These differences are all significantly larger than zero.

The predictions also receive some support with respect to the relative impact of user institutions and customer institutions, though the support is weaker. However, for three of the seven dependent variables the hypothesized differences were not to be found. And for one dependent variable ("difficult finding the right person") the direction of the difference was even opposite to the prediction. Still, for three of the seven dependent variables, exposure to user institutions does increase the negative experience odds more than exposure to customer institutions. These effect differences run in the predicted direction, but they are smaller than the differences between client institutions and user institutions, and they only approach significance.

The coefficients of the control variables reveal some interesting effects. These effects indicate that people exposed to a comparable institutional mix still differ systematically in their subjective reports of personal welfare state experiences. For instance, consistent with the assumption that individual bureaucratic capacity resources matter, political efficacy, education, and public sector employment all tend to decrease the odds of negative experiences. However, the same prediction is only partially confirmed with respect to class (the middle-class reports less difficulties only in "finding the right person" and in "understanding written messages"). Income and political sophistication were hardly related to negative experiences at all. Finally, it is evident that age often decreases the odds of reporting negative experiences. As discussed earlier, it has been shown that the oldest generations have lower expectations on their welfare state experiences, which is likely to produce more positive experience perceptions (Möller 1996). Also, it is likely that people develop more bureaucratic competence and confidence as life progresses (Goodsell 1981).

Does Welfare State Design Affect the Impact of Experiences on Political Orientations?

We have seen some evidence that welfare state design (as conceptualized in terms of citizen empowerment) has a certain impact on the nature of people's welfare state experiences (as conceptualized in terms of subjective reports of distributive and procedural justice). The lower the level of empowerment built into encountered institutional interfaces, the greater the odds of reporting negative welfare state experiences (at least for some aspects of experiences). Interestingly, this conclusion seems to hold for people with the same gender, age, education, sector employment, class, income, and political sophistication level.

I now turn to the more radical prediction that experiences are generalized into overarching political orientations. Do experiences with more empowering institutions yield more support for the political system, for politicians and for state intervention, than do experiences with less empowering institutions?

Four OLS regression models test these predictions. The first two models contain effects on satisfaction with democracy and trust in politicians, and can be observed in table 10.5. The by now familiar institutional experience scales are included as independent variables. In addition to the previously used socioeconomic controls, the model also includes judgments of the Swedish economy, subjective life satisfaction, as well as two dummy variables tapping whether or not respondents sympathize with the incumbent Social Democratic party, or with no party at all. Finally, we also control for whether the respondent resides in a rich or poor Göteborg district (with "others" as the reference group). These additional variables correlate with

Table 10.5 Experience effects on satisfaction with democracy and trust in politicians (unstandardized OLS estimates)

	Dependent variable: Satisfaction with democracy (higher value = greater satisfaction)	Dependent variable: Trust in politicians (higher value = greater trust)
Number of client experiences	−.08★★★	−.08★★★
Number of user experiences	.01	−.01
Number of customer experiences	.02★★	.02★★
Perception of Swedish economy	−.19★★★	−.19★★★
Preference for incumbent party	.31★★★	.36★★★
No party preference	−.18★★★	−.20★★★
Age in years	−.003★★	−.003★★
Education	.01	.04★★
Political sophistication	−.04★	.00
Political efficacy index	.13★★★	.17★★★
Subjective class affiliation	.06	.05
Household income	.00	−.03★★★
Life satisfaction	.15★★★	.11★★★
Poor Göteborg district	.20★★	.04
Rich Göteborg district	−.11	.00
Constant	.14	−.27★★
Adjusted R-squared	.15	.20
Number of respondents	2,438	2,515

★$p < .10$ ★★$p < .05$ ★★★$p < .01$

Notes: The data come from the 1999 West Sweden SOM Survey. The dependent variables were described in chapter 6. The client-, user-, and customer variables were described in table 10.3 and related text. The political efficacy scale is an additive index summing responses to two questions about the possibilities of affecting political decisions in Sweden and in the municipality, respectively. The political sophistication measure (higher values = higher sophistication) was obtained through a factor analysis. Both the efficacy measure and the sophistication measure are described in more detail in a footnote in chapter 9. For more information about other independent variables, see tables 6.3, 6.4, and 7.6.

both institutional experiences and political orientations and are therefore held constant in the analysis.[4]

Consistent with the prediction, experiences with empowering institutions yield more political trust, than do experiences with less empowering institutions. In fact, controlling for other independent variables in the models, experiences with customer institutions increase both satisfaction with democracy and trust in politicians (.02 in both cases), whereas client experiences tend to have negative effects ($-.08$ in both cases).

The user coefficients are substantively and statistically insignificant, indicating that user institutions neither build up nor decrease political trust. However, this shall not be interpreted as if specific information from user experiences does not spill over into general orientations. Rather, from an empowerment perspective, user institutions are compromises between the client and customer extremes. On one hand, poor exit-options decrease institutionalized empowerment and, in turn, make social justice aspects of experiences more negative. On the other hand, the absence of discretion increases institutionalized empowerment and, in turn, improves experiences. The interpretation, then, of the insignificant user coefficient is that absence of discretion and poor exit-options cancel out each other's political effects, not that political effects are absent.

To get a feeling for the magnitude of the effects we can compare different individuals with realistic sets of values along the three experience variables. Think for instance about a person who has recently been in contact with the three client institutions social welfare, job agency, and housing allowance, but not with any user or customer institutions; the effect of this "experience set" on trust in politicians is $-.08 \times 3 = -.24$. Now think about someone who enjoys the services of the four customer institutions public transportation, sports facilities, dental care, and public libraries, but not those of any user or client institutions; the effect of this experience set is $.02 \times 4 = .08$. Hence, the predicted trust difference between our two ideal typical citizens is $.08 + .24 = .32$. When comparing this effect with the coefficients for perceptions of the economy ($-.19$) and of incumbent party preference ($.36$), the design of experienced institutions appears to have a rather decent (although not dominant) effect.

Let us now probe these issues with respect to support for state intervention and left–right self-placement (table 10.6).[5] Analogous to the political trust pattern, client experiences appear to reduce state-intervention support ($-.11$), whereas customer experiences appear to increase it (.12). Again, the coefficient for user experiences is not significantly larger than zero. Furthermore, when comparing individuals in the same fashion as earlier, the predicted positive impact on intervention support of becoming a typical welfare customer instead of a client, is .81. This effect approaches the direct effects of the subjective class dichotomy ($-.90$) and public sector employment (.87). The finding is interesting as class and sector employment are emphasized in previous research as determinants of state-intervention orientations and voting behavior among the Swedish electorate (Oskarson 1992; Gilljam and Holmberg 1993; Svallfors 1996).

Table 10.6 Experience effects on state-intervention orientation and left–right self-placement (unstandardized OLS estimates)

	Dependent variable: State-intervention orientation (higher value = more support for state intervention)	Dependent variable: Left–right self-placement (higher value = further to the right)
Number of client experiences	−.11*	−.02
Number of user experiences	.02	.00
Number of customer experiences	.12***	−.06***
Education	−.17***	.04
Public sector employment	.87***	−.23***
Subjective class affiliation	−.90***	.65***
Household income	−.13***	.06***
Gender (1 = woman)	.09	−.04
Life satisfaction	−.18**	.06*
Political sophistication	.19***	−.12***
Political efficacy	.02	−.02*
Poor Göteborg district	.39**	−.16*
Rich Göteborg district	−.41**	.21***
Constant	6.98***	2.78***
Adjusted R-squared	.12	.14
Number of respondents	2,436	2,529

*$p < .10$ **$p < .05$ ***$p < .01$

Notes: The data come from the 1999 West Sweden SOM Survey. The dependent variables were described in chapter 7. The client, user, and customer variables were described in table 10.3 and related text. The political efficacy scale is an additive index summing responses to two questions about the possibilities of affecting political decisions in Sweden and in the municipality, respectively. The political sophistication measure (higher values = higher sophistication) was obtained through a factor analysis. Both the efficacy measure and the sophistication measure are described in more detail in a footnote in chapter 9. The Göteborg variables are described in a footnote in this chapter. For more information about other independent variables, see tables 6.3, 6.4, and 7.6.

Looking now at the second column of table 10.6, our expectations are only partially confirmed with respect to left–right self-placement. They are confirmed in the sense that customer institutions appear to be best at generating experiences that make people more inclined to place themselves further to the left. The regression coefficient for customer experiences amounts to −.06, whereas the client- and user-coefficients are not significantly different from zero. The latter observation means that the hypothesis is not supported with respect to client and user institutions.

Finally, let me clarify a potential source of confusion. As chapters 8 and 9 reported only weak effects of experienced distributive and procedural justice on ideological variables, it may seem strange that the impact of experiences on state-intervention orientations now appear to depend on the experienced institutional interface. More exactly, given the weak impact of experienced social justice on ideology, one may wonder through which causal mechanism the differences in table 10.6 operate.

Based on chapter 3, I think there are three possible answers. First, though the effects reported in chapters 8 and 9 were usually weak, they were not consistently equal to zero. Rather, the point was that effects on political trust variables were stronger, although in several instances both experienced distributive and procedural justice had certain effects on ideological variables. Second, chapter 9 looked at only one particular kind of procedural justice: experienced voice opportunities. It is still conceivable that if we tried to measure in a more detailed manner other procedural aspects such as for instance, polite treatment, there would be effects also on ideology. Third, experienced distributive and procedural justice are not the only mechanisms that we have identified as potential mediators of institutionalized empowerment effects. In particular, chapter 3 discussed the possibility that discretionary services have a higher probability than other institutions to stimulate suspicion concerning cheating and abuse. Exposure to discretionary services may therefore have a greater tendency to stimulate negative views on other peoples' morality and trustworthiness. Hence, in addition to experienced distributive and procedural justice, generalized trust might be an additional causal mechanism through which the negative effects of client experiences operate (see Kumlin and Rothstein, 2003).

Conclusion

Neo-institutionalist accounts of how welfare states affect citizens politically have slowly begun to influence empirical public opinion research. Chapter 3—*The Institutional Interface*—identified two ways of thinking about how differences across welfare state institutions influence political orientations among mass publics. First, there was the contention that welfare states have an impact through the quantity of welfare outcomes they distribute to various groups and individuals (Dunleavy 1979; Zetterberg 1985). From this point of view, welfare state size rather than welfare state design emerges as the important macro-level variable. Likewise, at the individual level the crucial variable is personal interests and outcome levels. Of course, *the self-interest perspective* is the label we have used for his way of thinking about how welfare state institutions intervene in processes of attitude formation. It was dealt with theoretically in chapter 2 and empirically in chapter 7.

In contrast, the welfare state design perspective on institutional impact draws attention to what people experience along the way to outcomes. It assumes that the structure of the contact interface between citizen and institution may be just as important as the generosity of the transfers and services that come out of the process. In support of the welfare state design perspective, we have seen that the ability of welfare state institutions to build support for state intervention and for the political system varies with the level of empowerment built into institutional designs. More exactly, client institutions tend to undermine support, whereas customer institutions tend to mobilize it. Somewhat ironically, it is the most market-like public institutions that excel at generating positive feelings about collective entities like the welfare state and the political system. The implications of this irony will be one of the topics in chapter 11.

Implications

CHAPTER ELEVEN

The Personal and the Political Revisited

The time has come to fulfill an old promise. More to the point, chapter 1 outlined the main research problems addressed by this study, and promised that this concluding chapter would reconsider them in greater depth in the light of the empirical findings. In fulfilling the promise, this chapter outlines the broader political, democratic, and scientific implications of the theories and results previously presented.

Our purpose is *not* to reiterate in great detail the empirical findings; for such repetition the reader may refer to concluding sections in the respective chapters. Nevertheless, before proceeding to implications, it may be useful to begin with just a minimal restatement of the most important findings that have emerged from the empirical analyses. Second, the chapter proceeds to a general discussion of a somewhat neglected—but important—research problem: the question of how and why basic political orientations gradually change in adult life. Third, we devote a couple of sections to the implications of the finding that the personal is more political in the welfare state territory than in the economic realm. Fourth, we ponder the finding that political effects of "the personal" appear constituted both by self-interest as well as by social justice. Fifth, we discuss what the findings imply for the question of how different ways of organizing and shaping welfare state institutions affect citizens politically.

In the final part of the chapter—the coda—we go well beyond these more immediately salient research problems. More specifically, we take on the challenge to think about ongoing democratic trends and reforms in the light of the empirical discoveries.

Findings in a Nutshell

Personal welfare state experiences have substantively significant effects on political orientations. This is a somewhat different conclusion than the one found in much previous research—especially the "economic voting" literature. By and large, this research has reinforced the notion that *the personal is separate from the political,* in that it has usually found relatively weak statistical relationships between, on the one hand, political attitudes and behavior, and personal economic hardship and personal unemployment on the other. In contrast, we have seen evidence that personal welfare state experiences are more politically important than personal economic experiences. Whereas the personal and the political are fairly separate in the economic realm, they seem to blend together in the welfare state.

Of course, as was emphasized in chapter 6, this does not mean we should throw the notion of *sociotropic animals* overboard when examining the political impact of welfare-state related government performance. On the contrary, perceptions of collective-level experiences matter also in the welfare state territory. But sociotropic public service perceptions are informed by personal experiences to a much greater extent than economic sociotropic perceptions. And sociotropic public service perceptions are to a quite large extent the causal mechanism of personal experience effects. Many seem to generalize their personal welfare state experiences into collective-level judgments of what the population as a whole is experiencing. In turn, collective-level perceptions have effects on the political orientations under study here.

Furthermore, personal welfare state experiences are not unidimensional events. Their political influence cannot be captured by any single master variable. Rather, the perspectives of self-interest, distributive justice, and voice opportunities all appear to capture different aspects of these experiences that are consequential for citizens' political orientations. Here, self-interest is influential mainly for political ideology, with those who gain personally from the welfare state being more likely to support state intervention and more likely to stand further to the left. In contrast, experienced distributive justice and experienced voice opportunities have an impact mainly on political trust, where those who have personally experienced injustice are less likely than others to be satisfied with the democratic system and to trust politicians. Finally, we have seen that the effects of personal welfare state experiences appear systematically structured by "the institutional interface." Customer institutions—where discretion is rare and exit-options frequent—are better at generating positive experiences, and in turn positive effects on welfare state support and political trust, than client institutions—where discretion is frequent and exit-options rare.

Having drawn these conclusions, a couple of caveats are worth repeating. First, we have drawn on cross-sectional data only, which means we can say little about possible reciprocal influences of political trust and ideology on measures of personal welfare state experiences. The extent to which people "select," "project," "resist," and "construct," personal welfare state experiences remains an issue for further exploration. Second, in contrast to what the most optimistic welfare state theorists sometimes assume, we have hardly found the holy explanatory grail of public opinion research. Not even in Sweden, where the welfare state occupies a large portion of political debate, and is a crucial source of party conflict, are personal welfare state experiences the sole or the most important causal factor behind political trust and ideology. In fact, in most of the statistical models presented throughout this book, there was usually some other independent variable that exercised about the same, or a greater influence compared to welfare state experiences. Judging from the estimates, then, welfare state experiences constitute but one of many factors that explain variation in political trust and ideology. But this is not bad, if the reader agrees that political orientations can only be understood by considering a multitude of perspectives, and that the holy grail is unlikely to exist.

Political Learning in Adulthood: A Blind Spot
in the Scientific Eye

What do these findings contribute to our knowledge about public opinion formation and political behavior? The most general answer is that it makes a small contribution to the filling of a quite large knowledge gap. That gap is constituted by the fact that we know surprisingly little—given the by now gargantuan dimensions of the research field—about *how and why citizens' general political orientations change in adult life.*

This state of affairs is not entirely easy to understand as there has been so much research on the sources, the nature, and the effects of general political orientations. As indicated in chapter 4, we know a lot about how preadult socialization lays a foundation for these orientations (Jennings and Niemi 1974; Westholm 1991), and there has been much research on their socioeconomic bases in adult life (Särlvik 1974; Franklin, Mackie, and Valen 1992; Oskarson 1994). Likewise, we know much about the internal structure of such orientations (especially when it comes to left–right related orientations), as well as about how orientations affect voting behavior (Holmberg 1981; Gilljam 1990; Oscarsson 1998), and interact into political information processing (Kinder 1998). Also, we know that general political orientations are relatively stable, so that there is certainly not an infinite amount of change in adult life to be explained (Sears and Funk 1999). Likewise, empirical studies have tended to support an "ageing-stability hypothesis," indicating that general political orientations are stabilized and reinforced further with age (Alwin and Krosnick 1991; Miller and Shanks 1996).

However, we would like to know much more about why, when, and how basic orientations nevertheless can gradually change in adult life. This desire should not be seen as a criticism against some unnamed scholars that are somehow denying that systematic political learning in adult life is going on, and that it is not worthwhile to explore the issue further. Rather, the point is that such learning in adulthood seems under-theorized and under-researched compared to other questions related to political orientations.[1] For sure, empirical results arousing one's curiosity are published at a regular rate. But they are rarely the main focus of research projects, and the findings come in the form of empirical side-products noted in passing, often as regression coefficients of control variables in models estimated for other purposes. Systematic knowledge about political learning in adulthood is therefore not accumulating as it should in a systematic and collective research program (Sigel 1989; Sapiro 1994).

John Zaller's theory of opinion formation—the so-called RAS model—is perhaps the prime example of how gradual political learning in adulthood has become a blind spot in the scientific eye. This model, most coherently presented in *The Nature and Origins of Mass Opinion* (Zaller 1992), is interesting for several reasons. For example, it is widely applied and appreciated by the scientific community, as reflected by James Stimson's (1995:182) judgment that it is "perhaps the best book ever written about public opinion." A more important reason, however, is that the model represents perhaps the most far-reaching and successful attempt to formulate a general theory about public opinion, an attempt that incorporates a large number of well-known (and some less well-known) empirical regularities uncovered by more than a half-century of research. Indeed, Donald Kinder's (1998:181) overview indicated that the model has been applied "with mostly smashing empirical success." So when thinking about the state-of-the-art of the research field, the RAS model is an excellent stimuli.

This is not the place for a detailed discussion on the subtleties of this sophisticated theory (see Zaller 1992:chapters 3 and 11). For our purposes it is enough to notice the important role assigned to *political predispositions* in the opinion formation process. Such predispositions include basic political values such as liberalism–conservatism, party identification, and race-related orientations. Political trust and ideology, as conceptualized and measured here, clearly fall into this category of political orientations.

Furthermore, the RAS model is a memory-based model. It states that opinions do not exist before a survey researcher asks for them. When prompted by an interviewer to form an opinion, the respondent manufactures it "on the spot" aided by the information that happens to be immediately available in memory. Indeed, "persons who have been asked a survey question [. . .] answer the question on the basis of whatever considerations are accessible 'at the top of the head.' In some cases, only a single consideration may be readily accessible, in which case people answer on the basis of that consideration; in other cases, two or more considerations may come quickly to mind, in which case people answer by averaging across accessible considerations" (Zaller 1992:49).

General political predispositions are predicted to have an effect on political opinions by virtue of regulating which considerations are accepted, memorized, and subsequently recalled for "on-the-spot" opinion formation. Although the model predicts that such effects vary in strength across individuals, issues, question wordings, and political contexts, it is clear that general political orientations such as political trust and ideology are very important factors behind opinion formation and political behavior.[2]

Therefore, it is not entirely satisfying that we know so little about how general political orientations are in turn formed, at least not beyond pre-adult socialization and location in the socioeconomic structure. Indeed, all its virtues notwithstanding, the Zaller model is almost completely silent on this matter. All we really learn is that, "The sources of variability in individuals' political predispositions are beyond the scope of this book. My assumption, however, is that predispositions are at least in part a distillation of a person's life-time experiences, including childhood socialization and direct involvement with the raw ingredients of policy issues, such as earning a living, paying taxes, racial discrimination, and so forth. Predispositions also depend on social and economic location and [...] on inherited and acquired personality factors" (Zaller 1992:23).

My aim here is not to unjustly bash Zaller's contribution, but rather to illustrate that the paths along which basic political orientations may travel during the life-course are under-researched. Not even in a study that incorporates into a general theory most of what we know about political attitudes—building a model of the "origins of mass opinion"—do we learn much about where the crucial political predispositions come from.

Instead, opinion change is reduced to short-term changes in the concrete considerations immediately available in citizen's memories. And according to the RAS model, when the salience of such short-term considerations drops, they do not leave much of an attitudinal imprint behind. There is little left for the possibility that citizens, alongside accepting, rejecting, recalling, and forgetting immediately available short-term information, actually manage to use information to gradually develop even their basic long-term political orientations.[3]

Granted, almost all researchers acknowledge the crucial impact of basic predispositions in the opinion formation process. But more often than not, these are assumed to exist rather than constituting the actual dependent variable in an empirical analysis; they are assumed at the outset to be the results of some half-mystical process that has occurred in the past and that is now to a great extent finished. The researcher can then safely go on to investigate how predispositions affect attitude formation, information processing, voting behavior, or some other important research topic. As a result, basic political learning in adulthood is far too seldom systematically theorized and investigated. This must be seen as problematic given the crucial role basic political predispositions have proven to play in public opinion formation and political behavior.

Clarifying the Political Time of Our Lives

Against this backdrop, Virginia Sapiro (1994) has made a forceful call for political scientists to "clarify the political time of our lives." She, too, argues that researchers are often too content with the sweeping assumption that basic political orientations are the results of preadult socialization, or of the usual socioeconomic suspects like class, education, and income: "As studies of electoral politics show, even some basic political identities such as partisanship can change during adulthood. Common sense, or at least experience, also suggests that we should look more closely at adulthood for political learning.

It is difficult to believe that those things that seem so important to day-to-day-experience would not affect our political persona: major life events, dramatic or persistent interaction with social institutions outside the family, the experience of historical events and changes, the biological process of ageing and the cumulative impact of acting, thinking, and being acted on over time. Nevertheless, rummaging through the relevant literature shows little coherent development of theory about political development over the life course" (Sapiro 1994:200). Consequently, she (1994:213) calls for more "conceptual and theoretical work in order to improve our understanding of the political implications of life-course development, especially if we are to move beyond the notion of life-course indicators as an untheorized set of 'demographic' or 'background' variables. What are the ways in which personal life-course events and experiences might take on political meaning, or become part of the process of political learning and development?"

The theoretical framework and the empirical results presented in this book provide some partial answers to these big questions. We have theorized and empirically investigated personal welfare state experiences as occasions for political learning in adulthood, occasions on which political trust and ideology are gradually updated in the light of new experienced facts about policies and politics. There are reasons to reinforce Soss's (1999:364) case for "studying welfare programmes as sites of adult political learning [...] I argue that as clients participate in welfare programs they learn lessons about how citizens and governments relate, and these lessons have political consequences beyond the domain of welfare agencies. [They] become the basis for broader orientations toward government and political action."

Inspired by authors like Sapiro (1994), Sigal (1989), and Soss (1999), as well as by my own research, I suggest that future public opinion research puts more energy into generating and testing theory-driven hypotheses about yet other sorts of political learning in adulthood. It is hard to believe that welfare state institutions are the only venues for such processes. But more focused theoretical and empirical work is needed if we are to find and make sense of these venues, thereby clarifying the political time of our lives.

The Personal is More Political in Welfare State Territory
Than in the Economic Realm

A somewhat more specific research program to which this study contributes is centered around the contention that personal experiences—or, in more dramatic parlance, people's independent observations of reality—tend to be of minor importance for political attitudes. In chapter 1, we even discovered that influential scholars assume at the outset of their studies that citizens do not have many politically relevant experiences in adult life from which they could draw political conclusions. Political issues and struggles are treated as if they were extraterrestrial phenomena located far up in the stratosphere, well beyond the personal life sphere. More than this, many empirical studies on especially economic voting have found that even when people do have relevant personal experiences from which they could draw political conclusions, they nevertheless fail to do it. Especially personal economic experiences such as unemployment and financial ups and downs in the pocketbook have proven to be of minor political importance. Rather than looking at personal experiences, much past research contends, citizens are driven politically by "sociotropic" perceptions of collective experiences. Thus, when forming attitudes they ask themselves, not "what has happened to me?" but "what has happened to people in the country." In turn, sociotropic economic perceptions have proven to originate mainly in information provided by elite actors such as journalists, experts, and politicians, rather than in independent observations of social and political reality. In sum, previous research suggests that the personal and the political lead rather separate lives among citizens in modern democracies. This, in turn, makes people more dependent on elite actors for politically relevant information.

Certainly, this study has not gone so far as to question the general notion that citizens to a large extent depend on the mass media and political elites for political information. Rather, it has made the more nuanced claim that there is a variance across policy domains. We predicted in chapter 1 and supported empirically in chapter 6 that the personal and the political are, to a degree, *reconnected* when we move out of the economic realm and into welfare state territory. Two explanations for the difference across policy domains have been suggested. First, the nature of available political information differs, with a better supply of general, sociotropic information about collective experiences in the economic realm compared to welfare state territory; this makes personal economic experiences less crucial from an informational point of view. Second, the nature of political responsibility varies across the two policy domains, with a clearer and closer link between responsible politicians and personal welfare state experiences, than between responsible politicians and ups and downs in the personal pocketbook. Judging from the results presented in chapter 6, this makes personal welfare state experiences more likely to trigger political thinking and attitude formation. They become a more important political information source than personal economic experiences. Whereas personal-level and collective-level judgments often fail to connect in the economic realm, they do so to a greater extent in the welfare state.

In sum, this suggests that citizens are not entirely dependent on politicians, the mass media, or experts, for information relevant to political learning in adulthood. Far away from the hustle and bustle of elite politics and mass media attention, there are other opinion formation processes going on where political trust and ideology are gradually updated in the light of new independent personal observations of welfare state arrangements and public services. Unfortunately, the tendency among researchers to investigate mainly the political impact of *economic* outcomes and performance—referred to in chapter 6 as the *economistic bias* in electoral research—has perhaps hidden this for a longer time than necessary.

Implications of Tighter Personal–Political Links

From a democratic point of view, how should we think about the variation in the strength of the personal–political link? As Diana Mutz explains in *Impersonal Influence* (1998), personal-experience based opinion formation has traditionally been regarded as something inherently positive for democratic processes. Building partly on the "mass society" tradition (Kornhauser 1955), Mutz identifies the danger that the information provided in the media does not accurately reflect what the collective has actually experienced. The information on which citizens' sociotropic perceptions are based may tell a different story than the sum of citizens' life situations. Hence, in contrast to personal-experience based opinion formation, "the sociotropic model suggests a potential for distortion and lack of accountability that personal-experience based politics appears to ensure. Personal concerns are anchored in real-world experience in a way that judgments of distant collectives are not. If the policies of current politicians are hurting enough people, voting on the basis of personal experience guarantees that the rascals will soon be thrown out of office. On the other hand, a citizenry forming political views on the basis of collective-level perceptions is vulnerable to manipulation. If mass media or other information sources lead people to form inaccurate perceptions, their political views cannot ensure the same level of accountability as aggregated personal experiences" Mutz (1998:109).

Of course, the quality of sociotropic information may vary greatly: The problem becomes smaller the more relevant, accurate, and multifaceted information about aggregated collective experience that journalists, politicians, and experts provide. However, to the extent that citizens do not draw political conclusions from their personal observations, there is always the suspicion of a gap between sociotropic information provided by elite discourse and actual collective experience.

In fact, the potential sources of distortion of collective-level perceptions are numerous. Prominent among them are the fact that the media can only focus on a limited number of aspects of collective experiences, as well as the fact that a "media logic" is said to give priority to negative, unusual, or dramatic events. Furthermore, not the least in election campaign coverage, journalists increasingly seem prone to report on the current political news of the day and neglect retrospective performance aspects altogether (Esaiasson and Håkansson 2002). On top of this, governments always have incentives to emphasize facts conducive to re-election, and avoid talking about those that are not, as manifested in strategies of blame avoidance (Weaver 1986; Lewin 2001).

Imagine a situation where a majority of citizens are somewhat dissatisfied with what they have experienced while in contact with public health care. In this situation, a government is nevertheless likely to put an emphasis on the few positive measures, increased spending, or otherwise positive reforms that have indeed been implemented. At the same time, selective journalists whose attention are driven by a media logic may be overly biased in the direction of exaggerated and dramatic health care events and trends, which are equally poor representatives of actual collective experience (see Eide and Hernes 1987).

For such reasons, sociotropic information provided in the mass media may not be an entirely satisfactory mirror of what is actually suggested by "the full" aggregated collective experience that the population has actually gone through.[4] From a democratic point of view, this is potentially problematic as people's sociotropic perceptions "become independent of their aggregated personal experiences, and democratic accountability breaks down. Those who do not have accurate perceptions of social conditions may punish politicians for problems that have not truly occurred or reward them for improvements that have no basis in collective individual realities." (Mutz 1998:285) Such informational biases are exacerbated if citizens do not manage to draw political conclusions from their personal observations of reality. Political accountability is obscured if sociotropic perceptions are not in accord with actual collective experience, at the same time as actually occurring personal experiences of societal trends and facts are not informing the opinion formation process.

Moreover, an absence of personal-experience based accountability would arguably be even more serious in the welfare state territory than in the economic realm. This is because the informational biases produced by media logic and blame avoidance may well be given greater leeway in the former policy domain. In chapter 1, we noted that economic perceptions have proven to be very responsive to a small subset of macroeconomic indicators (unemployment level, budget deficit, and inflation). Using such parsimonious and not terribly disputed information—typically provided by the mass media—it becomes a manageable task for citizens to form meaningful sociotropic perceptions. There is no need to consult personal experiences for political guidance. In contrast, the welfare state does not offer any small set of easily available and agreed-upon indicators, comparable to unemployment level and inflation. Whether welfare state institutions are improving or deteriorating becomes a more difficult, ambiguous, and subjective question for both citizens and journalists, than saying something about the state of the economy. Therefore, given that we value opinion formation based on perceptions that are as close as possible to actual collective experience, it seems healthy that people are more prone to use personal experiences as a political information source in the welfare state territory, compared to the economic realm.

Welfare State Experience Effects Reflect Both
Self-Interest and Social Justice

At this point, the reader may wonder if personal experiences are in fact a miracle medicine for unhealthy democratic processes. Not quite. In fact, while personal-experience based opinion formation may promote reality-based accountability, personal experiences are nevertheless increasingly seen as a rather poor source of political information. Many democratic theorists stress the importance of trying to make people look up from their narrow personal life spheres and consider a broader range of information that include other people's arguments, life situations, and experiences (see Mansbridge 1990:chapter 1).

Further, personal-experience based opinion formation is often regarded as dangerously close to short-term, material self-interest. As noted in chapter 2, self-interest based opinions are considered an obstacle to an enlightened politics striving for more collective and long-term rationality. Particularly proponents of deliberative democracy argue that the quality of political decisions increase if they were preceded by open conversation and debate between citizens with affected interests (see Fishkin 1995; Bohman and Rehg 1997; Elster 1998). Such deliberative processes, it is argued, encourage participants to develop their preferences so that they increasingly come to reflect also other people's experiences and points of view, not just strictly personal experiences and personal self-interest. The worry is that people's initial attitudes, which are presumably self-interest driven, do not correspond to the enlightened choices citizens would have made after more careful deliberation based on broader information. Therefore, self-interested attitudes, or other attitudes that have not been distilled through public deliberation, become an obstacle to the formation of an enlightened and true popular will.

Arguments of this sort build on the assumption that self-interest based attitudes typically do change as a result of a broader information intake; if the public would just engage in deliberation, the will of the people would often look considerably different than it does in the absence of such intense activities. Now, it has not been our purpose to examine whether political orientations become less affected by personal experiences as citizens engage more in deliberative activities. We do not really know to what extent deliberative democratic theorists have good reasons to suspect that short-term self-interest gradually loses whatever impact it has on public opinion as a result of public deliberation. Alternatively, one may open for the possibility that self-interest is often a resistant and exogenous force that is rarely reduced by a greater and broader information intake. Questions such as these are interesting issues for further research (see Luskin 2002).

What one can say based on the results, however, is that personal-experience based attitudes are not equivalent to self-interested attitudes. Rather, the question of whether personal experiences play a political role is a question of what information sources are used for opinion formation. It is not a question of what underlying motivation drives citizens, or what utility function they are typically maximizing.

This theoretical point has sometimes been made in the context of economic voting. For instance, Kinder and Kiewiet (1981:132) pointed out,

"The distinction between pocketbook and sociotropic politics is not equivalent to the distinction between a self-interested and an altruistic politics. [...] differences between the pocketbook and sociotropic characterizations of citizen politics should be regarded not as one of motivation, but as one of information." Sears and Funk (1991:65) add to this by explaining, "...apparently disinterested sociotropic judgments could be based in long-term self-interest. People who perceive the Republicans as having presided over a period of great national prosperity may support Republican candidates because they think that a party that is good for the national economy will ultimately benefit them as well..."

This distinction between personal experience effects and self-interest effects has not always been fully appreciated. For instance, in their theoretical work on self-interest and politics, Lewin (1988, 1991) and Udéhn (1996) interpret the relative absence of pocketbook voting, and the presence of sociotropic voting, as rather unproblematic evidence that voters are not driven by self-interest. But again, what such findings really show is that people are not inclined to use self-communicated economic information to form political preferences. Whether personal-experience based opinion formation also signals the presence of self-interested opinion formation, and whether sociotropic influence indicates its absence, must be regarded as empirical questions.

Here, chapter 7 found that short-term, material, personal self-interest is indeed one of the ingredients of welfare state experience effects on general political orientations. In contrast to what much past research contends, symbolic orientations such as political trust and ideology are not merely the results of preadult socialization, occupation, socioeconomic location, or group identities. They also seem to be significantly affected by current welfare-state related self-interest.

On the other hand, while the impact of welfare state self-interest is in all likelihood stronger than previous estimates based on sparse measures of self-interest, what we have at hand is not more than a half-full glass. Welfare state self-interest is not the most important explanation for political orientations, as manifested by the observation that a simple class identification dichotomy typically beats self-interest as a factor behind left–right self-identification and state-intervention orientations.

More than this, the self-interest perspective still only tells part of the true story about welfare state experiences. Consistent with the remarks of Kinder and Kiewiet earlier, this study has treated self-interest as merely one of several possibly influential dimensions of personal welfare state experiences: in addition to self-interest, the perspectives of distributive and procedural justice allow the possibility that the political impact of experiences is driven by a comparison between one's personal experience and an expectation as to what one has a right to experience in a given welfare state setting.

The empirical analyses in chapters 8 and 9 have supported these ideas with respect to political trust, though not with respect to political ideology.

Justice-related variables have an impact on political trust, which is to a large degree independent of self-interest. Further, justice-related considerations do not seem to be strongly affected by self-interest. The view that social justice concerns are just "self-interest in disguise" has received little empirical support. Likewise, in chapter 9 it was discovered that political reactions to judgments of procedures were also largely independent of the extent to which people were satisfied with outcomes of the procedures. Good voice opportunities in the process seem to enhance trust in the political system even among those already satisfied with service outcomes.

It seems, then, that the personal and the political are tied together by both self-interest and social justice concerns. Not even in the welfare state setting—where politics is so obviously about interests and redistribution—can the self-interest perspective account for nearly all of what is going on. Rather, the findings suggest that personal welfare state experiences are occasions when citizens not only react to narrow personal gain, but also ponder whether their personal outcomes can be regarded as socially just. The results suggest that people are concerned with what "a person such as me in this situation," has the right to expect in terms of outcomes and procedure. And if personal experiences fall short of social justice expectations, the welfare state experience has negative effects on political trust, even though it contributed substantially to personal, short-term, self-interest.

Taken together, the findings with respect to self-interest and social justice suggest that we ought to take a nuanced view of public opinion formation in general, and of personal welfare state experiences in particular. Not even the political effects of welfare state experiences—a setting where there is so much at stake for the individual—are only about short-term maximization of personal material gain. It seems that the worry raised by deliberative democrats and others—that personal-experience based opinion formation fosters mainly narrow self-interest based politics—does not do full justice to the reality of such opinion formation. Rather, our results suggest that citizens' faith in the democratic system does not necessarily hinge on the ability of the system to satisfy the self-interested wishes of a majority of citizens. Instead, the crucial issue seems to be whether most citizens see their personal outcomes, and the procedures by which outcomes were reached, as fair.

These findings raise a host of new questions that this study has not sought to answer. What is it that citizens expect, more exactly, in terms of procedure and service delivery from different concrete welfare state institutions? And what are the origins of expectations? If they are not "self-interest" in disguise, then what are they? Are they themselves mainly the result of previous experiences with an institution, opinion formation by political elites, or some other explanatory factor? And how variable and malleable are expectations across social groups and across time? Questions such as these should stand a chance of stimulating further research on public opinion formation in welfare states.

Path Dependence

Thus far, we have pondered mostly implications for why and how individual citizens develop their political orientations. But the implications of this study go beyond individual opinion formation: The findings also say something about the structural impact of some of the institutions on which political life is founded.

As a general backdrop for such a discussion, it is useful to invoke the notion of *path dependence*, which points to a reciprocal relationship between the organization of political institutions and individual behavior. Furthermore, as noted by scholars such as Pierson (2001) and Rothstein and Steinmo (2002), such a relationship can often, though not always, be described as "self-reinforcing over time." That is, institutional and organizational choices at a certain point in time gradually make citizens and major political actors adjust their knowledge, expectations, and attitudes, so as to become more consistent with the chosen organizational features of politics. In turn, such individual adjustment makes later political choices more likely to be in line with those that have already been made earlier. In this sense, different polities travel down different institutional paths, where initial institutional choices tend to constrain later choices, so as to reinforce the already chosen institutional path.

There are several mechanisms of path dependence. One is what March and Olsen (1989) call the logic of appropriateness. According to this logic, citizens and other political actors who must deal with a complex informational environment use already existing institutions, rules, and standard operating procedures for guidance as to what solutions and decisions are appropriate in a given situation. A second mechanism is that of increasing returns. As Pierson (2001:415) explains, this vehicle for path dependence "encourages actors to focus on a single alternative and to continue movement down a particular path once initial steps are taken. *Large set-up or fixed* costs are likely to create increasing returns to further investment in a given technology, providing individuals with a strong incentive to identify and stick with a single option. Substantial *learning effects* connected to the operation of complex systems provide an additional source of increasing returns. *Coordination effects* [. . .] occur when the individual receives increased benefits from a particular activity if others also adopt the same option" (see also Peters 1999).

Below I discuss a further factor that may at times be conducive to path dependence. More exactly, I discuss institutional effects on citizens' personal welfare state experiences and, in turn, their political orientations as one of the mechanisms by which welfare state institutions may—or may sometimes not—reinforce their own existence.

Path Dependence, Welfare State Reforms, and Public Opinion

Welfare state institutions have proven resilient to radical retrenchment. Unlike what is predicted by the more extreme versions of globalization theory, it has proven difficult to "roll back the welfare state" in most policy areas in Western countries. Recent research concludes that radical retrenchment policies have been implemented on a major scale only in a small number of countries (such as New Zealand, see Pierson 2001). Part of the typically offered explanation is that although welfare states face economic and demographic challenges, self-interested citizens are not keen to withdraw support for their services and entitlements. Retrenchment policies tend to highlight readily identifiable groups of "losers," whereas the potential gains are more diffuse, insecure, and long-term. Because so many voters have vested interests in the welfare state, the argument goes, large-scale welfare state retrenchment becomes "politically suicidal in most countries" (Pierson 2001:416; see also Lindbom 2001).

This storyline fits nicely into the general notion of path dependence. By gradually making greater portions of the electorate dependent on its products, the welfare state is believed to have gradually reinforced its own popular support. Returning to the dramatic parlance of Zetterberg (1985), electorates in developed nations are "in the grips of the welfare state," where the generosity of welfare state institutions coupled with the short-sighted egoism of individual citizens mean that seriously antiwelfare parties and ideological viewpoints will rarely win democratic battles. A self-reinforcing welfare state has closed its trap around self-interested voters.

As discussed earlier, we have found a certain amount of support for this line of reasoning in our analyses of self-interest and political orientations. At least to a greater extent than has usually been acknowledged in past individual-level political behavior research, support for state intervention, and left–right self-identification are partly products of the extent to which one benefits personally from welfare state institutions.

A corollary of this finding is that changes in institutions and policies that seriously reduce the extent to which citizens have vested welfare state interests will reduce welfare state support and left identification among affected groups. Of course, as we noted earlier, major efforts to roll back the state are not nearly as commonplace, popular, or radical as has been suggested by the more extreme variants of globalization theory. Nevertheless, significant institutional and policy changes clearly do occur, albeit in a more piecemeal fashion. In fall 2001, the Swedish parliamentary commission *Balance Sheet for the Welfare State in the 1990s* presented its main report (SOU 2001:79). Resulting in some 13 volumes of research, the purpose of this public investigation was to map a broad spectrum of welfare-state related lines of development during the 1990s, such as equality of opportunity, equality of condition, variations in individual resources, as well as institutional changes in welfare state services and transfers.

The commission found that, as a result of many piecemeal decisions at several political levels, significant institutional changes in the Swedish welfare state truly occurred in the 1990s. Interestingly, many of these seem to have reduced the extent to which people have a vested personal interest in welfare state institutions. Not least, the public social insurance system has undergone significant changes. Replacement rates in income-based insurances against unemployment, illness, and so on, are now considerably lower. At the same time, the replacement ceilings that indicate the maximum amount of income replacement have typically not been adjusted upward so as to keep up with actual wage increases. As a result, an increasing proportion of citizens in reality receive even lower benefits than what is suggested by (the gradually lowered) replacement rates. Parallel to these trends, private or other nonpublic insurances and solutions have become considerably more common in areas such as sick-leave, health care, and pensions (Grip 2001).

Also when it comes to certain public human services, changes have occurred that may affect the extent to which welfare state experiences contribute to self-interest. Not the least, the relative importance of direct user fees has increased compared to general taxes. That is, a greater financial burden has been placed on the citizens who themselves experience various institutions.[5] Moreover, following the economic crisis in the early 1990s, most welfare state services have been forced to deal with reductions in resources. The most important examples include fewer employees per child in public child care and schools, as well as significant staff reductions in public health care. As a final example, a smaller proportion of elderly are benefiting from elder care services now than before. Among those who do, resources are increasingly concentrated on a smaller and especially needy group. Services that were formerly provided by public employees (washing, cleaning, shopping, chatting, taking a walk) are increasingly considered nonpublic tasks. In these and other respects, there is an increasing reliance on family members, voluntary efforts, and market services.

None of these changes should be exaggerated. As Lindbom (2001) shows, the development is best described in terms of gradual and piecemeal changes on the fringe of a still mainly generous and universal welfare state. Nevertheless, many small changes currently point in the same direction: crucial welfare state institutions increasingly seem to generate personal welfare state experiences that do not contribute as much to personal, short-term, material, self-interest, as comparable experiences once did. Moreover, given that self-interest affects political orientations, and given that institutions and policies continue to change in the same direction, support for state intervention and identification with leftist politics may become weakened, all other things being equal. Of course, which institutional path that is actually chosen in this respect depends on both economic conditions and, ultimately, on political decisions.

One World of Welfare—Different Institutional Paths

Chapters 3 and 10 contrasted two ways of thinking about how differences across welfare state institutions, and across welfare states, influence political orientations among mass publics. According to one of these lines of thought—discussed at some length earlier—welfare states exercise a political influence on their publics by building a foundation of self-interest for themselves. The size and generosity of the welfare state is the important institutional variable; the more citizens that gain from such institutions, and the more they gain, the greater support for state intervention and the political left.

In contrast, the welfare state design perspective on institutional impact draws attention to the "institutional interfaces" that citizens experience along the way to outcomes. The idea is that the structure of the contact interface between citizen and institution may be as important as the extent to which experiences ultimately satisfy self-interest. In support of this idea, chapter 10 showed that the ability of welfare state experiences to build support for state intervention and for the political system varies with the level of empowerment built into institutional designs. Using the developed terminology, client institutions tend to undermine support, whereas customer institutions tend to mobilize it. The irony inherent in these findings is worth repeating: it is the most market-like and individualist public institutions that excel at generating positive attitudes toward collective entities like the welfare state and the political system.

These findings are interesting as it is customary to think about the impact of welfare state institutions on mass preferences in terms of differences across countries. Here, a particularly popular theoretical tool has been various variants of the welfare regime framework developed by Esping-Andersen (1990) and others. One assumption found in this discourse is that a popular welfare state is one that manages to include also the self-interested but politically ambivalent middle classes, not just the worse off social segments. However, as discussed in chapter 3, recent comparative analyses have not been entirely kind to the predictions of the regime framework. Overall differences in welfare state support, or differences in welfare-state related group conflict, cannot be entirely accounted for by classifying countries into social democratic, liberal, and conservative worlds of welfare (Papadakis and Bean 1993; Svallfors 1993, 1997; Papadakis 1993; Bean and Papadakis 1998; Lapinski et al. 1998).

Our findings underscore the notion that the regime approach is not the only tool for thinking about attitudinal impact of welfare state institutions. We have seen that there is much individual-level variation within welfare states as to the design of personally experienced institutions. A significant portion of institutional influence on opinion seems to operate *inside welfare regimes*. Depending on whether Swedes are customers, users, or clients in the social democratic world of welfare, they appear to travel down different institutional and attitudinal paths.

More than this, within-regime variation appears to be increasing in several European welfare states. On the one hand, there is a trend toward more means-testing. Faced with external challenges such as globalized markets, as well as with internal challenges such as demographic change, targeted social services have become increasingly popular in many countries (Ferrara and

Rhodes 2000). Based on trends such as these, Cox (1998:3) has even made the radical suggestion that, "the post-war idea of the welfare state, based on the principle of universal entitlement derived from citizenship, is giving way to a less formal, more discursive notion of social entitlement."

Sweden—usually seen as a universalist stronghold—is a good example of this trend. The economic crisis of the 1990s caused a surge in the use of means-tested services such as social assistance, housing allowance, and early retirement (Svallfors 1996; SOU 2001:79). Similarly, a firmer emphasis on active labor market policies and individual-oriented rehabilitation schemes in order to combat absenteeism and work-related illness (see Kuhnle 2000; Lindqvist 1998) means more citizens get in contact with street-level bureaucrats making discretionary decisions. Of course, more means-testing and selectivity hampers the level of citizen empowerment and, judging by data presented here, general support for state intervention and political trust among citizens that are in contact with such institutions.

But at the same time we see counter-balancing changes that increase citizen empowerment. For instance, market-oriented reforms involving competition between service providers and freedom of choice for citizens have been introduced in countries such as Britain, Australia, the Netherlands, and Sweden (Blomqvist and Rothstein 2000). Such reforms have been especially popular in areas such as education and health care. Typically, market-like competition and freedom of choice are combined with public regulation and public financing through "vouchers." This trend in the direction of better exit-options in important public service areas will probably increase the level of citizen empowerment among those experiencing these institutions.

The growing within-regime institutional heterogeneity underscores the point that institutional influence on opinion might operate inside welfare regimes. Different citizens in the same world of welfare are *increasingly* experiencing very different parts of the welfare state, which should mean that they are also *increasingly* traveling down different institutional and attitudinal paths. Our results indicate that if within-regime institutional variation is conceptualized and measured, we learn useful things about the impact of welfare state design on opinion formation. The reported findings connect to one growing empirical literature indicating that citizen empowerment is one fruitful tool for thinking about within-regime institutional effects on political preferences (Hoff 1993). It seems that empowering welfare state designs are more likely to generate experiences that in turn build support for the welfare state and the existing political system.

CODA: Thinking About Democratic Change

The final mission is to think about ongoing democratic changes from the perspective of our findings. This task is of a different nature than the previous sections, as they addressed the more direct political, democratic, and scientific implications of the study. This preceding discussion was directly structured around the political science research problems outlined in chapter 1. In contrast, our final topic probably bears a more nonobvious relation to the empirical results, and it has so far largely been left out of the presentation. Nevertheless, because the presented results do shed a certain amount of light on some very important democratic lines of development, I think this book would be incomplete without the following remarks.

Inspired by much contemporary democratic debate, our starting point is that traditional party-based representative democracy appears troubled. Underlying this judgment are a number of trends that are explained in more detail later. These trends are typically seen as products of a continuous modernization process in advanced Western societies, involving raised living standard, educational and cognitive mobilization, increasing social and geographical mobility, as well as labor market differentiation and individualization.

The democratic consequences of modernization are manifold. One is decreasing attachment to the institutions and actors of traditional party-based representative democracy. Party membership and activity have been decreasing in most countries for several decades (Widfeldt 1995; Scarrow 2000; Petersson et al. 2000). Likewise, the proportion of citizens who feel emotionally attached to a party—the level of party identification—is on a long-term decrease (Schmitt and Holmberg 1995; Dalton, McAllister, and Wattenberg 2000). In the 1990s, more negative news was added to these long-standing downward trends: general distrust in democratic institutions and politicians became more widespread, and voter turnout decreased in many countries (Klingemann 1999; Dalton 1999; Dalton, McAllister, and Wattenberg 2000).

However, while attachment to traditional political institutions and actors is declining, modernization is also gradually giving birth to a new form of citizen, one who is more educated, knowledgeable, and often more interested in societal issues than her predecessors. This citizen is anything but unable or unwilling to participate politically. However, she is not necessarily keen on expressing preferences through collectivist inventions such as parties and elections. The worldwide emergence of "critical citizens" (Norris 1999) is a case in point. As discussed in chapter 4, critical citizens are deeply committed to democratic values. But on the other hand they have less respect for traditional authorities than previous generations. They are skeptical about the collectivist hierarchical institutions of representative democracy, as these do not sufficiently allow individual political participation and influence (see also Inglehart 1990, 1999).

In fact, it has become customary to speak of a general individualization of political behavior. Rather than engaging in political parties, or perhaps even vote, the modern citizen uses her improved skills and confidence for more individual forms of exercising influence in specific issues; examples include contacting journalists and public employees, consumer boycotts, signing petitions, and so on (Petersson, Westholm, and Blomberg 1989;

Petersson et al. 1998). Also, single-issue organizations appear to grow in popularity at the expense of political parties (Goul Andersen and Hoff 2001). In a related vein, researchers have uncovered a normalization of protest activities that were once thought of as unconventional (Barnes, Kaase et al. 1979; Jennings and van Deth 1989). As Dalton, McAllister, and Wattenberg (2000:61) explain, "Whereas elections were once seen as the focal point of political activity, it is often argued that elections are being displaced by unconventional forms of participation, such as petitions, protests, and demonstrations [...] These new forms of participation have emerged as a result of value change, the rise of new social movements and new issue concerns, and increasing cognitive mobilization within the electorates of the advanced societies."

In conclusion, it is not so much democracy itself that is facing challenges. Rather, what is increasingly questioned is the ability of the party-based representative system to integrate a more individualized and more capable demos into the democratic process.

Democratic Reforms

To a larger extent than usually appreciated, democratic systems are currently reforming themselves to meet the challenges. Moreover, while some distinct remedies are aimed at improving parties and elections, many of the most popular democratic reforms are about further enhancing opportunities for direct, individualized, single-issue participation in the political process. This development was clearly reflected in the main conclusions of the Swedish *Democracy Commission* (SOU 2000:1). Drawing on more than 40 research volumes and reports, this parliamentary commission came down strongly in favor of "a participatory democracy with deliberative qualities" (23). It was stated that "our notion of democracy does not refer to just any participation. It builds on the idea that each citizen can be assured of influence, in other words participation with real influence in sight [...] political participation is valuable because it develops the personalities of the participants. Gradually, a public spirit and a concern for the common good is developed" (35).[6]

Inspired by scholars such as Pateman (1970), Mansbridge (1990), and Barber (1984), many concrete democratic reforms now under way in Sweden and elsewhere embody the participatory ideal. We have already noted welfare-state related institutional changes such as resources for user influence, vouchers, and freedom-of-choice, which are meant to empower citizens vis-à-vis public services. In January 2002 the Swedish government submitted its *Democracy Proposition*[7] which suggested yet other reforms along participatory lines. For instance, legislative changes were proposed so as to expand decision-making rights in collective user boards in for instance, public schools. Individual voice opportunities are also to be improved, not least through enhanced Internet-based opportunities to communicate views and opinions about personally experienced public services to administrations. Moreover, it was proposed that citizens' opportunities to initiate local referenda be further expanded, thus reinforcing the growing use of direct democracy (Butler and Ranney 1994; Hadenius 2001). It was also suggested that municipalities should be able to decide that individual citizens may initiate issues in the local parliament. Finally, inspired by for instance, Fishkin (1995), it was envisioned that "deliberative polls" (medborgarpaneler) should be increasingly offered as a form of political participation for those who do not want to be active in traditional party politics, but are nevertheless interested in local issues.

Reforms and trends such as these underscore that at the beginning of the twenty-first century, participatory democracy is no longer a remote philosophical fiction. On the contrary, there are very real democratic reforms under way, many of which imply that people will increasingly exercise political influence in an *individualized* fashion in *specific* issues. At the same time, traditional and more collective channels for exercising political influence are declining in popularity.

Democratic Reforms, Voice Opportunities, and Political Trust

Party-based representative channels and individualized participatory channels are not communicating vessels. Just because one increases in popularity does not mean the other will decline in any automatic fashion. In fact, proponents of participatory democracy argue that those who engage in really concrete matters—by signing a petition, by participating in a user board or in a deliberative poll, or by activism in a single-issue organization—will develop a concern and an understanding also for other and potentially larger issues. Traditional collectivist channels like party activism and voting may thus be stimulated by individualistic participation trends. In Warren's (1992:8) formulation, "were individuals more broadly empowered, especially in the institutions that have most impact on their everyday lives [...] their experiences would have transformative effects: they would become more public-spirited, more tolerant, more knowledgeable, more attentive to the interests of others, and more probing of their own interests. These transformations would improve the workings of higher-level representative institutions."

More empirical research is needed here. As previously emphasized, we know too little about the actual extent of, and conditions for, positive spillover effects between individualist participation in specific issues and areas, and collectivist representative democracy. Most empirical studies so far conclude that effects on engagement and knowledge are typically limited to the particular setting and issue in which participation occurs (see Goul Andersen and Hoff 2001; Jarl 2001).

This study, however, has reported the presence of one such positive spillover effect. Chapter 9 reported that satisfaction with the way democracy works and trust in politicians grows among those who experience good voice opportunities in contacts with welfare state institutions. And these effects appear to indicate something more than just effects of opportunities to steer strictly personal outcomes in a self-interested direction. Furthermore, chapter 10 showed that empowering customer experiences tend to generate political trust, whereas more powerless client experiences tend to undermine it.

These findings suggest that citizens generalize the democratic lessons learned from personal experiences with the implementation stage of the political process. If such experiences indicate that the political system is interested in and responsive to citizens' views, then trust in the whole political system appears to be strengthened. In turn, higher levels of general trust in the democratic system should also increase the prospects for participation also in arenas such as parties and elections.

Democratic Reforms and the Variable Impact of Self-Interest

This sounds great. But the increasing popularity of individualized modes of participation and deliberation also has potentially negative democratic implications, which could outweigh potential positive spillover effects.[8] One such problem is highlighted by our analyses of *self-interest*. We have found support for the hypothesis that the relative importance of self-interest as an ingredient in personal experience effects varies across political trust and ideology. Whereas self-interest is the main ingredient of experience effects on left–right related orientations, social justice concerns are at least as important (often more important) when it comes to political trust. Moreover, in chapter 7 it was discovered that self-interest effects are stronger for experiences with public transfer systems than for experiences of public human services.

These results are consistent with a greater pattern that is beginning to emerge in empirical research on self-interest and political behavior. Although generally speaking the impact of self-interest is rarely enormous, it seems to increase when political choices are more concrete, and when the personal stakes associated with different alternatives are large and visible (Sears and Citrin 1982; Green 1988). Other things equal, such choices seem to raise the likelihood that citizens recognize, calculate, and choose on the basis of consequences for personal, short-term, material interest.

From a normative point of view, it is hardly self-evident how to evaluate self-interested popular attitudes (see Warren 1992). Then again, it has not been the purpose of this study to solve such normative problems. However, if the reader shares my hunch that self-interested attitudes—especially in the narrow sense that we have conceptualized them here—do not always equal the attitudes people would hold after greater information intake, and after becoming aware of all the involved trade-offs, for instance, through an extensive open debate on equal terms—then the emerging pattern causes concern. The problem is that many increasingly popular individualized modes of participation present citizens with exactly the kind of choices that are most likely to stimulate self-interest. Participation channels such as single-issue organizations, user influence, individually experienced voice opportunities, local referenda, citizen initiatives in local councils, deliberative polls, and many others, very often facilitate participation in local and specific matters where personal stakes are high and visible. Moreover, because such choices do not necessarily involve simultaneous trade-offs between many issues, they often make self-interest easier to notice and calculate. We have empirical reasons to believe, then, that individualist participation in specific issues has a potential for turning into egoism. In stark contrast to the hope that participatory reforms can transform otherwise self-interested citizens in the direction of "a public spirit and a concern for the common good," such reforms may instead stimulate the potency of personal, material, short-term self-interest as a decisive factor in the opinion formation process.

Now, it would be unfair to lump all participatory and deliberative reforms together without pointing out important internal differences. Some reforms are in all likelihood worse than others when it comes to stimulating self-interest. Particularly voice in individual welfare state experiences is an extreme example in that the influence provided typically concerns extremely concrete issues, that is, services that are directly related to one welfare state institution in a limited geographical area. And such voice opportunities rarely involve being confronted with trade-offs, conflicting arguments and interests (except perhaps for the interests and arguments of the encountered public official).

This qualification is important as deliberative theorists typically argue that the *open-minded debate* involved in settings such as deliberative polls provides participants with the views and arguments of other interests and areas. By weighing such information against self-interested views and arguments, an enlightened attitudinal synthesis is hoped to emerge. Another mechanism that disarms self-interest supposedly kicks in when participating citizens are equipped with real *decision-making rights* or at least a large influence on decisions, such as user boards in public schools. When participation is no longer only about expressing opinions and interests, but also about directly affecting real decisions, a sense of responsibility to consider other factors than self-interest is thought to develop. To these caveats one may add that it is by no means self-evident that the issues raised by individual citizens in local councils, or the issues debated in deliberative polls, will always be concrete and local. When deliberating, say, the future of health care, the conveners can to some extent decide whether to frame the issue as one of ideological principles, or as one where it should be decided which hospital in the region should be protected from cutbacks.

Nevertheless, when compared to the political choices offered by traditional party-based democracy, most participatory and deliberative reforms stick out in the same self-interested direction. Many scholars have emphasized that a main function of political parties is to elevate political choices to a more abstract and aggregated level. Because parties formulate general political cal programs covering many areas, they must make trade-offs between interests and issues. Parties take general ideological positions that can be summarized in overarching concepts such as left, right, pro-public sector, pro-market, pro-family, and so on. When parties in this way bundle issues into a smaller set of abstract alternatives it also becomes more difficult for citizens to discover and calculate consequences of choosing an alternative for personal, short-term, material self-interest. In other words, whereas it is quite easy to say whether you would gain personally from increased spending on child care in your part of the city, a similar calculus becomes difficult when the choice is between more leftist or more rightist policies in society.

These arguments square well with the empirical evidence. Self-interest has previously proven to be a crucial explanation for very concrete attitudes toward spending on very concrete services (Green 1988; Sannerstedt 1981; Nilsson 1997; Johansson, Nilsson, and Strömberg 2001). By contrast, chapter 7 discovered that while welfare state self-interest is probably somewhat more consequential for left–right related ideological orientations than most research has concluded, it is nevertheless but one of many contributing variables. Based on results such as these (see further Sears and Funk 1991), one may venture that collectivist party-based democracy—by virtue of presenting citizens with general ideological choices—is not as bad at creating a public spirit as some theorists would have it. Likewise, the increasingly popular individualist modes of exercising political influence, by virtue of presenting citizens with concrete choices that are free of trade-offs, and where personal stakes are high and visible, could very well be detrimental to such a spirit.

A more benevolent version of this criticism accepts the (typically unsupported) participatory and deliberative contentions that open-minded debate, direct influence, and decision-making responsibility, do have a potential to disarm narrow self-interest. Still, this does not change the fact that most conceivable participatory and deliberative reforms facilitate participation and deliberation in rather specific, local, or otherwise limited matters. Therefore, whatever the abilities of such solutions to transform self-interest, the transformation starts out from a worse initial position compared to a democracy where citizens choose between overarching ideological alternatives in the first place.

The Personal, the Political, and the Future

The clock cannot be turned back. Neither the citizens nor the institutional and organizational landscapes of the twentieth century will return in the foreseeable future. The real issue is how to design democratic reforms that can combine individualized and issue-specific modes of citizen deliberation and participation, with a concern for more long-term and more collective interests. Here, I do not think it will suffice just to reiterate the largely untested theoretical mantras of deliberative and participatory theory, and then transform the democratic process accordingly. Rather, our task as constructive political scientists must now be to develop and test empirically oriented theories that specify the individual, contextual, and institutional circumstances under which positive democratic effects of increased participation and deliberation outweigh the negative ones. Expressed differently, we need to answer the question of how to improve opportunities for individualist modes of political participation, at the same as we are faithful to the principle of popular rule based on informed preferences. If we suspect that specific self-interested preferences do not always equal the preferences that people *would hold* when presented with more abstract and "bundled" choices with simultaneous trade-offs, then many ongoing democratic changes are cause for concern.

If we do not take these issues seriously, maybe we are heading for a democratic order where citizens increasingly think about politics in terms of specific close-to-home issues, and to a greater extent than before base their preferences on narrow self-interest. Conversely, especially if party identification, trust in representative democracy, and voter turnout continue to decline, citizens might become less prone to think about politics in terms of long-term, coherent, and viable ideological courses of action.

If we are not careful, the political might become more personal than we ever wanted it to be.

Notes

Chapter One   The Personal and the Political

1. As quoted in Goodsell (1981:3).
2. For two accessible introductions to the twentieth-century welfare state expansion, see Tarschys (1978) and Goldsmith (1995).
3. My translation from original Swedish. Parts of this popular quote can also be found in Assarson (1995:166–7), and in Dahlberg and Vedung (2001:11–12).
4. The quote can also be found in Strömbäck (2000:148).
5. Very similar arguments have been made by Lane (1962), Sniderman, Brody and Tetlock (1991), and Zaller (1992).
6. Westerståhl introduced the concept in a 1956 newspaper article (see Nilsson 1996a). It has also inspired publications such as Westerståhl and Johansson (1981), and Johansson, Nilsson, and Strömberg 2001. For an in-depth analysis of Westerståhl's democratic thought in general, and of service democracy in particular, see Boström (1988:chapter 8; see also Strandberg 1998:chapter 6).
7. Here, the notion of service democracy has something in common with the "end-of-ideology" argument. Both build on the idea that ideological conflict in developed democracies became less severe as postwar affluence was gradually generated. Instead, as authors like Bell (1960) and Tingsten (1966) argued, political debate shifted its main focus from ideological goals to practical methods for reaching certain goals that were largely uncontested. The delivery of satisfactory public services could very well be seen as such a goal. For a discussion, see Håkansson (1999:17–19).
8. The economic voting literature is gigantic. Lewis-Beck and Paldam (2000:113) identify more than 200 books and articles that are relevant to the field. Some examples are: Campbell et al. 1960:391; Kinder and Kiewiet 1981; Weatherford 1983; Miller and Listhaug 1984; Holmberg 1984; Lewis-Beck 1988; Conover and Feldman 1986; Markus 1988; Aardal and Valen 1989, 1995; Mutz 1992, 1994; Gilljam and Holmberg 1993, 1995; Hibbs 1993; Mondak, Mutz, and Huckfeldt 1996; Borre and Goul Andersen 1997; Jenssen 1998; Evans 1999; Bengtsson 2002. For studies examining the (typically weak) impact of personal unemployment on various political attitudes, see Schlozman and Verba 1979; Garcia de Polavieja 1999; Adman 1999.
9. The notion that the personal is weakly related to the political applies only to *short-term changes* in the personal economic situation, rather than to people's locations in relatively stable long-term socioeconomic structures. This is an important remark: while short-term ups and downs in the private economy have usually turned out to have rather weak effects on political attitudes and behavior, we know that variables such as occupational class, education, and income level have quite a strong impact in this regard (see Franklin, Mackie, and Valen 1992; Oskarson 1994; and the cited literature in chapter 4). A similar but more general point will be made in chapter 2, where the definition of a personal experience will include strictly personal observations of politically relevant phenomena, but not interpersonal communication concerning those phenomena. Of course, we know that much of the effects of stable social structure on attitudes and behavior are brought about by a good deal of interpersonal communication and socialization in primary groups. Therefore, such effects should not be thought of as personal experience effects in the sense that the term is used in this study.
10. As it stands, the literature seems to indicate that economic perceptions are less influential for political trust variables than for party choice, or at least that the effects are quite unstable and inconsistent (see McAllister 1999:201). Recently however, a number of scholars have tried, with some

success, to account for the instability in economic effects on political trust by including contextual interaction variables measuring the clarity of responsibility for economic failure. The hypothesis is that the fuzzier the political responsibility, the more likely it is that economic discontent reduces support for the whole political system, rather than just support for the incumbent party or candidate (see further Powell and Whitten 1993; Huseby 1999; Taylor 2000; Bengtsson 2002).

11. This does not mean that personal economic experiences are always unimportant for political trust. For instance, Aardal and Valen (1995:210–20) and Aardal (1999) found relatively strong effects in Norway.

12. Experiences of such events still have strong effects on perceptions of the extent to which one thinks they are important as *personal* problems (Mutz 1998:73).

13. For a Swedish discussion on the topic, see Strömbäck (2001).

14. The finding that personal economic experiences have weak effects on political attitudes is a relatively stable result that has proven to pertain to most developed Western states including Sweden (see Holmberg 1984; Gilljam and Holmberg 1993; Adman 1999), not just to the United States (Lewis-Beck 1988). Exceptions have been reported, especially in Denmark and Britain (Lewis-Beck 1988; Jordahl 2002).

15. These findings corroborate studies indicating that the correlation between economic perceptions and government popularity increases when the measures of economic perceptions tap views on whether the government has actually been able to influence the economic situation (Gilljam and Holmberg 1993; Aardal and Valen 1989).

16. For similar arguments, see Weatherford (1983) and Mondak, Mutz, and Huckfeldt (1996).

17. Tyler (1980) also found that the *affectivity* of information matters. If information has the power to evoke stronger emotional reactions among people it is more likely to affect sociotropic perceptions and, in turn, political preferences. However, I leave this factor outside the discussion as I see no reason why the level of affectivity should differ across welfare state information and economic information.

Chapter Two   Self-Interest and Social Justice

1. Miller and Listhaug (1999) also use essentially the same three conceptual distinctions.

2. Nilsson (1995, 1996b) identifies four "citizen roles" in which citizens can have personal contacts with welfare state institutions. First, citizens may be "users" or "consumers" of welfare state services and transfers, a role that is essentially the same thing as the welfare state experiences that are at focus here. Second, citizens may also encounter the public sector as public employees, as taxpayers, and as voters.

3. As suggested by Downs (1960), there are important differences between citizens' relations to public sector inputs and outputs respectively (see also Peters 1991:55–56). He noted that whereas there is usually a direct link between costs and benefits in the market, the two are often divorced in the public sphere. This may reduce support for public spending among the ordinary citizen: "since his payments to the government are not related to the benefits he receives from it, he finds himself contributing to things that do not benefit him" (Downs 1960:548). Further, he argued that whereas the costs of the public sector become very well known to most people through an annual and painful taxpaying experience, many of the products of the public sector are both remote and uncertain to all those who are not extremely well informed about government matters. According to Downs, these characteristics of public sector transactions mean that the support for a large public sector will be *lower* the less information about government outputs the electorate possesses. In contrast, according to a very different hypothesis, uninformed citizens tend to *underestimate* the costs of public service provision, and their support for public spending on various services tends to go down if they are informed about the real costs for taxpayers (for a more detailed discussion, further references, and some empirical support for this latter hypothesis, see Winter and Mouritzen 2001).

4. For in-depth descriptions of the Swedish public sector and welfare state, see Ringqvist (1996), Edebalk, Ståhlberg, and Wadensjö (1998), and Olsson (1993).

5. My translation from original Swedish.

6. Therefore, it is not surprising that there are few empirical studies on long-term self-interest and political attitudes and behavior (Sears and Funk 1991:65). In one of the rare exceptions, it was shown that whereas expectations about personal finances in the next year influenced presidential

voting in the 1984 U.S. election, expectations concerning the next five years did not have a significant impact (Lewis-Beck 1988:121).

7. Having said this, it should be pointed out that "other" versions of self-interest are in no way rejected theoretically or empirically. On the contrary, to the extent that the self-interest perspective as conceptualized here is not supported empirically, one possible explanation may very well be that citizens are still interest-driven, but more inclined to consider group- and long-term interests.

8. See Svallfors (1996:30–33) for critical comments on especially Baldwin's treatment of the social class concept.

9. See Clayton and Pontusson (1998) for an attempt to modify Pierson's view that welfare retrenchment largely failed in these countries, and Lindbom (2001) for an analysis of the extent of welfare state retrenchment in Sweden in the 1990s. For a similar overall Scandinavian analysis, see Kuhnle (2000).

10. Sectoral cleavage theory assumes that the main causal mechanism at the individual level is self-interested and rational comparison of political alternatives. The sectoral perspective thus builds on a different micro-theoretical foundation than traditional cleavage theory, which emphasizes various group-oriented socialization mechanisms. Such mechanisms make people from the same social environment to adopt similar political preferences (see Franklin and Page 1984, for a similar point). Instrumental cost–benefit calculation, on the other hand, has a less prominent position in traditional cleavage theory.

11. Svensson (1994) shows that the Social Democratic party elite developed important welfare state institutions with this model of Swedish voters in mind.

12. The symbolic politics literature dealt with the impact of self-interest in a wider context than does this study. Many areas that lie outside the scope of the welfare state were covered, for instance attitudes toward the Vietnam War.

13. Interestingly, in one of the few Swedish analyses that have been set up in this particular way, Holmberg (1981:264–65) found a slightly different pattern. Drawing on the 1979 Swedish Election Study, Holmberg found that opinions on "reducing tax deductions for house-owners" were affected *both* by left–right ideology and by self-interest (as measured by a home-ownership dummy variable). Here it may be noted that issues related to home-ownership were especially salient in the 1979 election (see Esaiasson 1990).

14. For further references to research on the stability of general "symbolic" political orientations, see Krosnick (1991), Sapiro (1994), and Sears and Funk (1999).

15. In contrast, Gilljam and Nilsson (1985) found somewhat stronger effects of various variables representing the self-interest perspective (especially among nonsocialist voters). Their dependent variable was opinions on "reducing the public sector" among the Swedish electorate.

16. This contention has received empirical support in the context of public service provision. Biel, Eek, and Gärling (1997) analyzed Swedish survey data and found that equality was by far the most preferred distribution principle for public child care. Equity was the least popular one.

17. Also quoted in Rothstein (2001:217).

18. Distributive justice is not the only factor that is believed to be conducive to compliance in social dilemmas. Indeed, Levi's (1993, 1997) "theory of contingent consent" assumes that support for the production of public goods also depends on whether individuals actually value the public good in question, on procedural justice factors, and on what Rothstein calls "a just distribution of burdens."

19. Empirical studies emphasize variables such as personal outcomes, procedural fairness, group size, perceptions of other group members' behavior, and basic value orientations, as explanations for willingness to contribute and otherwise support common institutions (see Eek 1999:18–23).

20. See also Biel, Eek, and Gärling 1997.

21. See Grimes (2001), for a Swedish analysis on the impact of different types of procedural aspects.

22. For more detailed discussions about the pros and cons of user influence and voice opportunities, see Dahlberg and Vedung (2001:chapter 4) and Jarl (2001:54–57).

23. My translation from original Swedish.

24. Note that this study investigates the effects of voice opportunities during *individual* personal welfare state experiences. Unlike for instance Jarl (2001), we do not analyze participation in collective resources for voice and user influence such as representative user boards. It should be pointed out that some of the alleged positive democratic effects—especially those on citizens' political involvement and knowledge—are built on the notion that users of public services are actually provided with real decision-making responsibilities and that they "deliberate" with each other in collective settings such as user boards, not just that they individually experience voice

opportunities in their personal service contacts. In contrast, the predictions about how voice opportunities affect political orientations do not seem as sensitive to whether we are talking about participation in collective user influence, or about experienced voice opportunities in strictly personal contacts with services. Given that people value voice opportunities, and given that they update political orientations as a result of personal experiences, reasonably there should be an impact of voice also in strictly personal contacts.

Chapter Three   The Institutional Interface

1. More than this, in order for such measurement to be meaningful, one needs clear conceptual yardsticks for the social justice variables in various welfare state situations. And as discussed in chapter 2, the purpose of this study is not to analyze exactly what citizens mean, or should mean, by distributive justice and experienced voice opportunities in various situations.
2. For an extensive discussion on how political institutions should be defined, see Rothstein (1996).
3. My translation from original Swedish.
4. There has been a vigorous debate on whether the regime framework should be expanded and/ or reconstructed so that it comes to reflect institutional circumstances and effects not originally incorporated by the regime framework. This discussion lies outside the purposes of this study, and interested readers may want to take a look at e.g. Sainsbury (1996) and Castles and Mitchell (1992).
5. Following Rothstein, I do not include decisions made on more informal professional grounds in the concept of discretion. Rothstein (1998:20–21) points out that it is "a different thing to be denied a certain medical treatment because the responsible physician deems it medically unsuitable, and to be denied a certain public service because the responsible official judges one to possess sufficient means to purchase it on the open market." Hence, when referring to discretion, what I have in mind is not professionals applying occupation-specific norms (as in the case of the physician). Rather, the concept refers to means-testing of an economic kind, or when a bureaucrat applies other more or less formalized rules and policy instructions to determine whether a citizen belongs to a target category.
6. Note that Hoff (1993) and Möller (1996) use the word "autonomy" in their respective Scandinavian languages for what is here called empowerment.

Chapter Four   Political Trust and Ideology

1. Also quoted by Lodge and Stroh (1993:226).
2. In addition, while media exposure may (at times) strengthen the direct personal–political link, it often simultaneously undermines the indirect link flowing through sociotropic perceptions. This occurs because media exposure tends to increase one's general level of information and knowledge about a problem. And as discussed in chapter 1, more general and accurate information tends to decrease the need to fall back on personal experiences as an information source for the formation of sociotropic perceptions. Personal experience becomes more politically important the lower the knowledge about relevant macro conditions (Conover, Feldman, and Knight 1986; Weatherford 1983).
3. Of course, people still need to notice the political relevance of an experience at the time it occurs. As discussed in chapter 1, a suspicion in this study is that welfare state experiences, by virtue of their direct links to public policies and responsible politicians, are more likely to stimulate political thinking compared to personal economic experiences. However, beyond these basic differences between the two policy domains, it is still likely that increased media attention on a particular welfare state institution would to an even greater extent politicize people's experiences of that institution, at least if media reports fit with many people's experiences. This possibility is discussed further in chapter 5.
4. Throughout I use "political trust" and "political support" interchangeably. This seems to be a common practice in the current literature. In the original formulation, however, trust was considered a particular version of what Easton called "diffuse" support. (See later for a discussion on "diffuse" versus "specific" support.)
5. However, based on Canadian data, Kornberg and Clarke (1992:121) reported that evaluations of the economy were more strongly related to support for the political community than to attitudes

toward leaders. Moreover, attitudes toward the European Union (EU) is an interesting exception. Past analyses have shown that macroeconomic concerns and evaluations affect Swedes' attitudes toward the European Union (Jenssen 1998; Oskarson and Ringdal 1998; Kumlin 2001a).

6. At the same time, there are studies indicating that the rhetoric and messages of Swedish parties and politicians have remained surprisingly stable over time (Esaiasson 1996; Håkansson 1999).

7. My translation from original Swedish.

8. Converse's (1964) publication stimulated a vigorous debate on the extent to which American voters were in fact "innocent of ideology." For introductions to this very large literature, see Nie, Verba, and Petrocik 1979; Smith 1989; Niemi and Weissberg 1993; Dalton 2002.

9. It should be pointed out that citizens' welfare state attitudes are considerably more complex than what we can hope to capture with general measures of state-intervention orientations and left–right self-identification (see Borre and Scarbrough 1995; Pettersen 1995; Roller 1995; Huseby 1995; Svallfors 1989, 1996, 1999). Still, we have good reason to stick to a small set of general dependent variables in the context of the present study, as the purpose is not to describe and explain all conceivable aspects of welfare state attitudes. Instead, we are interested in political effects of welfare state experiences, and given this choice, ideological orientations (and political trust) offer good places to look. These orientations are so generally useful for interpretation and evaluation of political information, that citizens may update them in an on-line fashion as a result of new relevant personal welfare state experiences.

10. For similar findings in Sweden, see Holmberg (1981) and Bennulf (1994).

11. In support of overload theories, Birgersson (1975) reported the existence of a "service paradox." That is, evaluations of public services were more negative, and demands for more public efforts higher, in Swedish municipalities whose services were already more developed. However, in a later analysis that was also extended to the individual level, Sannerstedt (1981:132–53) could not find support for the service paradox. Similarly, in a Danish study, Lolle (1999) found virtually no effects at all of the level of public spending on different service areas and citizens' satisfaction with those areas (see also Johansson, Nilsson, and Strömberg 2001:177–78).

12. As Svallfors (1996) demonstrates, this trend in general ideological orientations was not necessarily paralleled by similar changes in concrete attitudes toward specific programs or aspects of the welfare state.

13. See Green (1988:chapter 2) for more information about these variables. Furthermore, self-interest is believed to grow in importance when countries are struck by recessions. Some studies strongly suggest that as a "crisis awareness" develops among the electorate, individuals temporarily come to value material well-being more than usual (Inglehart 1981). Parallel to this development, self-interest political concerns might gain in legitimacy.

14. My translation from original Swedish.

Chapter Five   The Data and the Case

1. Note that this presupposes that personal experiences and media/elite coverage convey similar pictures of the experienced welfare state institutions. As discussed in chapter 4, and as shown by Mutz (1998), media coverage can at times weaken the impact of personal experiences, provided that what has been personally experienced does not fit with the image conveyed by the media.

2. All datasets used in this study will be available for scientific purposes from the Swedish Social Science Data Archive (SSD) at Göteborg University (http://www.ssd.gu.se).

3. The SOM Institute is directed by a steering committee consisting of Professor Sören Holmberg, Department of Political Science, Professor Lennart Weibull, Department of Journalism and Mass Communication, and Senior Lecturer Lennart Nilsson, School of Public Administration. For more information about the SOM Institute and its surveys, see Holmberg and Weibull (1997, 1999, 2000, 2002; Nilsson 2000a), or visit its website at http://www.som.gu.se/.

4. For more information about the Swedish Election Studies Program, see Holmberg 2000; Esaiasson and Holmberg 1996; or visit http://www.pol.gu.se/sve/vod/vustart.htm.

5. The 1992 Swedish Living Standard Survey data were distributed to the author by the Swedish Social Science Data Archive ("Svensk Levnadsstandard 1992," SSD 0492). Neither the archive nor the primary investigator bear any responsibility for the analyses and interpretations presented here.

6. For an introduction, see Eagly and Chaiken (1993:595–99).

7. A related remark is that resistance should be more widespread when people *expect* to encounter persuasive messages and to engage in political thinking. When people follow political debates and issues at the elite level, they know that different political interests will present pros and cons for their positions. Moreover, citizens know that they like some of those interests and actors more than others. They therefore have good reason not to automatically accept all information they encounter, but to turn resistance filters on. In contrast, personal welfare state experiences often occur in a seemingly harmless everyday context in which politically relevant information may catch people off-guard (see Katz and Lazarsfeld 1955).
8. The viability of this possibility is discussed further in chapter 8.

Chapter Six   The Welfare State and the Economy

1. The phone-in was reported in Göteborgs-Posten, August 25, 2001 ("Många berättade om sina skräckupplevelser på akuten").
2. Whereas the economic questions refer to "the last twelve months," the public service questions in the SOM Survey ask about "the last two, three years." The reason is that economic information tends to be more quantifiable and periodically exact than information about public services. Therefore, I felt it would be somewhat strange to ask about public services during a very recent and exactly specified period of time. In the Swedish European Election Study, however, all retrospective questions referred to the last 12 months. It turned out that this had little effect on the results.
3. See Kumlin and Oskarson (2000), and Kumlin (2001a), for in-depth analyses of these differences.
4. For the satisfaction with democracy items, the alternatives were very satisfied (coded 1), rather satisfied (2), not very satisfied (3), not at all satisfied (4). For the trust in politicians items, alternatives were very much trust (coded 1), quite some trust (2), neither much nor little trust (3), quite little trust (2), very little trust (1), and don't know (3). The loadings on the satisfaction with democracy factor were as follows: satisfaction with democracy in Sweden (.78), in Västra Götaland (.80), in the municipality (.77). The loadings on trust in politicians were: trust in national politicians (.72), trust in Västra Götaland politicians (.66), trust in municipality politicians (.75). Finally, the correlation between the two factors was $r = .50$, which indicates that although satisfaction with democracy and trust in politicians are kept separate conceptually, they are nevertheless empirically related; people who are satisfied with democracy are more likely to also trust politicians.
5. The models in table 6.3 allow for these effects to be estimated. This means that a small part of the indirect effect of one personal experience variable is channeled by sociotropic perceptions in "the other" policy domain. However, it should be pointed out that because the effects in question are relatively minor they do not change any substantive conclusions compared to models that exclude them.
6. These probabilities were calculated using the formula for logistic regression (see Long 1997:49): Prob (social democrat) = exp $(a + b_1x_1 \ldots b_ix_i)/1 + \exp (a + b_1x_1 \ldots b_ix_i)$. The nonlinearity of the logit model means the effect of an independent variable on the probability of supporting the incumbent party varies somewhat depending on the level of the other independent variables in the model. Figures 6.2 and 6.3 show the effects when other variables in the model are held at their means.
7. Some may feel that our independent variables are less relevant in the context of European Parliament Elections as the goal of these elections is to appoint representatives dealing mainly with issues related to the EU and European integration. For this reason, and because the Parliament is not the most influential assembly within the EU, it would make less sense to hold such representatives accountable for mainly national policies and social trends, such as national public services and the national economy. However, previous research shows convincingly that voters send signals to the national government although, formally, more Europe-oriented issues "should" be at focus in European elections. This pattern, together with the fact that interest and turnout in these elections are low, has led researchers to characterize them as "second-order national elections" (see van der Eijk and Franklin 1996). This characterization has proven valid also in Sweden although European issues are more important to Swedish voters in European Parliament elections than in most other countries (see Gilljam and Holmberg 1998; Holmberg et al. 2001).
8. There are two differences. First, we include people's opinions on Swedish membership in the European monetary union (EMU), because EU-related opinions are especially salient and influential in these elections. Second, the election study does not contain any measure of subjective life satisfaction. Judging from the West Sweden survey, however, this seems to be a small problem: the coefficients of the central

independent variables remained unaltered when I dropped subjective life satisfaction from the model in table 6.4.

9. Like before, the effects are calculated holding other variables in the model at their means.

Chapter Seven   Self-Interest

1. See Taylor-Gooby (1986:594) for a similar point.

2. Note the limited sense in which interest is regarded as "objective." It only means that it is the researcher who, based on a particular conceptual definition, decides values along the variable, not the respondent herself. Of course, among researchers, the question of how objective interests should be defined may still be a highly subjective matter.

3. Distinctions between objective characteristics as determined by the researcher, and subjective perceptions of characteristics, are ubiquitous in the social sciences. For instance, our distinction is analogous to that between objective occupational/social class and subjective class identification (Lipset and Rokkan 1967; Petersson 1982; Oskarson 1994). Another example is the separation found in the economic voting literature between objective economic conditions—as measured by e.g., unemployment and income—and subjective perceptions of the situation (see Mutz 1992).

4. More exactly, the measure covers usage of the following public institutions: public child care, public schools (gymnasium and grundskola), children's health care (barnavårdscentral), local health care (vårdcentral), hospitals, public dental care, elder care, social welfare, transportation subsidies (färdtjänst), handicap care, housing allowance, public transportation, public sport facilities, public libraries, public leisure time activities, job agencies and participation in unemployment schemes (AMS-arbete, AMS-utbildning, kunskapslyftet etc.), and early retirement benefits. Cases were coded as missing if they had invalid answers on all the items following the head question "Please indicate below which of the following services you yourself or a family member use." Finally, it should be pointed out that, in the case of public schools, I have allowed both parents and pupils to define themselves as users of an institution. The logic is that the interests of both categories are affected by their relation to schools, and that both actually experience the school environment directly.

5. A nice aspect of this variable is that it is based on a larger number of institutions than has been used in much previous research. Still however, we are not dealing with a perfect measure of the extent to which welfare state arrangements satisfy one's short-term self-interest. In particular, there is variation among users of the same institution as to how much and how often one receives service. Of course, our variable does not record that variation as it is based only on usage versus nonusage.

6. When answering these questions it might be difficult to separate between personal and collective losses and gains. After all, if I believe that a smaller public sector will generate some collective gain (such as a more efficient market economy), this should benefit most people in society including myself. Hence, I might answer that I will in fact benefit personally from a public sector reduction, even if I perceive my personal interest in the welfare state to be high. Of course, the logic is that I, as well as everyone else, will enjoy the positive effects of a more efficient market economy. To avoid such confusion, I incorporated items into the question battery that explicitly differentiate between personal benefits and benefits for the Swedish people in general. To make the distinction clearer, items concerning personal and collective gains respectively were placed immediately next to each other in the questionnaire.

7. More exactly, the measure covers usage of the following public institutions: housing allowance, unemployment insurance, sick-leave benefits, parental benefit (föräldrapenning), unemployment support (KAS), student aid, social assistance, child allowance, early retirement benefits, and old-age pension.

8. One might discern a second circumstance that would give us reason to mistrust subjective interest effects. It occurs when objective and subjective measures are largely independent of one another. Reasonably, the risk of objective interest being reactive in relation to ideological variables is smaller than the corresponding risk for subjective perceptions. If subjective interest is firmly rooted in objective interests, then, subjective variables become increasingly credible as measures of meaningful perceptions rather than as second-rate indicators of the dependent variable.

9. Both items offered the following response alternatives: very good suggestion (coded 1), rather good suggestion (2), neither good nor bad suggestion (3), rather bad suggestion (4), and very bad suggestion (5).

10. The first item was "it's better to raise taxes than to cut social reforms" (loading .56). Here, respondents answered along a balanced five-point scale (1 = agree completely, 3 = neither/nor, 5 = do not agree). The second and third items respectively were "work towards a society with more private enterprise" (loading −.56) and "work towards a society with small income differences" (loading .53). The response alternatives for these two items were very good suggestion (coded 1), rather good suggestion (2), neither good nor bad suggestion (3), rather bad suggestion (4), very bad suggestion (5), and don't know (3).

11. As can be seen in table 7.1, about 5 percent used 10 or more institutions.

12. I have also experimented with larger versions of this model, including variables such as occupational class, age, education, and unemployment. The inclusion of these variables did not change any of the observations made.

13. The simple class dichotomy is a crude measure compared to the more fine-tuned classifications used in studies that specifically examine class effects on political attitudes and behavior (see Oskarson 1994; Svallfors 1996). However, it turns out that this simpler measure is generally sufficient for purposes of statistical control in the context of this study. In fact, all analyses throughout this book have been performed under control for the original five-category subjective class variable (split into four dummy variables), and these "tougher" controls only produce insignificant changes in estimates of experience effects. I reached the same conclusion when I controlled, not for subjective class identification, but rather for a more elaborate occupational class variable containing the following categories: non-skilled worker, skilled worker, lower white-collar, middle white-collar, higher white-collar, and self-employed (including the few farmers in the data set). Having said this, it should also be pointed out that more elaborate class controls generally reveal stronger class effects, as they allow large differences between relatively unusual extreme groups such as industrial workers and the self-employed. This means that effect comparisons between a variable such as objective self-interest and the subjective class dichotomy is rather kind to the impact of the former. Finally, there is another reason why effect comparisons between objective self-interest and class variables are somewhat kind to the impact of self-interest. The reason is that no attempt has been made to model the internal structural relations between the "control variables" in figure 7.1. In other words, the total class effects reported in tables 7.6–7.8 denote the impact of class holding other control variables constant. It may be argued that this is somewhat unfair to the impact of class as one would expect class to exercise indirect effects also through variables such as education and income. In practice, however, including these additional portions of class effects in the effect comparisons do not make that much of a difference. In fact, the bivariate effects of class on state intervention orientations are −.95 (West Sweden SOM) and −.46 (SLEV), coefficients that are not radically different to the total effects reported in tables 7.6–7.8. Similarly, the bivariate impact of class on left–right ideology is .67 (West Sweden SOM).

14. Holmberg and Asp (1984:355) provided an interesting parallel to these findings in their study of the 1980 Swedish referendum on nuclear power. They found that very little of the variance in voting behavior could be accounted for by perceptions of how different referendum alternatives affected one's personal job market interests. The reason was that "most people did not perceive a concrete connection between their jobs and the alternatives in the referendum." Rather, the data showed that some 60 percent of respondents were piled up on the midpoint ("neither improve nor worsen"), and where another 5 percent chose the don't know alternative.

15. As can be seen in table 7.3, about 5 percent of the respondents have received service from 4 or more of the included institutions.

Chapter Eight   Distributive Justice

1. What is the justification for treating noncontact along the experience variable, and don't know along the sociotropic variable, as neutral middle categories? While there are no strict theoretical reasons I found empirically that these categories actually tend to function as middle categories with respect to the dependent variables. In other words, although noncontact/don't know must still be regarded as "categories apart" on a conceptual level, no empirical information is lost by simply treating them as middle categories in analyses of the dependent variables used here. Expressed differently, no significant increases in model fit are gained by splitting the two variables into subsets of dummy variables, thus avoiding the theoretically arbitrary restriction that values on the dependent variables change linearly when moving from negative experiences, to no

experiences/don't know, to positive experiences. Because of this finding, and because I see a value in expressing results as parsimoniously as possible, I have chosen the simpler way of treating the independent variables.

2. See chapter 6 for more detailed descriptions of these variables.

3. This correlation was also included in table 6.2.

4. See chapter 7 for more information about the variables tapping objective and subjective welfare state interest respectively.

5. Out of the six institutions for which experienced distributive justice was measured, five were included in the subjective self-interest battery. Job agencies were not included.

6. Note that the analyses reported in table 8.5 are performed only among users of the institution in question, which reduces the variation in the independent interest perception variables somewhat. On average, a dichotomy indicating whether one uses a service or not explains 14 percent of the variation in the extent to which one perceives that increased spending would be of personal benefit. (Interestingly, this observation is consistent with the argument made in chapter 4 that memory-based opinion formation is more influential when it comes to concrete and specific opinions.)

7. There are no theoretical reasons to equate noncontact with neutral experience. Hence, on a conceptual level, they should be kept apart. However, the chosen procedure is justified by analyses showing that, in terms of the political orientations of interest here (satisfaction with democracy and trust in politicians), those reporting "no contact" tend to be very similar to those who tick the mid-points along the experienced distributive justice scales. More specifically, this was checked by splitting each five-point item into five dummy variables using "have not been in contact" as the reference category. The measures of satisfaction with democracy and trust in politicians were then regressed on the five dummy variables together with the controls used throughout this chapter. In most cases, the dummy representing the mid-point in terms of experienced distributive justice had an insignificant or modest regression coefficient. In summary, although there are no theoretical reasons to equate noncontact with neutral experience, little empirical information is actually lost by doing so when it comes to effects on the political orientations examined here.

8. See further the discussion in chapter 5.

Chapter Nine   Voice

1. For accessible introductions to, and some critical comments on, Hirschman's reasoning, see Möller (1996:chapter 9) and Goul Andersen, Torpe, and Andersen (2000:chapters 1 and 4).

2. See the literature cited in Niemi, Craig, and Mattei (1991).

3. My translation from the original Danish text.

4. It should be pointed out that the distinction between informal and formal voice opportunities is by no means equivalent to the distinction between collective resources for user influence (such as user boards), and voice opportunities in the strictly personal experiences with services that are at focus in this study. For instance, in many collective user influence settings, users have mainly an advisory function, thus making it possible that participants perceive good possibilities to communicate opinions and views (informal voice), whereas they may very well think that the opportunities to actually affect services are poor.

5. See chapter 8 for more details on this question battery.

6. The correlation between the two experienced voice items was rather low (Pearson's $r = .13$).

7. As in chapter 8, this coding is justified by analyses showing that virtually nothing is gained in terms of model fit by relaxing this particular type of linearity constraint on the effects on the dependent variables. In these analyses, I compared models using the independent variables described in the text, with models that do not make any assumptions whatsoever about the form of effects (i.e., models that split the five-category voice items into four dummy variables each).

8. For instance, Petersson, Westholm, and Blomberg (1989:191) report a correlation of .31 between education and a measure of subjective "administrative competence."

9. Admittedly, this formulation blurs the distinction between internal and external efficacy.

10. The political efficacy scale is an additive index (Cronbach's alpha $= .83$) summing responses to two questions about the possibilities of affecting political decisions in Sweden and in the municipality, respectively. Respondents indicated whether they perceived very good (coded 1), rather good (2), neither good nor bad (3), rather bad (4) or very bad opportunities (5), or whether they did not know (3). The index was scored so that it varies between 1 and 9, higher

values = higher efficacy. Cronbach's alpha was .82. An alternative index where don't know answers were coded as missing did not yield different conclusions about effects on political orientations. The political sophistication variable (mean = 0, standard deviation = 1) was generated by factor analyzing three variables: (1) an additive political interest index based on three items tapping interest in national, regional, and local politics respectively, (2) a measure of the extent to which the respondent discusses politics, (3) a variable counting the number of don't know answers across 11 political attitude items (Q24, Q25, Q26a, Q26b, Q26d, Q41a, Q41b, Q41c, Q41d, Q44, and Q45; see Nilsson 2000a). The factor analysis yielded a strong unidimensional solution. See Luskin (1987) for an introduction to the concept of political sophistication.

11. There is a very slight tendency ($r = .06$) for people receiving service from many institutions to respond more positively to "employees listened." On the other hand, the pattern was the opposite, though still weak, for "affect services" ($r = -.09$). The same unexpected negative relation was found for subjective self-interest and "employees listened" ($r = -.08$). Finally, there was no statistically significant correlation between subjective self-interest and "affect services."

12. Regression analyses show that this difference was not due to the fact that the "affect services" item has a smaller variance than "employees listened."

13. Take the word challenge with a grain of salt. These researchers usually challenge the universal model of procedural justice without knowing it, as voice opportunities are rarely thought about in the broader context of procedural justice research.

14. My translation from Swedish.

15. Three other types of public services were included: social welfare, elder care, and environmental protection. However, these have been left out of the analysis as the number of respondents having experienced social welfare and elder care respectively was too low for meaningful analysis ($n < 50$ in the multivariate regressions), and because there was no information about whether people had been in contact with public services involving environmental protection.

16. More precisely, in tables 9.4 and 9.5, "among users" means the following. *Child care*: Respondent indicated that she personally uses municipality child care. *Leisure time activities/culture*: Respondent indicated that she personally uses either or both of these public services. *Health care*: Respondent uses either hospitals, children's health care (barnavårdscentral), or local health care (vårdcentral). *Public transportation*: Respondent indicated that she personally uses public transportation. *Schools*: Respondent indicated that she personally uses public primary schools (kommunal grundskola) or public secondary schools (kommunal gymnasieskola).

17. Again, child care and schools stick out (7 and 12 percent respectively). One speculation about this difference has to do with the duration and frequency of citizen' personal contacts with institutions: Contacts with schools and child care may, in contrast to many experiences with e.g., culture and health, involve frequent contacts extending over several years. The more frequent and long-lasting contacts are the more prone should people be to express views on experiences.

18. While there are no strict theoretical reasons to equate the mid-point with "don't know," the chosen procedure is justified in this context by analyses in which the voice items were split into dummy variables, using "neither nor" as the reference category. The dependent variables were then regressed on the dummies together with the controls used throughout this chapter. The analysis showed that the "don't know" dummy had no significant effects. Hence, little explanatory power is lost by collapsing the mid-point and the "don't know" category.

19. There is only one exception to this generalization. Strangely enough, poor voice opportunities in contacts with health care services significantly increase (!) support for state intervention among users of health care (.09). Given the theoretical framework, and given the previous results, this finding is indeed difficult to understand. However, although the finding is in conflict with the hypothesis, one should perhaps not make too much of it. Given how many regression analyses that have been, and will be, performed in this study, one or two instances of seemingly unexplainable coefficients could very well be produced by pure sampling error, although taken on their own these coefficients are statistically significant. Be that as it may, the basic conclusion must nevertheless be that institution-specific voice items do not affect intervention orientations.

20. These interaction terms were: voice $\times$ dissatisfaction with child care on satisfaction with democracy, voice $\times$ dissatisfaction with leisure time/culture on satisfaction with democracy, voice $\times$ dissatisfaction with public transportation on trust in politicians. In all these equations there was a significant main effect, and a sizable but not significant interaction coefficient suggesting that the impact of experienced voice is increased by approximately 50 percent among those dissatisfied with services.

Chapter Ten   The Customer, the User, and the Client

1. These results indicate that "correct treatment" ("korrekt behandlad") means something different to Swedish respondents, than "fair treatment" to American respondents. While the latter has proven to trigger procedural concerns in U.S. studies, the former appears to trigger mainly distributive concerns among Swedes.
2. The three variables build on the same information, procedure, and principles for missing data as the objective self-interest measure in chapter 7. Information on contacts with social assistance, housing allowance, and job agency, was taken from answers to the question on correct treatment in contacts with these institutions (see table 10.1).
3. Table 10.4 only reports one of the odds contrasts generated by the multinomial logit model. The reason was that only this contrast was directly addressed by theoretically driven expectations. Specifically, effects on the odds of positive experiences relative to the odds of not having been in contact, and the odds of negative experiences relative to the odds of not having been in contact, were left out of the table. An inspection of these effects showed that all three institutional variables increase the odds of reporting both negative and positive experiences (relative to reporting not having been in contact). This is logical (and trivial) since the odds of reporting *some* kind of experience always ought to grow as the number of actual contacts with institutions increases. What we are interested in, and what table 10.4 informs us about, is how the risk of negative experiences, relative to positive experiences, changes as a function of exposure to different types of institutions.
4. The categorization of Göteborg districts has previously been used by e.g., Lennart Nilsson (1996b), and is based on average household income, the proportion receiving social assistance, and the proportion of immigrants in the district. Five percent live in poor Göteborg districts as defined here, whereas seven percent live in rich districts. Twenty-nine percent of respondents live in Göteborg, which is the urban center of the Västra Götaland region and the second largest city in Sweden. The reference category "others" thus contains Göteborg residents living in neither rich nor poor districts as well as non-Göteborg residents.
5. Table 10.6 includes subjective "life satisfaction" as a control variable. While this control was not included in models of ideological orientations in other chapters, it was seen as desirable in this particular analysis. The reason is that low life satisfaction is correlated with both exposure to different welfare state designs (clients are more dissatisfied), as well as with ideological variables (as can be seen in the table, low life satisfaction is associated with greater support for state intervention and with leftist self-identification).

Chapter Eleven   The Personal and the Political Revisited

1. There are obviously prominent exceptions to this simplification. For instance, a vigorous research program has been devoted to investigating the extent to which party identification—a political orientation originally believed to be mainly, though not entirely, influenced by early socialization (Campbell et al. 1960)—is affected by issue stands and retrospective evaluations of government performance in adult life (see further Converse 1975; Fiorina 1981; Franklin and Jackson 1983; Franklin 1984; Miller and Shanks 1996).
2. One of the cornerstones of the RAS model is that, in order for predispositions to affect opinions, people need contextual information about how information surrounding the issue in question relates to basic predispositions. One of the contextual sources that citizens draw on is the pattern of party conflict on an issue: when there is elite consensus, many people have a hard time figuring out how different stands and arguments fit with their basic orientations. Conversely, such value-driven information processing becomes considerably easier when there are clear differences between parties. These findings are interesting as they point to systematic differences between America and many West European systems. The latter are typically marked by a more issue-based, polarized, and stable mode of party conflict. It has been shown that more of such conflict has a tendency to make ideological predispositions more well developed and frequently used among the citizenry (see Niemi and Westholm 1984; Granberg and Holmberg 1988; van der Eijk, Franklin, and Oppenhuis 1996; van Wijnen 2001; Kumlin 2001b). These findings thus suggest that especially ideological orientations are more important for opinion formation and political behavior in many West European political

systems, than they are in the United States. Naturally, if this is correct, it becomes even more interesting to explore the processes by which such orientations develop in adult life.

3. Zaller pursues a similar line of reasoning when he (1992:280) recognizes "a general weakness of the entire RAS framework, namely its failure to provide any mechanism for integration of information that has been acquired. By its axioms, people screen information at the point of first encountering it, but once internalized, each bit of information becomes just another consideration in a mental 'bin' full of such atomized cognitions."

4. For more in-depth discussions about the meaning and impact of media logic, see McQuail 1994, Westerståhl and Johansson 1981, Eide and Hernes 1987, Petersson and Carlberg 1990, Strömbäck 2001.

5. It should be pointed out that this trend has been combated by means of cost ceilings in especially child care and elder care.

6. My translation from original Swedish.

7. Prop. 2001/02:80.

8. For example, research shows that resource-demanding modes of exercising political influence such as encounters with public employees are less compatible with the principle of *political equality* than not so resource-demanding forms of participation such as voting (see Verba, Nie, and Kim 1978; Lijphart 1997; Sanders 1997).

References

Aardal, Bernt. 1999. "Politikerforakt og politisk misstillit." In *Velgere i 90-årene*, edited by Bernt Aardal in cooperation with Henry Valen, Hanne Marthe Narud, and Frode Berglund. Oslo: NKS-forlaget.

Aardal, Bernt and Henry Valen. 1989. *Velgere, partier og politisk avstand*. Oslo: Statistisk sentralbyrå.

Aardal, Bernt and Henry Valen. 1995. *Konflikt og opinion*. Oslo: NKS-forlaget.

Adman, Per. 1999. "Arbetslöshetens effekter på politiskt deltagande i Sverige." Paper delivered at the Nordic Political Science Association conference in Uppsala, August 1999.

Alber, Jens. 1998. "Continuities and Change in the Idea of the Welfare State." *Politics & Society* 16:451–68.

Almond, Gabriel A. and Sidney Verba. 1963. *The Civic Culture. Political Attitudes and Democracy in Five Nations*. Princeton: Princeton University Press.

Alwin, Duane F. and Jon A. Krosnick. 1991. "Aging, Cohorts, and the Stability of Sociopolitical Orientations over the Life Span." *American Journal of Sociology* 97:169–95.

Asp, Kent. 1986. *Mäktiga massmedier*. Stockholm: Akademilitteratur.

Assarsson, Jan. 1995. "Systemtilltro och brukarmissnöje." *Statsvetenskaplig Tidskrift* 98:157–84.

Baldwin, Peter. 1990. *The Politics of Social Solidarity. Class Bases of the European Welfare State 1875–1975*. Cambridge: Cambridge University Press.

Barber, Benjamin. 1984. *Strong Democracy. Participatory Politics for a New Age*. Berkely: University of California Press.

Barnes, Samuel H. and Max Kaase et al. 1979. *Political Action: Mass Participation in Five Western Democracies*. Beverly Hills: Sage.

Barr, Nicholas. 1992. "Economic Theory and the Welfare State: A Survey and Interpretation." *Journal of Economic Literature* 30:741–803.

Barret-Howard, Edith and Tom R. Tyler. 1986. "Procedural Justice as a Criterion in Allocation Decisions." *Journal of Personality and Social Psychology* 50:296–304.

Bartels, Larry M. 1996. "Uninformed Votes: Information Effects in Presidential Elections." *American Journal of Political Science* 40:194–230.

Bean, Clive and Elim Papadakis. 1998. "A Comparison of Mass Attitudes Towards the Welfare State in Different Institutional Regimes, 1985–1990." *International Journal of Public Opinion Research* 10:211–36.

Bell, Daniel. 1960. *The End of Ideology*. Glencoe: The Free Press.

Bengtsson, Åsa. 2002. *Ekonomisk röstning och politisk kontext. En studie av 266 val i parlamentariska demokratier*. Åbo: Åbo Akedemis förlag.

Bennulf, Martin. 1994. *Miljöopinionen i Sverige*. Lund: Dialogos.

Bennulf, Martin and Sören Holmberg. 1990. "The Green Breakthrough in Sweden." *Scandinavian Political Studies* 13:165–84.

Berelson, Bernard, Paul F. Lazarsfeld, and William N. McPhee. 1954. *Voting. A Study of Opinion Formation in a Presidential Campaign*. Chicago: University of Chicago Press.

Biel, Anders, Daniel Eek, and Tommy Gärling. 1997. "Distributive Justice and Willingness to Pay For Municipality Child Care." *Social Justice Research* 10:63–80.

Birgersson, Bengt Owe. 1975. *Kommunen som serviceproducent: Kommunal service och serviceattityder i 36 svenska kommuner*. Stockholm: Stockholms Universitet.

Bleiklie, Ivar. 1990. *Service Regimes. A Comparative Organizational Study of Client-Official Relations and Political Steering in Two Service Agencies*. Bergen: Department of Administration and Organization Theory, University of Bergen.

Blomqvist, Paula and Bo Rothstein. 2000. *Välfärdens nya ansikte. Demokrati och marknadsreformer inom den offentliga sektorn*. Stockholm: Agora.

Bohman, James and William Rehg (Eds.). 1997. *Deliberative Democracy. Essays on Reason and Politics*. Cambridge: The MIT Press.

Borre, Ole. 1995. "Scope-of-Government Beliefs and Political Support." In *The Scope of Government*, edited by Ole Borre and Elinor Scarbrough. Oxford: Oxford University Press.

Borre, Ole and Elinor Scarbrough (Eds.). 1995. *The Scope of Government*. Oxford: Oxford University Press.

Borre, Ole and José Manuel Viegas. 1995. "Government Intervention in the Economy." In *The Scope of Government*, edited by Ole Borre and Elinor Scarbrough. Oxford: Oxford University Press.

Borre, Ole and Jørgen Goul Andersen. 1997. *Voting and Political Attitudes in Denmark. A Study of the 1994 Election*. Aarhus: Aarhus University Press.

van den Bos, Kees, Henk A.M. Wilke, and Allan E. Lind. 1998. "When Do We Need Procedural Fairness? The Role of Trust in Authority." *Journal of Personality and Social Psychology* 75:1449–58.

Boström, Bengt-Ove. 1988. *Samtal om demokrati*. Lund: Doxa.

Brants, Kees and Hetty van Kempen. 2002. "The Ambivalent Watchdog: The Changing Culture of Political Journalism and Its Effects." In *Political Journalism. New Challenges, New Practices*, edited by Raymond Kuhn and Erik Neveu. London/New York: Routledge.

Brody, Richard A. and Paul M. Sniderman. 1977. "From Life Space to Polling Place: The Relevance of Personal Concerns for Voting Behavior." *British Journal of Political Science* 7:337–60.

Butler, David and Austin Ranney (Eds.). 1994. *Referendums Around the World: The Growing Use of Direct Democracy*. London: MacMillan.

Campbell, Angus, Gerald Gurin, and Warren E. Miller. 1954. *The Voter Decides*. Evanston: Row, Peterson & Comp.

Campbell, Angus, Philip E. Converse, Warren E. Miller, and Donald E. Stokes. 1960. *The American Voter*. New York: Wiley.

Capella, Joseph N. and Kathleen Hall Jamieson. 1997. *Spiral of Cynicism. The Press and the Public Good*. New York: Oxford University Press.

Castles, Francis. 1989. *The Comparative History of Public Policy*. Cambridge: Polity Press.

Castles, Francis G. and Deborah Mitchell. 1992. "Identifying Welfare State Regimes: The Links Between Politics, Instruments and Outcomes." *Governance* 5:1–26.

Chanley, Virginia A., Thomas J. Rudolph, and Wendy M. Rahn. 2000. "The Origins and Consequences of Public Trust in Government." *Public Opinion Quarterly* 64:239–56.

Clarke, Harold C., Nitish Dutt, and Allan Kornberg. 1993. "The Political Economy of Attitudes Toward Polity and Society in Western European Democracies." *Journal of Politics* 55:998–1021.

Clayton, Richard and Jonas Pontusson. 1998. "Welfare State Retrenchment Revisited: Entitlement Cuts, Public Sector Restructuring, and Inegalitarian Trends in Advanced Capitalist Societies." *World Politics* 51:67–98.

Conover, Pamela Johnston and Stanley Feldman. 1986. "Emotional Reactions to the Economy: I'm Mad as Hell and I'm Not Going to Take It Anymore." *American Journal of Political Science* 30:50–78.

Conover, Pamela Johnston, Stanley Feldman, and Kathleen Knight. 1986. "Judging Inflation and Unemployment: The Origins of Retrospective Evaluations." *Journal of Politics* 48:565–88.

Converse, Philip E. 1964. "The Nature of Belief Systems in Mass Publics." In *Ideology and Discontent*, edited by David E. Apter. New York: Free Press.

Converse, Philip E. 1975. "Public Opinion and Voting Behavior." In *Handbook of Political Science*, edited by Fred I. Greenstein and Nelson W. Polsby. Reading, Massachusetts: Addison-Wesley.

Coughlin, Richard M. 1980. *Ideology, Public Opinion, and Welfare Policy: Attitudes Toward Taxes and Spending in Industrialized Societies*. Berkeley: Institute of International Studies, University of California.

Cox, Robert Henry. 1998. "The Consequences of Welfare Reform: How Conceptions of Social Rights are Changing." *Journal of Social Policy* 27:1–16.

Crozier, Michel, Samuel P. Huntington, and Joji Watanuki. 1975. *The Crisis of Democracy*. New York: New York University Press.

Dahlberg, Magnus and Evert Vedung. 2001. *Demokrati och brukarutvärdering.* Lund: Studentlitteratur.

Dalton, Russell J. 2002. *Citizen Politics. Public Opinion and Political Parties in Advanced Industrial Democracies.* New York: Chatham House.

Dalton, Russel J., Ian McAllister, and Martin P. Wattenberg. 2000. "The Consequences of Partisan Dealignment." In *Parties without Partisans. Political Change in Advanced Industrial Democracies,* edited by Russel J. Dalton and Martin P. Wattenberg. Oxford: Oxford University Press.

Dalton, Russell J. 1999. "Political Support in Advanced Industrial Democracies." In *Critical Citizens. Global Support for Democratic Governance,* edited by Pippa Norris. Oxford: Oxford University Press.

Dalton, Russell J., Scott C. Flanagan, and Paul Allen Beck (Eds.). 1984. *Electoral Change in Advanced Industrial Democracies. Realignment or Dealignment?* Princeton: Princeton University Press.

Delli Carpini, Michael and Scott Keeter. 1996. *What Americans Know About Politics and Why it Matters.* New Haven: Yale University Press.

van Deth, Jan W. and Elinor Scarbrough (Eds.). 1995. *The Impact of Values.* Oxford: Oxford University Press.

Deutsch, Morton. 1985. *Distributive Justice. A Social-Psychological Perspective.* New Haven: Yale University Press.

Djerf-Pierre, Monika and Lennart Weibull. 2001. *Spegla, Granska, Tolka. Aktualitetsjournalistik i svensk radio och TV under 1900-talet.* Stockholm: Prisma.

Downs, Anthony. 1960. "Why the Government Budget is Too Small in a Democracy." *World Politics* 12:541–63.

Duit, Andreas and Tommy Möller. 1997. *Demokrati på prov. Erfarenheter av försök med föräldrastyrda skolor.* Stockholm: Skolverket.

Dunleavy, Patrick. 1979. "The Urban Basis of Political Alignment: Social Class, Domestic Property Ownership and State Intervention in Consumption Processes." *British Journal of Political Science* 9:409–43.

Dunleavy, Patrick. 1980a. "The Political Implications of Sectoral Cleavages and the Growth of State Employment: Part 1, The Analysis of Production Cleavages." *Political Studies* 28:364–83.

Dunleavy, Patrick. 1980b. "The Political Implications of Sectoral Cleavages and the Growth of State Employment: Part 2, Cleavage Structures and Political Alignment." *Political Studies* 28:527–49.

Dunleavy, Patrick. 1980c. *Urban Political Analysis: The Politics of Collective Consumption.* London: Macmillan.

Dunleavy, Patrick. 1991. *Democracy, Bureaucracy and Public Choice. Economic Explanations in Political Science.* Hemel Hempstead: Harvester Wheatsheaf.

Dunleavy, Patrick and Christopher T. Husbands. 1985. *British Democracy at the Crossroads. Voting and Party Competition in the 1980s.* London: George Allen & Unwin.

Eagly, Alice H. and Shelly Chaiken (Eds.). 1993. *The Psychology of Attitudes.* New York: Harcourt Brace Jovanovich College Publishers.

Easton, David. 1965. *A Systems Analysis of Political Life.* New York: Wiley.

Easton, David. 1975. "A Re-Assessment of the Concept of Political Support." *British Journal of Political Science* 5:435–57.

Edebalk, Per Gunnar, Ann-Charlotte Ståhlberg, and Eskil Wadensjö. 1998. *Socialförsäkringarna.* Stockholm: SNS förlag.

Edlund, Jonas. 1999a. *Citizens and Taxation. Sweden in Comparative Perspective.* Umeå: Department of Sociology, Umeå University.

Edlund, Jonas. 1999b. "Trust in Government and Welfare Regimes: Attitudes to Redistribution and Financial Cheating in the USA and Norway." *European Journal of Political Research* 35:341–70.

Eek, Daniel. 1999. *Distributive Justice and Cooperation in Real-Life Social Dilemmas.* Göteborg: Department of Psychology, Göteborg University.

Eide, Martin and Gudmund Hernes. 1987. *Død og pine! Om massemedia og helsepolitikk.* Oslo: FAFO.

van der Eijk, Cees and Mark N. Franklin (Eds.). 1996. *Choosing Europe? The European Electorate and National Politics in the Face of Union.* Ann Arbor: University of Michigan Press.

van der Eijk, Cees, Mark N. Franklin, and Erik Oppenhuis. 1996. "The Strategic Context: Party Choice." In *Choosing Europe? The European Electorate and National Politics in the Face of Union,* edited by Cees van der Eijk and Mark N. Franklin. Ann Arbor: University of Michigan Press.

Elster, Jon (Ed.). 1998. *Deliberative Democracy.* Cambridge: Cambridge University Press.

Esaiasson, Peter. 1990. *Svenska valkampanjer 1866–1988*. Stockholm: Allmänna Förlaget.

Esaiasson, Peter. 1996. "Käbblar politikerna? Om skryt, attacker och bortförklaringar i partiernas valbudskap." In *Vetenskapen om politik. Festskrift till professor emeritus Jörgen Westerståhl*, edited by Bo Rothstein and Bo Särlvik. Göteborg: Statsvetenskapliga institutionen, Göteborgs universitet.

Esaiasson, Peter and Sören Holmberg. 1996. *Representation from Above. Members of Parliament and Representative Democracy in Sweden*. Aldershot: Dartmouth.

Esaiasson, Peter and Nicklas Håkansson. 2002. *Besked ikväll! Valprogrammen i svensk radio och TV*. Värnamo: Stiftelsen Etermedierna i Sverige.

Esping-Andersen, Gøsta. 1985. *Politics Against Markets: The Social Democratic Road to Power*. Princeton: Princeton University Press.

Esping-Andersen, Gøsta. 1990. *The Three Worlds of Welfare Capitalism*. Cambridge: Polity Press.

Evans, Geoffrey. 1999. "Economics and Politics Revisited. Exploring the Decline in Conservative Support 1992–1995." *Political Studies* 47:139–51.

Feld, Lars P. and Gebhard Kirchgässner. 2000. "Official and Hidden Unemployment and the Popularity of the Government: An Econometric Analysis for the Kohl Government." *Electoral Studies* 19:333–47.

Feldman, Stanley. 1995. "Answering Survey Questions: The Measurement and Meaning of Public Opinion." In *Political Judgment: Structure and Process*, edited by Milton Lodge and Kathleen McGraw. Ann Arbor: The University of Michigan Press.

Fernlund, Siegrun. 1988. "Möte med myndighet. Formella och informella mönster i förvaltningsarkitekturen." In *Hej, det är från försäkringskassan! Informaliseringen av Sverige*, edited by Orvar Löfgren. Stockholm: Natur och Kultur.

Ferrara, Maurizio and Martin Rhodes. 2000. "Recasting European Welfare States: An Introduction." *West European Politics* 23:1–10.

Finkel, Steven E., Edward N. Muller, and Mitchell A. Seligson. 1989. "Economic Crisis, Incumbent Performance and Regime Support: A Comparison of Longitudinal Data from West Germany and Costa Rica." *British Journal of Political Science* 19:329–51.

Fiorina, Morris P. 1981. *Retrospective Voting in American National Elections*. New Haven: Yale University Press.

Fishkin, James S. 1995. *The Voice of the People. Public Opinion and Democracy*. New Haven: Yale University Press.

Fiske, Susan T. 1986. "Schema-Based Versus Piecemeal Politics: A Patchwork Quilt, But not a Blanket, of Evidence." In *Political Cognition*, edited by Richard R. Lau and David O. Sears. Hillsdale, NJ: Lawrence Erlbaum Associates.

Flora, Peter and Arnold J. Heidenheimer. 1981. *The Development of Welfare States in Europe and America*. New Brunswick: Transaction Books.

Franklin, Charles H. 1984. "Issue Preferences, Socialization, and the Evolution of Party Identification." *American Journal of Political Science* 28:459–78.

Franklin, Charles H. and John E. Jackson. 1983. "The Dynamics of Party Identification." *American Political Science Review* 77:957–73.

Franklin, Mark N. 1985. *The Decline of Class Voting in Britain. Changes in the Bases of Electoral Choice 1964–1983*. Oxford: Clarendon Press.

Franklin, Mark N. and Edward C. Page. 1984. "A Critique of the Consumption Cleavage Approach in British Voting Studies." *Political Studies* 32:521–36.

Franklin, Mark N., Tom Mackie, and Henry Valen (Eds.). 1992. *Electoral Change. Responses to Evolving Social and Attitudinal Structures in Western Countries*. Cambridge: Cambridge University Press.

Fuchs, Dieter and Hans-Dieter Klingemann. 1989. "The Left–Right Schema." In *Continuities in Political Action. A Longitudinal Study of Political Orientations in Three Western Democracies*, edited by M. Kent Jennings and Jan W. van Deth. Berlin: Walter de Gruyter & Co.

Gamson, William A. 1992. *Talking Politics*. Cambridge: Cambridge University Press.

Garcia de Polavieja, Javier. 1999. "How Do Labour Market Experiences Affect Political Attitudes? Analysing the Political Effects of Labour Market Dualisation in Spain." Working Paper 1999/142, Juan March Institute, Madrid.

Gerber, Alan and Donald Philip Green. 1999. "Misperceptions about Perceptual Bias." *Annual Review of Political Science* 2:189–210.

Gilljam, Mikael. 1988. *Svenska folket och löntagarfonderna.* Lund: Studentlitteratur.

Gilljam, Mikael. 1990. "Sex förklaringar till valet av parti." In *Rött, Blått, Grönt. En bok om 1988 års riksdagsval,* edited by Mikael Gilljam and Sören Holmberg. Stockholm: Bonniers.

Gilljam, Mikael and Lennart Nilsson. 1985. "Svenska folkets åsikter om den offentliga sektorn—två förklaringsansatser." *Statsvetenskaplig tidskrift* 88:123–39.

Gilljam, Mikael and Sören Holmberg (Eds.). 1990. *Rött, blått, grönt. En bok om 1988 års riksdagsval.* Stockholm: Bonniers.

Gilljam, Mikael and Sören Holmberg. 1993. *Väljarna inför 1990-talet.* Stockholm: Norstedts.

Gilljam, Mikael and Sören Holmberg. 1995. *Väljarnas val.* Stockholm: Norstedts.

Gilljam, Mikael and Sören Holmberg. 1998. *Det första Europaparlamentsvalet.* Stockholm: Norstedts.

Goldsmith, Michael. 1995. "The Growth of Government." In *The Scope of Government,* edited by Ole Borre and Elinor Scarbrough. Oxford: Oxford University Press.

Goodsell, Charles T. 1977. "Bureaucratic Manipulation of Symbols: An Empirical Study." *American Journal of Political Science* 21:79–91.

Goodsell, Charles T. (Ed.). 1981. *The Public Encounter. Where State and Citizen Meet.* Bloomington: Indiana University Press.

Goodsell, Charles T. 1983. *The Case for Bureaucracy. A Public Administration Polemic.* Chatham, NJ: Chatham House Publishers.

Goul Andersen, Jørgen. 1993. "Sources of Welfare State Support in Denmark: Self-Interest or Way of Life?" In *Welfare Trends in the Scandinavian Countries,* edited by Erik Jørgen Hansen, Stein Ringen, Hannu Uusitalo, and Robert Erikson. London: M.E. Sharpe.

Goul Andersen, Jørgen. 1999. "Changing Labour Markets, New Social Divisions and Welfare State Support." In *The End of the Welfare State,* edited by Stefan Svallfors and Peter Taylor-Gooby. London: Routledge.

Goul Andersen, Jørgen. 2000. "Magt og afmagt: Nytt perspektiv på 'political efficacy.'" In *Hvad folket magter. Demokrati, magt og afmagt,* edited by Jørgen Goul Andersen, Lars Torpe, and Johannes Andersen. København: Jurist- og økonomiforbundets forlag.

Goul Andersen, Jørgen and Jens Hoff. 2001. *Democracy and Citizenship in Scandinavia.* New York: Palgrave.

Goul Andersen, Jørgen, Lars Torpe, and Johannes Andersen (Eds.). 2000. *Hvad folket magter. Demokrati, magt og afmagt.* København: Jurist- og økonomiforbundets forlag.

Granberg, Donald and Sören Holmberg. 1988. *The Political System Matters. Social Psychology and Voting Behavior in Sweden and the United States.* Cambridge: Cambridge University Press.

Granberg, Donald and Sören Holmberg. 1996. "Attitude Constraint and Stability Among Elite and Mass in Sweden." *European Journal of Political Research* 29:59–72.

Green, Donald Philip. 1988. *Self-interest, Public Opinion and Mass Political Behavior.* Doctoral Dissertation, University of California, Berkely.

Green, Donald Philip and Ian Shapiro. 1994. *Pathologies of Rational Choice Theory: A Critique of Applications in Political Science.* New Haven: Yale University Press.

Grimes, Marcia. 2001. "Procedural Justice and its Policy Implications." Department of Political Science, Göteborg University.

Grip, Gunvall. 2001. "Social, avtalad och privat försäkring i Sverige under 1990-talet." In *Välfärdens finansiering och fördelning, SOU 2001:57,* edited by Johan Fritzell and Joakim Palme. Stockholm: Fritzes.

Hadenius, Axel. 1986. *A Crisis of the Welfare State?* Uppsala: Almquist & Wiksell.

Hadenius, Axel. 2001. *Demokrati. En jämförande analys.* Malmö: Liber.

Halleröd, Björn. 1994. *Poverty in Sweden: A New Approach to the Direct Measurement of Consensual Poverty.* Umeå: Sociologiska institutionen, Umeå universitet.

Halleröd, Björn, Staffan Marklund, Anders Nordlund, and Mikael Stattin. 1993. *Konsensuell fattigdom— en studie av konsumtion och attityder till konsumtion.* Umeå: Sociologiska institutionen, Umeå universitet.

Hastie, Reid and Bernadette Park. 1986. "The Relationship Between Memory and Judgment Depends on Whether the Judgment Task is Memory-Based or On-Line." *Psychological Review* 93:258–68.

Hedberg, Per. 2000. *Europaparlamentsvalundersökning 1999. Variabelförteckning, marginalfördelningar, bilagor.* Statsvetenskapliga institutionen, Göteborgs universitet.

Held, David. 1987. *Models of Democracy*. Cambridge: Polity Press.

Hetherington, Marc J. 1998. "The Political Relevance of Political Trust." *American Political Science Review* 92:791–808.

Heunks, Felix J. 1989. "From Personal to Political." In *Continuities in Political Action. A Longitudinal Study of Political Orientations in Three Western Democracies*, edited by M. Kent Jennings and Jan W. van Deth. Berlin: Walter de Gruyter & Co.

Hibbs, Douglas. 1993. *Solidarity or Egoism? The Economics of Sociotropic and Egocentric Influences on Political Behavior: Denmark in International and Theoretical Perspective*. Aarhus: Aarhus University Press.

Hirschman, Albert O. 1970. *Exit, Voice and Loyalty. Responses to Decline in Firms, Organizations and States*. Cambridge, MA: Harvard University Press.

Hochschild, Jennifer L. 1981. *What's Fair: American Beliefs About Distributive Justice*. Cambridge: Harvard University Press.

Hoff, Jens. 1993. "Medborgerskab, brukerrolle og magt." In *Medborgerskab—Demokrati och politisk deltagelse*, edited by Johannes Andersen, A.-D. Christensen, K. Langberg, Birte Siim, and Lars Torpe. Viborg: Systeme.

Hofferbert, Richard I. and David Louis Cingranelli. 1996. "Public Policy and Administration: Comparative Policy Analysis." In *A New Handbook of Political Science*, edited by Robert E. Goodin and Hans-Dieter Klingemann. Oxford: Oxford University Press.

Holmberg, Sören. 1981. *Svenska väljare*. Stockholm: Liber.

Holmberg, Sören. 1984. *Väljare i förändring*. Stockholm: Liber.

Holmberg, Sören. 1996. "Svensk åsiktsöverensstämmelse." In *Vetenskapen om politik. Festskrift till professor emeritus Jörgen Westerståhl*, edited by Bo Rothstein and Bo Särlvik. Göteborg: Statsvetenskapliga institutionen, Göteborgs universitet.

Holmberg, Sören. 1999. "Down and Down We Go: Political Trust in Sweden." In *Critical Citizens. Global Support for Democratic Governance*, edited by Pippa Norris. Oxford: Oxford University Press.

Holmberg, Sören. 2000. *Välja parti*. Stockholm: Norstedts juridik.

Holmberg, Sören and Kent Asp. 1984. *Kampen om kärnkraften. En bok om väljare, massmedier och folkomröstningen 1980*. Stockholm: Liber.

Holmberg, Sören and Lennart Weibull (Eds.). 1997. *Trends in Swedish Opinion*. Göteborg: The SOM Institute, Göteborg University.

Holmberg, Sören and Lennart Weibull (Eds.). 1999. *Ljusnande framtid*. Göteborg: SOM-institutet, Göteborgs universitet, SOM-rapport 22.

Holmberg, Sören and Lennart Weibull (Eds.). 2000. *Det nya samhället*. Göteborg: SOM-institutet, Göteborgs universitet, SOM-rapport 24.

Holmberg, Sören and Lennart Weibull (Eds.). 2002. *Det våras för politiken*. Göteborg: SOM-institutet, Göteborgs universitet, SOM-rapport 30.

Holmberg, Sören and Mikael Gilljam. 1987. *Väljare och val i Sverige*. Stockholm: Bonniers.

Holmberg, Sören, Per Hedberg, Henrik Oscarsson, Martin Bennulf, Staffan Kumlin, Maria Oskarson, Rutger Lindahl, and Martin Brothén. 2001. *EuropaOpinionen*. Göteborg: Statsvetenskapliga institutionen, Göteborgs universitet.

Huckfeldt, Robert and John Sprague. 1995. *Citizens, Politics and Social Communication*. Cambridge: Cambridge University Press.

Huckfeldt, Robert, Jeffrey Levine, William Morgan, and John Sprague. 1999. "Accessibility and the Political Utility of Partisan and Ideological Orientations." *American Journal of Political Science* 43:888–911.

Huseby, Beate M. 1995. "Attitudes Towards the Size of Government." In *The Scope of Government*, edited by Ole Borre and Elinor Scarbrough. Oxford: Oxford University Press.

Huseby, Beate M. 1999. "Government Economic Performance and Political Support." In *Challanges to Representative Democracy. Parties, Voters and Public Opinion*, edited by Hanne Marthe Narud and Toril Aalberg. Bergen: Fagbokforlaget.

Huseby, Beate M. 2000. *Government Performance and Political Support. A Study of How Evaluations of Economic Performance, Social Policy and Environmental Protection Influence the Popular Assessments of the Political System*. Trondheim: Department of Sociology and Political Science, Norwegian University of Technology (NTNU).

Håkansson, Nicklas. 1999. *Valretorik. Om politiskt språk i partipropagandan*. Göteborg: Statsvetenskapliga institutionen.

Immergut, Ellen M. 1998. "The Theoretical Core of the New Institutionalism." *Politics & Society* 26:5–34.

Inglehart, Ronald. 1977. *The Silent Revolution: Changing Values and Political Styles Among Western Publics.* Princeton: Princeton University Press.

Inglehart, Ronald. 1981. "Postmaterialism in an Environment of Insecurity." *American Political Science Review* 75:880–900.

Inglehart, Ronald. 1990. *Cultural Shift in Advanced Industrial Society.* Princeton: Princeton University Press.

Inglehart, Ronald. 1997. "Postmaterialist Values and the Erosion of Institutional Authority." In *Why People Don't Trust Government*, edited by Joseph S. Jr. Nye, Philip D. Zelikow, and David C. King. Cambridge, MA: Harvard University Press.

Inglehart, Ronald. 1999. "Postmodernization Erodes Respect for Authority, but Increases Support for Democracy." In *Critical Citizens. Global Support for Democratic Governance*, edited by Pippa Norris. Oxford: Oxford University Press.

Inglehart, Ronald and Hans-Dieter Klingemann. 1976. "Party Identification, Ideological Preference, and the Left–Right Dimension among Western Mass Publics." In *Party Identification and Beyond*, edited by Ian Budge, Ivor Crewe, and Dennis Farlie. London: John Wiley.

Iyengar, Shanto and Donald R. Kinder. 1987. *News that Matters. Television and American Opinion.* Chicago: The University of Chicago Press.

Jacobs, Lawrence R. and Robert Y. Shapiro. 1994. "Studying Substantive Democracy." *Political Science & Politics* 27:9–17.

Jarl, Maria. 2001. "Erfarenheter av ett utbrett brukarinflytande. En utredning om brukarinflytandet i Sverige 2001." In *Ds 2001:34 Ökade möjligheter till brukarinflytande.*

Jennings, M. Kent and Jan W. van Deth (Eds.). 1989. *Continuities in Political Action. A Longitudinal Study of Political Orientations in Three Western Democracies.* Berlin: Walter de Gruyter & Co.

Jennings, M. Kent and Richard G. Niemi. 1974. *The Political Character of Adolescence: The Influence of Families and Schools.* Princeton: Princeton University Press.

Jenssen, Anders Todal. 1998. "Personal Economies and Economic Expectations." In *To Join or Not to Join*, edited by Anders Todal Jenssen, Pertti Pesonen, and Mikael Gilljam. Oslo: Scandinavian University Press.

Jenssen, Anders Todal, Pertti Pesonen, and Mikael Gilljam (Eds.). 1998. *To Join or Not to Join.* Oslo: Scandinavian University Press.

Johansson, Bengt. 1998. *Nyheter mitt ibland oss. Kommunala nyheter, personlig erfarenhet och lokal opinions-bildning.* Göteborg: Institutionen för journalistik och masskommunikation, Göteborgs universitet.

Johansson, Bengt. 2000. "Medierna och krisen i hälso—och sjukvårdsstyrelsen." In *Den nya regionen*, edited by Lennart Nilsson. Göteborg: SOM-institutet, Göteborgs universitet, SOM-rapport 25.

Johansson, Folke, Lennart Nilsson, and Lars Strömberg. 2001. *Kommunal demokrati under fyra decennier.* Malmö: Liber.

Johansson, Sanna and Åsa Nilsson. 2002. "Riks- och Väst-SOM 2001: En jämförelse i svarsmönster." Presenterat vid SOM-institutets utvärderingskonferens, Gdansk, mars 2002.

Jordahl, Henrik. 2002. *Essays on Voting Behavior, Labor Market Policy, and Taxation.* Uppsala: Department of Economics, Uppsala University.

Kaase, Max and Kenneth Newton. 1995. *Beliefs in Government.* Oxford: Oxford University Press.

Karlsson, Lars. 2003. *Konflikt eller harmoni? Individuella rättigheter och ansvarsutkrävande i svensk och brittisk sjukvård.* Göteborg: Göteborg Studies in Politics 81.

Katz, Elihu and Brenda Danet (Eds.). 1973. *Bureaucracy and the Public. A Reader in Official-Client Relations.* New York: Basic Books.

Katz, Elihu and Paul F. Lazarsfeld. 1955. *Personal Influence. The Part Played by People in the Flow of Mass Communications.* New York: The Free Press.

Katz, Daniel, Barbara A. Gutek, Robert L. Kahn, and Eugenia Barton. 1975. *Bureaucratic Encounters. A Pilot Study in the Evaluation of Government Services.* Ann Arbor: Survey Research Center, Institute for Social Research, The University of Michigan.

Kelley, Stanley Jr. and T. Mirer. 1974. "The Simple Act of Voting." *American Political Science Review* 68:572–91.

Kinder, Donald R. 1998. "Communication and Opinion." *Annual Review of Political Science* 1:167–97.

Kinder, Donald R. and David O. Sears. 1985. "Public Opinion and Political Action." In *Handbook of Social Psychology*, edited by Gardner Lindzey and Elliot Aronson. New York: Random House.

Kinder, Donald R. and D. Roderick Kiewiet. 1981. "Sociotropic Politics: The American Case." *British Journal of Political Science* 11:129–61.

Klapper, Joseph T. 1960. *The Effects of Mass Communication*. New York: Free Press.

Klingemann, Hans-Dieter. 1999. "Mapping Political Support in the 1990s: A Global Analysis." In *Critical Citizens. Global Support for Democratic Governance*, edited by Pippa Norris. Oxford: Oxford University Press.

Klingemann, Hans-Dieter and Dieter Fuchs (Eds.). 1995. *Citizens and the State*. Oxford: Oxford University Press.

Knutsen, Oddbjørn. 1995. "Value Orientations, Political Conflicts and Left–Right Identification: A Comparative Study." *European Journal of Political Research* 28:63–93.

Knutsen, Oddbjørn. 1998a. "Europeans Move Towards the Center: A Comparative Longitudinal Study of Left–Right Self-Placement in Western Europe." *International Journal of Public Opinion Research* 10:292–316.

Knutsen, Oddbjørn. 1998b. *Social Class, Sector Employment and Gender as Political Cleavages in the Scandinavian Countries. A Comparative Longitudinal Study, 1970–95*. University of Oslo, Faculty of Social Sciences.

Knutsen, Oddbjørn. 1998c. "The Strength of the Partisan Component of Left–Right Identity. A Comparative Longitudinal Study of Left–Right Party Polarisation in Eight West European Countries." *Party Politics* 4:5–31.

Kornberg, Allan and Harold D. Clarke. 1992. *Citizens and Community. Political Support in a Representative Democracy*. Cambridge: Cambridge University Press.

Kornhauser, William. 1959. *The Politics of Mass Society*. Glencoe: Free Press.

Korpi, Walter. 1980. "Social Policy and Distributional Conflict in the Capitalist Democracies." *West European Politics* 3:296–316.

Korpi, Walter. 1983. *The Democratic Class Struggle*. London: Routledge.

Kristensen, Niels Nørgaard. 1998. *Skolbestyrelser og demokratisk deltagelse*. København: Jurist- og økonomiforbundets forlag.

Krosnick, Jon A. 1991. "The Stability of Political Preferences: Comparisons of Symbolic and Nonsymbolic Attitudes." *American Journal of Political Science* 35:547–76.

Krosnick, Jon A. 2002. "The Challenges of Political Psychology: Lessons to be Learned from Research on Attitude Perception." In *Thinking About Political Psychology*, edited by James H. Kuklinski. Cambridge: Cambridge University Press.

Kuhnle, Stein. 2000. "The Scandinavian Welfare State in the 1990s: Challenged but Viable." *West European Politics* 23:209–28.

Kumlin, Staffan. 1997. "Folket och högervågen. Om opinionsbildning, samhällsstrukturer och ideologisk förändring i 1980-talets Sverige." *Statsvetenskaplig tidskrift* 100:411–40.

Kumlin, Staffan. 2001a. "Missnöje på hemmaplan." In *EuropaOpinionen*, edited by Sören Holmberg, Per Hedberg, Henrik Oscarsson, Martin Bennulf, Staffan Kumlin, Maria Oskarson, Rutger Lindahl, and Martin Brothén. Göteborg: Statsvetenskapliga institutionen, Göteborgs universitet.

Kumlin, Staffan. 2001b. "Ideology-Driven Opinion Formation in Europe: The Case of Attitudes towards the Third Sector in Sweden." *European Journal of Political Research* 39:487–518.

Kumlin, Staffan. 2002. "Government Performance and Political Legitimacy." Chapter draft presented at the conference of the TMR network on "Political Representation in Europe," Cadenabbia, Italy, May 2002.

Kumlin, Staffan and Bo Rothstein 2003. "Staten och det sociala kapitalet." In *Välfärdsstat i otakt*, edited by Jon Pierre and Bo Rothstein. Malmö: Liber.

Kumlin, Staffan and Maria Oskarson. 2000. "Opinionsbildning som dragkamp: företaget Sverige möter den svenska välfärdsstaten." In *Den nya regionen*, edited by Lennart Nilsson. Göteborg: SOM-institutet, Göteborgs universitet, SOM-rapport 25.

Lane, Robert E. 1962. *Political Ideology. Why the American Common Man Believes What He Does*. New York: The Free Press.

Lane, Robert E. 1986. "Market Justice, Political Justice." *American Political Science Review* 80:383–402.

Lapinski, John S., Charles R. Riemann, Robert Y. Shapiro, Matthew F. Stevens, and Lawrence R. Jacobs. 1998. "Welfare State Regimes and Subjective Well-Being: A Cross-National Study." *International Journal of Public Opinion Research* 10:2–24.

Lau, Richard R. and David O. Sears (Eds.). 1986. *Political Cognition*. Hillsdale, NJ: Lawrence Erlbaum Associates.

Lavine, Howard. 2002. "On-Line Versus Memory-Based Process Models of Political Evaluation." In *Political Psychology*, edited by Kristen Renwick Monroe. Mahwah: Lawrence Erlbaum Associates.

Levi, Margaret. 1993. "Are There Limits to Rationality?" *Archives Européennes de Sociologie* 32:130–41.

Levi, Margaret. 1997. *Consent, Dissent, and Patriotism*. New York: Cambridge University Press.

Lewin, Leif. 1988. *Det gemensamma bästa. Om egenintresset och allmänintresset i västerländsk politik*. Stockholm: Carlssons Bokförlag.

Lewin, Leif. 1991. *Self-Interest and Public Interest in Western Politics*. Oxford: Oxford University Press.

Lewin, Leif. 2001. "Att utkräva politiskt ansvar." *Politologen*.

Lewis-Beck, Michael S. 1988. *Economics & Elections. The Major Western Democracies*. Ann Arbor, MI: The University of Michigan Press.

Lewis-Beck, Michael S. and Martin Paldam. 2000. "Economic Voting: An Introduction." *Electoral Studies* 19:113–21.

Lijphart, Arend. 1997. "Unequal Participation: Democracy's Unresolved Dilemma." *American Political Science Review* 91:1–14.

Lind, Allan E. and Tom R. Tyler. 1988. *The Social Psychology of Procedural Justice*. New York: Plenum Press.

Lind, E. Allan, Ruth Kanfer, and P. Christopher Earley. 1990. "Voice, Control, and Procedural Justice: Instrumental and Noninstrumental Concerns in Fairness Judgments." *Journal of Personality and Social Psychology* 59:952–59.

Lindbom, Anders. 1995. *Medborgarskapet i välfärdsstaten. Föräldrainflytande i skandinavisk grundskola*. Uppsala: Acta Universitatis Upsaliensis.

Lindbom, Anders. 1998. "Institutional Legacies and the Role of Citizens in the Scandinavian Welfare State." *Scandinavian Political Studies* 21:109–28.

Lindbom, Anders. 2001. "Dismantling the Social Democratic Welfare Model? Has the Swedish Welfare State Lost Its Defining Characteristics." *Scandinavian Political Studies* 24:171–93.

Lindqvist, Rafael (Ed.). 1998. *Organisation och välfärdsstat*. Lund: Studentlitteratur.

Lindqvist, Rafael and Klas Borell. 1998. "Inledning: Organisation och välfärdspolitik." In *Organisation och välfärdsstat*, edited by Rafael Lindqvist. Lund: Studentlitteratur.

Lippman, Walter. 1922. *Public Opinion*. London: George Allen & Unwin.

Lipset, Seymour Martin and Stein Rokkan (Eds.). 1967. *Party Systems and Voter Alignments*. New York: The Free Press.

Lipsky, Michael. 1980. *Street-Level Bureaucracy. Dilemmas of the Individual in Public Services*. New York: Russell Sage Foundation.

Listhaug, Ola. 1995. "The Dynamics of Trust in Politicians." In *Citizens and the State*, edited by Hans-Dieter Klingemann and Dieter Fuchs. Oxford: Oxford University Press.

Listhaug, Ola and Arthur H. Miller. 1985. "Public Support for Tax Evasion: Self-interest or Symbolic Politics?" *European Journal of Political Research* 13:265–82.

Lodge, Milton and Patrick Stroh. 1993. "Inside the Mental Voting Booth: An Impression-Driven Process Model of Candidate Evaluation." In *Explorations in Political Psychology*, edited by Shanto Iyengar and William J. McGuire. Durham: Duke University Press.

Lodge, Milton, Kathleen M. McGraw, and Patrick Stroh. 1989. "An Impression-Driven Model of Candidate Evaluation." *American Political Science Review* 83:399–419.

Lodge, Milton, Marco R. Steenbergen, and Shawn Brau. 1995. "The Responsive Voter: Campaign Information and the Dynamics of Candidate Evaluation." *American Political Science Review* 89:309–26.

Lolle, Henrik. 1999. *Serviceudgifter og brugertilfredshed i danske kommuner*. Aalborg: Aalborg Universitetsforlag.

Long, J. Scott. 1997. *Regression Models for Categorical and Limited Dependent Variables*. Thousands Oaks: Sage.

Lupia, Arthur. 1994. "Shortcuts versus Encyklopedias: Information and Voting Behavior in California Insurance Reform Elections." *American Political Science Review* 88:63–76.

Luskin, Robert C. 1987. "Measuring Political Sophistication." *American Journal of Political Science* 31:857–89.

Luskin, Robert C. 2002. "From Denial to Extenuation (and Finally Beyond): Political Sophistication and Citizen Performance." In *Thinking About Political Psychology*, edited by James H. Kuklinski. Cambridge: Cambridge University Press.

MacKuen, Michael B., Robert S. Erikson, and James A. Stimson. 1992. "Peasants or Bankers? The American Electorate and the US Economy." *American Political Science Review* 86:597–611.

Manin, Bernhard. 1997. *The Principles of Representative Government*. Cambridge: Cambridge University Press.

Mansbridge, Jane J. (Ed.). 1990. *Beyond Self-Interest*. Chicago: The University of Chicago Press.

March, James G. and Johan P. Olsen. 1984. "The New Institutionalism: Organizational Factors in Political Life." *American Political Science Review* 78:734–49.

March, James G. and Johan P. Olsen. 1989. *Rediscovering Institutions. Organizational Basis of Politics*. New York: The Free Press.

March, James G. and Johan P. Olsen. 1996. "Institutional Perspectives on Political Institutions." *Governance* 9.

Markus, Gregory B. 1988. "The Impact of Personal and National Economic Conditions on the Presidential Vote: A Pooled Cross-Sectional Analysis." *American Journal of Political Science* 32:137–54.

Marshall, T.H. 1950. *Citizenship and Social Class*. Cambridge: Cambridge University Press.

McAllister, Ian. 1999. "The Economic Performance of Governments." In *Critical Citizens. Global Support for Democratic Governance*, edited by Pippa Norris. Oxford: Oxford University Press.

McCombs, Maxwell. 1999. "Personal Involvement with Issues on the Public Agenda." *International Journal of Public Opinion Research* 11:152–68.

McCombs, Maxwell and Donald L. Shaw. 1972. "The Agenda-Setting Function of the Mass Media." *Public Opinion Quarterly* 36:176–87.

McGraw, Kathleen M. and Clark Hubbard. 1996. "Some of the People Some of the Time: Individual Differences in Acceptance of Political Accounts." In *Political Persuasion and Attitude Change*, edited by Diana C. Mutz, Paul M. Sniderman, and Richard A. Brody. Ann Arbor: The University of Michigan Press.

McGuire, William J. 1985. "Attitudes and Attitude Change." In *Handbook of Social Psychology. Volume II. Special Fields and Applications*, edited by Gardner Lindzey and Elliot Aronson. New York: Random House.

McQuail, Denis. 1994. *Mass Communication Theory. An Introduction*. London: Sage.

Miller, Arthur. 1974. "Political Issues and Trust in Government: 1964–1970." *American Political Science Review* 68:951–72.

Miller, Arthur and Ola Listhaug. 1984. "Economic Effects on the Vote in Norway." *Political Behavior* 6:301–19.

Miller, Arthur and Ola Listhaug. 1999. "Political Performance and Institutional Trust." In *Critical Citizens. Global Support for Democratic Governance*, edited by Pippa Norris. Oxford: Oxford University Press.

Miller, Joanne M. and Jon A. Krosnick. 1996. "News Media Impact on the Ingredients of Presidential Evaluations: A Program of Research on the Priming Hypothesis." In *Political Persuasion and Attitude Change*, edited by Diana C. Mutz, Paul M. Sniderman, and Richard A. Brody. Ann Arbor: The University of Michigan Press.

Miller, Warren E. and Merrill J. Shanks. 1996. *The New American Voter*. Cambridge: Harvard University Press.

Minkenberg, Michael and Ronald Inglehart. 1989. "Neoconservatism and Value Change in the USA: Tendencies in the Mass Public of a Postindustrial Society" in *Contemporary Political Culture*, edited by John Gibbins. London: Sage.

Mondak, Jeffery J., Diana C. Mutz, and Robert Huckfeldt. 1996. "Persuasion in Context: The Multilevel Structure of Economic Evaluations." In *Political Persuasion and Attitude Change*, edited by Diana C. Mutz, Paul M. Sniderman, and Richard A. Brody. Ann Arbor: The University of Michigan Press.

Monroe, Kristen and Lynda Erickson. 1986. "The Economy and Political Support: The Canadian Case." *Journal of Politics* 48:617–47.

Mutz, Diana C. 1992. "Mass Media and the Depoliticization of Personal Experience." *American Journal of Political Science* 36:483–508.

Mutz, Diana C. 1994. "Contextualizing Personal Experience: The Role of the Mass Media." *Journal of Politics* 56:689–714.

Mutz, Diana C. 1998. *Impersonal Influence. How Perceptions of Mass Collectives Affect Political Attitudes*. Cambridge: Cambridge University Press.

Möller, Tommy. 1996. *Brukare och klienter i välfärdsstaten. Om missnöje och påverkansmöjligheter inom barn- och äldreomsorg*. Stockholm: Publica.

Nadeau, Richard, Richard G. Niemi, and Timothy Amato. 2000. "Elite Economic Forecasts, Economic News, Mass Economic Expectations, and Voting Intentions in Great Britain." *European Journal of Political Research* 38:135–70.

Nadeau, Richard, Richard G. Niemi, David P. Fan, and Timothy Amato. 1999. "Elite Economic Forecasts, Economic News, Mass Economic Judgments, and Presidential Approval." *Journal of Politics* 61:109–35.

Neuman, Russell W., Marion R. Just, and Ann N. Crigler. 1992. *Common Knowledge. News and the Construction of Political Meaning*. Chicago: University of Chicago Press.

Newton, Kenneth. 1999. "Social and Political Trust in Established Democracies." In *Critical Citizens. Global Support for Democratic Governance*, edited by Pippa Norris. Oxford: Oxford University Press.

Newton, Kenneth and Pippa Norris. 2000. "Confidence in Public Institutions: Faith, Culture, or Performance?" in *Disaffected Democracies. What's Troubling the Trilateral Countries?* edited by Susan J. Pharr and Robert D. Putnam. Princeton: Princeton University Press.

Nie, Norman H., Sidney Verba, and John R. Petrocik. 1979. *The Changing American Voter*. Cambridge: Harvard University Press.

Niemi, Richard G. and Anders Westholm. 1984. "Issues, Parties, and Attitudinal Stability: A Comparative Study of Sweden and the United States." *Electoral Studies* 3:65–83.

Niemi, Richard G. and Herbert F. Weisberg (Eds.). 1993. *Controversies in Voting Behavior*. Washington: CQ Press.

Niemi, Richard G., Stephen C. Craig, and Franco Mattei. 1991. "Measuring Internal Political Efficacy in the 1988 National Election Study." *American Political Science Review* 85:1407–13.

Nilsson, Lennart. 1995. "Att spara eller inte spara." In *Det gamla riket*, edited by Sören Holmberg and Lennart Weibull. Göteborg: SOM-institutet, Göteborgs universitet, SOM-rapport 13.

Nilsson, Lennart. 1996a. "Medborgarna och servicedemokratin." In *Vetenskapen om politik. Festskrift till professor emeritus Jörgen Westerståhl*, edited by Bo Rothstein and Bo Särlvik. Göteborg: Statsvetenskapliga institutionen, Göteborgs universitet.

Nilsson, Lennart. 1996b. "Medborgarna och den lokala välfärdsstaten." In *Västsvenska perspektiv*, edited by Lennart Nilsson. Göteborg: SOM-institutet, Göteborgs universitet, SOM-rapport 14.

Nilsson, Lennart. 1997. "Välfärd och lycka i Västsverige." In *Nya landskap*, edited by Lennart Nilsson. Göteborg: SOM-institutet, Göteborgs universitet, SOM-rapport 19.

Nilsson, Lennart (Ed.). 1999. *Region i omvandling*. Göteborg: SOM-institutet, Göteborgs universitet, SOM-rapport 23.

Nilsson, Lennart (Ed.). 2000a. *Den nya regionen*. Göteborg: SOM-institutet, Göteborgs universitet, SOM-rapport 25.

Nilsson, Lennart. 2000b. "Välfärd i obalans." In *Det nya samhället*, edited by Sören Holmberg and Lennart Weibull. Göteborg: SOM-institutet, Göteborgs universitet, SOM-rapport 24.

Nilsson, Åsa and Peder Olsson. 2000. "Samhälle Opinion Massmedia Västra Götaland 1999." in *Den nya regionen*, edited by Lennart Nilsson. Göteborg: SOM-institutet, Göteborgs universitet, SOM-rapport 25.

Norpoth, Helmuth. 1996. "The Economy." In *Comparing Democracies. Elections and Voting in Comparative Perspective*, edited by Lawrence LeDuc, Richard G. Niemi, and Pippa Norris. Thousand Oaks: Sage.

Norris, Pippa (Ed.). 1999. *Critical Citizens. Global Support for Democratic Governance*. Oxford: Oxford University Press.

Nye, Joseph S. Jr. 1999. "Foreword." In *Critical Citizens. Global Support for Democratic Governance*, edited by Pippa Norris. Oxford: Oxford University Press.

Nye, Joseph S. Jr., Philip D. Zelikow, and David C. King (Eds.). 1997. *Why People Don't Trust Government*. Cambridge: Harvard University Press.

Olsson, Sven E. 1993. *Social Policy and Welfare State in Sweden*. Lund: Arkiv.

Oscarsson, Henrik. 1998. *Den svenska partirymden. Väljarnas uppfattningar av konfliktstrukturen i partisystemet 1956–1996*. Göteborg University: Department of Political Science.

Oskarson, Maria. 1990. "Klassröstning på reträtt." In *Rött, blått, grönt. En bok om 1988 års riksdagsval*, edited by Mikael Gilljam and Sören Holmberg. Stockholm: Bonniers.

Oskarson, Maria. 1992. "Sweden." In *Electoral Change. Responses to Evolving Social and Attitudinal Structures in Western Countries*, edited by Mark N. Franklin, Tom Mackie, and Henry Valen. Cambridge: Cambridge University Press.

Oskarson, Maria. 1994. *Klassröstning i Sverige. Rationalitet, lojalitet eller bara slentrian*. Stockholm: Nerenius & Santerus.

Oskarson, Maria and Kristen Ringdal. 1998. "The Arguments." In *To Join or Not to Join*, edited by Anders Todal Jenssen, Pertti Pesonen, and Mikael Gilljam. Oslo: Scandinavian University Press.

Ostrom, Elinor. 1995. "New Horizons in Institutional Analysis." *American Political Science Review* 89:174–78.

Paldam, Martin and Peter Nannestad. 2000. "Into Pandoras's Box of Economic Evaluations: A Study of the Danish Macro VP-function, 1986–1997." *Electoral Studies* 19:123–40.

Papadakis, Elim. 1993. "Class Interests, Class Politics, and Welfare State Regime." *British Journal of Sociology* 44:249–70.

Papadakis, Elim and Clive Bean. 1993. "Popular Support for the Welfare State: A Comparison Between Institutional Regimes." *Journal of Public Policy* 13:227–54.

Pateman, Carole. 1970. *Participation and Democratic Theory*. Cambridge: Cambridge University Press.

Patterson, Thomas E. 1993. *Out of Order*. New York: Knopf.

Peters, B. Guy. 1991. *The Politics of Taxation. A Comparative Perspective*. Cambridge: Blackwell.

Peters, B. Guy. 1999. *Institutional Theory in Political Science. The New Institutionalism*. London: Pinter.

Peters, B. Guy and Jon Pierre. 2000. "Citizens Versus the New Public Manager: The Problem of Mutual Empowerment." *Administration & Society* 32:9–28.

Petersson, Olof. 1977. *Väljarna och valet 1976*. Stockholm: Statistiska centralbyrån.

Petersson, Olof. 1982. "Klassidentifikation." In *Väljare Partier Massmedia. Empiriska studier i svensk demokrati*, edited by Kent Asp, Stig Hadenius, Sören Holmberg, Rutger Lindahl, Björn Molin, Olof Petersson, and Lennart Weibull. Stockholm: Liber.

Petersson, Olof and Ingrid Carlberg. 1990. *Makten över tanken*. Stockholm: Carlssons.

Petersson, Olof, Anders Westholm, and Göran Blomberg. 1989. *Medborgarnas makt*. Stockholm: Carlssons Bokförlag.

Petersson, Olof, Jörgen Hermansson, Michele Micheletti, Jan Teorell, and Anders Westholm. 1998. *Demokrati och medborgarskap. Demokratirådets rapport 1998*. Stockholm: SNS förlag.

Petersson, Olof, Gudmund Hernes, Sören Holmberg, Lise Togeby, and Lena Wängnerud. 2000. *Demokrati utan partier. Demokratirådets rapport 2000*. Stockholm: SNS förlag.

Pettersen, Per Arnt. 1995. "The Welfare State: The Security Dimension." In *The Scope of Government*, edited by Ole Borre and Elinor Scarbrough. Oxford: Oxford University Press.

Pettersen, Per Arnt. 2001. "Welfare State Legitimacy: Ranking, Rating, Paying." *Scandinavian Political Studies* 24:27–49.

Petty, Richard T. and John E. Cacioppo. 1986. *Communication and Persuasion*. New York: Springer-Verlag.

Pharr, Susan J. and Robert D. Putnam (Eds.). 2000. *Disaffected Democracies. What's Troubling the Trilateral Countries?* Princeton: Princeton University Press.

Pierson, Paul. 1994. *Dismantling the Welfare State?* Cambridge: Cambridge University Press.

Pierson, Paul (Ed.). 2001. *The New Politics of the Welfare State*. Oxford: Oxford University Press.

Pitkin, Hanna F. 1967. *The Concept of Representation*. Berkeley: University of California Press.

Popkin, Samuel L. 1991. *The Reasoning Voter: Communication and Persuasion in Presidential Campaigns*. Chicago: University of Chicago Press.

Powell, G. Bingham and Guy D. Whitten. 1993. "A Cross-national Analysis of Economic Voting: Taking Account of the Political Context." *American Journal of Political Science* 37:391–414.

Przeworski, Adam, Susan C. Stokes, and Bernard Manin (Eds.). 1999. *Democracy, Accountability, and Representation*. New York: Cambridge University Press.

Rahn, Wendy M., Jon A. Krosnick, and Marijke Breuning. 1994. "Rationalization and Derivation Processes in Survey Studies of Political Candidate Evaluation." *American Journal of Political Science* 38:582–600.

Rasinski, Kenneth. 1987. "What's fair is fair . . . or is it? Value Differences Underlying Public Views about Social Justice." *Journal of Personality and Social Psychology* 53:201–11.

Ringqvist, Margareta. 1996. *Om den offentliga sektorn. Vad den ger och vad den tar*. Stockholm: Fritzes.

Roller, Edeltraud. 1995. "The Welfare State: The Equality Dimension." In *The Scope of Government*, edited by Ole Borre and Elinor Scarbrough. Oxford: Oxford University Press.

Rothstein, Bo (Ed.). 1991. *Politik som organisation: förvaltningspolitikens grundproblem*. Stockholm: SNS förlag.

Rothstein, Bo. 1996. "Political Institutions: An Overview." In *A New Handbook of Political Science*, edited by Robert E. Goodin and Hans-Dieter Klingemann. Oxford: Oxford University Press.

Rothstein, Bo. 1998. *Just Institutions Matter. The Moral and Political Logic of the Universal Welfare State*. Cambridge: Cambridge University Press.

Rothstein, Bo. 2001. "The Universal Welfare State as a Social Dilemma." *Rationality and Society* 13:213–33.

Rothstein, Bo and Sven Steinmo (Eds.). 2002. *Restructuring the Welfare State. Political Institutions and Policy Change*. New York: Palgrave-Macmillan.

Ryghaug, Marianne. 1998. "Opinionens oppfatninger om rettferdig fordeling av goder og byrder." *Tidskrift for samfunnsforskning* 39:516–40.

Sabato, Larry J. 1991. *Feeding Frenzy: How Attack Journalism Has Transformed American Politics*. New York: The Free Press.

Sainsbury, Diane. 1996. *Gender, Equality, and Welfare States*. Cambridge: Cambridge University Press.

Sanders, Lynn M. 1997. "Against Deliberation." *Political Theory* 25:347–76.

Sannerstedt, Anders. 1981. *Attityder till kommunal service*. Stockholm: Ds Kn 1981:22, Rapport 9 från kommunaldemokratiska forskningsgruppen.

Sapiro, Virginia. 1994. "Political Socialisation in Adulthood: Clarifying the Political Time of Our Lives." *Research in Micropolitics* 4:197–223.

Scarrow, Susan E. 2000. "Parties without Members? Party Organization in a Changing Electoral Environment." In *Parties without Partisans. Political Change in Advanced Industrial Democracies*, edited by Russel J. Dalton and Martin P. Wattenberg. Oxford: Oxford University Press.

Schierenbeck, Isabell. 2003. *Bakom välfärdsstatens dörrar*. Umeå: Boréa.

Schlozman, Kay Lehman and Sidney Verba. 1979. *Injury to Insult*. Cambridge: Harvard University Press.

Schmitt, Hermann. 2001. *Politische Repräsentation in Europa. Eine empirische Studie zur Interessenvermittlung durch allgemeine Wahlen*. Frankfurt am Main: Campus Verlag.

Schmitt, Hermann and Sören Holmberg. 1995. "Political Parties in Decline?" In *Citizens and the State*, edited by Hans-Dieter Klingemann and Dieter Fuchs. Oxford: Oxford University Press.

Schneider, Anne Larason and Helen Ingram. 1997. *Policy Design for Democracy*. Lawrence: University Press of Kansas.

Schumpeter, Joseph A. 1942. *Capitalism, Socialism, and Democracy*. New York: Harper & Shaw.

Sears, David O. 1993. "Symbolic Politics: A Socio-Psychological Theory." In *Explorations in Political Psychology*, edited by Shanto Iyengar and William J. McGuire. Durham: Duke University Press.

Sears, David O. and Carolyn L. Funk. 1990. "Self-Interest in Americans' Political Opinions." in *Beyond Self-Interest*, edited by Jane J. Mansbridge. Chicago: The University of Chicago Press.

Sears, David O. and Carolyn L. Funk. 1991. "The Role of Self-Interest in Social and Political Attitudes." *Advances in Experimental Social Psychology* 24:1–91.

Sears, David O. and Jack Citrin. 1982. *Tax Revolt. Something for Nothing in California*. Cambridge: Harvard University Press.

Sears, David O. and Carolyn L. Funk. 1999. "Evidence of the Long-Term Persistence of Adults' Political Predispositions." *Journal of Politics* 61:1–28.

Sears, David O., Carl P. Hensler, and Leslie K. Speer. 1979. "Whites' Opposition to 'Busing': Self-interest or Symbolic Politics?" *American Political Science Review* 73:369–84.

Sears, David O., Richard R. Lau, Tom R. Tyler, and Harris M. Allen Jr. 1980. "Self-interest vs. Symbolic Politics in Policy Attitudes and Presidential Voting." *American Political Science Review* 74:670–84.

Sigel, Roberta S. (Ed.). 1989. *Political Learning in Adulthood. A Sourcebook of Theory and Research*. Chicago: The University of Chicago Press.

Sjoberg, Gideon, Richard A. Brymer, and Buford Farris. 1966. "Bureaucracy and the Lower Class." *Sociology and Social Research* 50:325–37.

Skocpol, Theda. 1994. "From Social Security to Health Security? Opinion and Rhetoric in U.S. Social Policy Making." *Political Science & Politics* 27:21–25.

Smith, Eric R.A.N. 1989. *The Unchanging American Voter*. Los Angeles: University of California Press.

Smith, Steven Rathgeb. 2002. "Privatization, Devolution, and the Welfare State: Rethinking the Prevailing Wisdom." In *Restructuring The Welfare State*, edited by Bo Rothstein and Sven Steinmo. New York: Palgrave.

Sniderman, Paul M. and Richard A. Brody. 1977. "Coping: The Ethic of Self-Reliance." *American Journal of Political Science* 21:501–21.

Sniderman, Paul M., Richard A. Brody, and Philip E. Tetlock (Eds.). 1991. *Reasoning and Choice. Explorations in Social Psychology.* Cambridge: Cambridge University Press.

Soss, Joe. 1999. "Lessons of Welfare: Policy Design, Political Learning, and Political Action." *American Political Science Review* 93:363–80.

SOU 2000:1. *En uthållig demokrati.* Stockholm: Fritzes.

SOU 2001:79. *Välfärdsbokslut för 1990-talet.* Stockholm: Fritzes.

Starrin, Bengt and Ronny Svensson. 1998. *Sverige efter välfärdskrisen. Mellan hot och hopp.* Umeå: Boréa.

Steinmo, Sven, Kathleen Thelen, and Frank Longstreth (Eds.). 1992. *Structuring Politics. Historical Institutionalism in a Comparative Perspective.* New York: Cambridge University Press.

Stimson, James A. 1995. "Opinion and Representation." *American Political Science Review* 89:179–83.

Strandberg, Urban. 1998. *Debatten om den kommunala självstyrelsen.* Hedemora: Gidlunds förlag.

Strömbeck, Jesper. 2000. *Makt och medier. En bok om samspelet mellan medborgarna, medierna och de politiska makthavarna.* Lund: Studentlitteratur.

Strömbäck, Jesper. 2001. *Gäster hos verkligheten: en studie av journalistik, demokrati och politisk misstro.* Eslöv: Brutus Östlings bokförlag Symposion.

Svallfors, Stefan. 1989. *Vem älskar välfärdsstaten.* Lund: Arkiv förlag.

Svallfors, Stefan. 1993. "Dimensions of Inequality: A Comparison of Attitudes in Sweden and Britain." *European Sociological Review* 9:267–87.

Svallfors, Stefan. 1996. *Välfärdsstatens moraliska ekonomi. Välfärdsopinionen i 90-talets Sverige.* Umeå: Boréa.

Svallfors, Stefan. 1997. "Worlds of Welfare and Attitudes to Redistribution: A Comparison of Eight Western Nations." *European Sociological Review* 13:283–304.

Svallfors, Stefan. 1999. *Mellan risk och tilltro: Opinionsstödet för en kollektiv välfärdspolitik.* Umeå: Sociologiska institutionen, Umeå universitet.

Svallfors, Stefan. 2001. "Kan man lita på välfärdsstaten?—Risk, tilltro och betalningsvilja i den svenska välfärdsopinionen 1997–2000." In *Välfärdens finansiering och fördelning, SOU 2001:57,* edited by Johan Fritzell and Joakim Palme. Stockholm: Fritzes.

Svensson, Torsten. 1994. *Socialdemokratins dominans. En studie av den svenska socialdemokratins partistrategi.* Uppsala: Statsvetenskapliga föreningen.

Särlvik, Bo. 1974. "Sweden: The Social Bases of the Parties in a Developmental Perspective." In *Electoral Behavior: A Comparative Handbook,* edited by Richard Rose. New York: Free Press.

Sørensen, Eva. 1997. "Democracy and Empowerment." *Public Administration* 75:553–67.

Sørensen, Eva. 1998. "New Forms of Democratic Empowerment: Introducing User Influence in the Primary School System in Denmark." *Statsvetenskaplig Tidskrift* 100:129–43.

Tarschys, Daniel. 1978. *Den offentliga revolutionen.* Stockholm: Liber förlag.

Taylor, Michaell A. 2000. "Channeling Frustrations: Institutions, Economic Fluctuations, and Political Behavior." *European Journal of Political Research* 38:95–134.

Taylor-Gooby, Peter. 1985. *Public Opinion, Ideology, and State Welfare.* London: Routledge & Kegan Paul.

Taylor-Gooby, Peter. 1986. "Consumption Cleavages and Welfare Politics." *Political Studies* 34:592–606.

Thelen, Kathleen. 1999. "Historical Institutionalism in Comparative Politics." *Annual Review of Political Science* 2:369–404.

Thibaut, John and Laurens Walker. 1975. *Procedural Justice: A Psychological Analysis.* Hillsdale: L. Erlbaum Associates.

Tingsten, Herbert. 1966. *Från idéer till idyll: Den lyckliga demokratin.* Stockholm: Norstedts.

Titmuss, Richard M. 1974. *Social Policy: An Introduction.* London: Allen and Unwin.

Tyler, Tom R. 1980. "Impact of Directly and Indirectly Experienced Events: The Origin of Crime-Related Judgments and Behaviors." *Journal of Personality and Social Psychology* 39:13–28.

Tyler, Tom, R. 1990. "Justice, Self-Interest, and the Legitimacy of Legal and Political Authority." In *Beyond Self-Interest,* edited by Jane J. Mansbridge. Chicago: The University of Chicago Press.

Tyler, Tom R., Jonathan D. Casper, and Bonnie Fisher. 1989. "Maintaining Allegiance toward Political Authorities: The Role of Prior Attitudes and the Use of Fair Procedures." *American Journal of Political Science* 33:629–52.

Tyler, Tom R., Kenneth A. Rasinski, and Kathleen M. McGraw. 1985. "The Influence of Perceived Injustice on the Endorsement of Political Leaders." *Journal of Applied Social Psychology* 15:700–25.

Tyler, Tom R., Robert J. Boeckmann, Heather J. Smith, and Yuen J. Huo. 1997. *Social Justice in a Diverse Society*. Boulder: Westview Press.

Udéhn, Lars. 1996. *The Limits of Public Choice. A Sociological Critique of the Economic Theory of Politics*. London: Routledge.

Vedung, Evert. 1998. *Utvärdering i politik och förvaltning*. Lund: Studentlitteratur.

Verba, Sidney, Norman H. Nie, and Jae-on Kim. 1978. *Participation and Political Equality: A Seven-Nation Comparison*. Cambridge: Cambridge University Press.

Vinzant, Janet Coble and Lane Crothers. 1998. *Street-Level Leadership: Discretion and Legitimacy in Front-Line Public Service*. Washington DC: Georgetown University Press.

Warren, Mark. 1992. "Democratic Theory and Self-Transformation." *American Political Science Review* 86:8–23.

Weatherford, M. Stephen. 1983. "Economic Voting and the 'Symbolic Politics' Argument: A Reinterpretation and a Synthesis." *American Political Science Review* 77:158–74.

Weatherford, M. Stephen. 1984. "Economic 'Stagflation' and Public Support for the Political System." *British Journal of Political Science* 14:187–205.

Westerståhl, Jörgen and Folke Johansson. 1981. *Medborgarna och kommunen: Studier av medborgerlig aktivitet och representativ folkstyrelse*. Ds Kn 1981:12.

Westholm, Anders. 1991. *The Political Heritage: Testing Theories of Family Socialization and Generational Change*. Uppsala Universitet: Statsvetenskapliga institutionen.

Weaver, Kent R. 1986. "The Politics of Blame Avoidance." *Journal of Public Policy* 6:371–98.

Widfeldt, Anders. 1995. "Party Membership and Party Representativeness." In *Citizens and the State*, edited by Hans-Dieter Klingemann and Dieter Fuchs. Oxford: Oxford University Press.

van Wijnen, Pieter. 2001. *Policy Voting in Advanced Industrial Democracies. The Case of the Netherlands 1971–1998*. Enschede: University of Twente, Faculty of Public Administration and Public Policy.

Wilensky, Harold. 1975. *The Welfare State and Equality. Structural and Ideological Roots of Public Expenditures*. Berkely, CA: University of California Press.

Wilke, Henk A.M. 1991. "Greed, Efficiency, and Fairness in Resource Management Situations." *European Review of Social Psychology* 2:165–87.

Winter, Søren and Poul Erik Mouritzen. 2001. "Why People Want Something for Nothing: The Role of Assymetrical Illusions." *European Journal of Political Research* 39:109–43.

Zaller, John R. 1992. *The Nature and Origins of Mass Opinion*. Cambridge: Cambridge University Press.

Zetterberg, Hans L. 1985. "An Electorate in the Grips of the Welfare State." Stockholm: Swedish Institute for Opinion Polls.

INDEX

Entries in *italics* refer to figures and tables.